高职高专商务英语、应用英语专业规划教材

跨文化交际

（第3版）

主　编　郑晓泉

副主编　蔡　红　郑　斌　汤　莉

　　　　何雅叶　朱伟芳　赵　平

INTERCULTURAL COMMUNICATION

(3rd Edition)

ZHEJIANG UNIVERSITY PRESS

浙江大学出版社

第三版前言

随着交通、信息、通信、旅游业的高速发展，以及国家与国家之间贸易额、投资额的不断扩大，不同文化背景的个体和群体之间的交流日益增多，跨文化的交际在广度、密度和深度上都发展迅速。不管愿意与否，几乎所有人都不可避免地要与来自不同文化背景的人进行交流，跨文化交际已成为"地球村"每个公民的必然。然而存在于地区之间、国家之间的文化差异甚至文化沟壑必将导致相互间的误解、隔阂甚至冲突，阻碍了来自不同文化背景下人们之间的有效交际。因此，培养对文化差异的敏感性，发展跨文化意识，学会与来自不同文化背景的人进行交流，已成为新时代的迫切需求。党的二十大报告中指出，要"加强国际传播能力建设，全面提升国际传播效能，形成同我国综合国力和国际地位相匹配的国际话语权。深化文明交流互鉴，推动中华文化更好走向世界"。外语教学界要以党的二十大报告为指引，注重增强学生对文化差异的敏感性、宽容性以及处理文化差异的灵活性，培养学生跨文化交际的能力，更好地形成文化自信，主动成为中华优秀文化的传播者、继承者与践行者。

本教材在内容上，针对高职高专教育人才培养目标、知识结构和能力要求，充分体现理论知识够用为度，着重培养学生跨文化交际技能的目的。第一章以基本知识和理论为主，介绍文化、交际、跨文化交际的定义及概念，阐述交际与文化的关系、文化价值观对跨文化交际的影响。第二、第三、第四、第五、第六章通过对跨文化交际案例的分析，向学生展示文化差异在跨文化交际中的种种表现，以及在特定的国际商务语境中的文化差异。

在体例和编写手法上，本教材各个单元的构成形式多样，不求整齐划一，以适合不同需求与兴趣的学生，并给教师留有一定的选择余地，教师可以结合具体情况更加生动活泼地组织教学。每个章节都配有思考题，给学生留有思考、探讨的空间。同时，本教材配备了电子课件。附录中提供了部分讨论题及课堂任务的参考答案。

在选材上，本教材选材广泛，编排合理，广泛发掘来自不同文化的人们在进行跨文化交际过程中出现问题、遭遇障碍的案例，以及成功进行跨文化交际的案例。这些案例既有趣味性，又有实用性，给学生大量直观的、感性的体验，帮助学生建构跨文化交际的真实场景。教材适合于高职高专英语教师、高职高专英语专业学生，以及英语翻译、导游和英语爱好者。

本教材主编为郑晓泉（丽水职业技术学院），副主编为蔡红（绍兴托普信息职业技术学院）、郑斌（浙江艺术职业学院）、汤莉（浙江育英职业技术学院）、何雅叶（金华职业技术学院）、朱伟芳（绍兴托普信息职业技术学院）、赵平（平顶山工业职业技术学院），参加编写的人员还有梅雪（丽水职业技术学院）、王芬（浙江长征职业技术学院）、王培辉（衢州职业技术学院）、吴丽云（浙江商业职业技术学院）、谢红月（绍兴托普信息职业技术学院）、徐谨（浙江工商职业技术学院）。全书由郑晓泉总纂。本教材配有 PPT 课件以及配套练习答案，可扫二维码获取。

本教材于 2010 年初版，2013 年第二版，2021 年再次修订。在编撰的过程中，参考了大量专著、教材和论文，得到了有关专家和学者的支持、鼓励和帮助。在此书问世之际，谨表达我们衷心的感谢。由于我们的理论水平和实践经验有限，书中疏漏之处在所难免，竭诚希望得到读者批评指正。谢谢！

编　者

2023 年 7 月

Contents

CHAPTER 1   Understanding Culture and
                Intercultural Communication

Human beings draw close to one another by their common
nature, but habits and customs keep them apart.
                                    —Analects of Confucius

Studying a second language without learning the culture is
like learning how to drive a car by studying a driver's manual
and never getting behind a steering wheel.
                                    —K. J. Irving

1.1　Understanding Culture

1.1.1　Pre-reading

Have you ever encountered foreigners? Have you tried to speak English with native speakers? If not, you may at least have watched some foreign films and been struck by behavior which made you feel uncomfortable, puzzled, surprised, or even shocked. Communicating with people from different countries can be fascinating precisely because of different cultures. Yet such different cultures can all too easily give rise to misunderstandings.

Read the following story told by a Chinese student in Britain about her first invitation to have dinner in an English family. Then find some cultural differences in it.

A month after I had settled down at Warwick University for my M.A. course, I was invited to give a talk to a professional women's organization about my first impressions of Britain. After the talk, quite a few participants gave me their addresses and invited me to visit their families. They were really very friendly and helpful. The first visit left a lasting memory because it was my first time to have dinner at an English home. My hostess picked me up at the university and showed me around the city till sunset. I was very excited about the visit, but at the same time I was wondering who would cook the meal. Her husband? In China, if I'm going to have some visitors to dinner, it usually takes me at least three hours to prepare eight courses. As soon as we arrived at the house, the lady asked me to sit at the table and said everything was in the oven and ready to serve. She told me she had put food in the oven before she went to the university and after two hours of touring the city, dinner was ready. Can you imagine how many dishes I had? Only one—a stew with meat and vegetables. The meat was overdone and too hard to eat; green vegetables were no longer green. Compared with Chinese food, they were tasteless. I was very much disappointed at their hospitality. However, after I had stayed in Britain for a year and visited many different families, I became more used to the British way of showing hospitality. In Britain, hospitality is not measured by how many dishes are provided as in China. It is shown by giving you freedom to choose whatever you really want. They never press you. They never put food on your plate but just ask you to help yourself. If you, as a guest, are shy or modest, waiting for the food to be put on your plate, you will remain half-starved.

（1）为什么这个中国学生在看到英国主人给她准备的晚餐后很失望？

（2）你是不是认为英国人不够客气？

围绕这两个问题我们可以展开思考：第一，这个中国学生感到失望是因为在中国，人们为了表示客气，通常会花好几个小时来准备一大桌的美味佳肴，而在英国，女主人却简单地准备了一锅肉煮蔬菜，而且已经煮过了头；第二，英国人不看中招待客人时的饮食是因为在他们的文化中，人们用不同的方式来表达客气，他们注重招待时对客人的重视，会不停地找节目与话题让客人不觉得被冷落，但在饮食上他们比较随意。

不同的国家有不同的文化，不同的文化导致不同的风俗、行为与习惯，那到底什么是文化呢？

1.1.2　What Is Culture?

As we all know, different countries have different cultures. "Culture is the collective programming of the mind which distinguishes the members of one category of people from another."

The word "culture" has numerous meanings. For example, we sometimes say that people who know about art, music, and literature are cultured. However, it has a different meaning for anthropologists (people who study humankind). To an anthropologist it means all the ways in which a group of people act, dress, think, and feel. People have to learn the cultural ways of their communities: they are not something that the people in the group are born with.

Instinctive behaviour, on the other hand, is a pattern of behaviour that an animal is born with. Spiders' spinning their webs is an example of instinctive behaviour. The mother spider does not teach her babies how to spin webs. In fact, she is not even there when they are born. They know how to do it when they are born. This is what we mean by instinctive behaviour.

As humans, we learn some of the ways of our culture by being taught by our teachers or parents. We learn more of the ways of our culture by growing up in it. We see how other people in our culture do things, and we do them in the same way. We even learn how to think and feel in this way.

All human beings have certain basic needs, such as eating, drinking, keeping warm and dry, and so on. However, the way in which they take care of their needs depends on the culture in which they grow up. All cultures have ways of eating, dressing, finding shelter, marrying, and dealing with death. The foods that we think are good to eat, the kind of clothes we wear, and how many people we can marry at one time are all parts of our culture.

Our own culture seems very natural to us. We feel in our hearts that the way that we do things is the only right way to do them. Other people's culture often makes us laugh or feels disgusted or shocked. We may laugh at clothing that seems ridiculous to us. Many people think that eating octopus or a piece of red juicy roast beef is disgusting. The idea that a man can have  more than one wife or that brothers and sisters can marry each other may shock people from other cultures.

Ideas of what is beautiful differ from one culture to another. The Flathead Indian of North America used to bind the heads of babies between boards so they would have long

sloping foreheads. In the Flathead culture, long sloping foreheads were beautiful. Other cultures might think that they are strange-looking and unattractive. Many people cut scars into their bodies or tattoo themselves so that others in their culture will think they are beautiful. Objects are inserted in holes in the nose, lips, and ears in a number of different cultures in many twentieth-century societies. Rouge, lipstick, eye shadow, perfume, and hair spray are all used to increase attractiveness.

When people die, different cultures dispose of their bodies in different ways. Sometimes bodies are burnt. Sometimes bodies are buried in the ground. In many cultures in the past, people were buried with food, weapons, jewellery, and other things that might be useful in the next life. For example, the ancient Egyptians buried people with little human figures made from clay. These clay figures were supposed to work for the death person in the other world. A religious group called the parses exposed their dead on platforms for birds to eat. Some people practice a second burial. After the bodies have been in the earth for several years, the bones are dug up and reburied, sometimes in a small container.

These are just a few of the many different customs that are found in different cultures. Most of the time, the different ways that stand for the customs of different cultures are neither right nor wrong. It is simply that different people do the same things in different ways.

The Characteristics of Culture

From the definition of culture, we can generate the basic characteristics of culture as following.

Culture is holistic

As a holistic system, culture can be broken down into several subsystems, including a kinship system, an educational system, a religious system, an economic system, a political system, a food system, a corporate system, a sports system, and so on, but the various systems of culture are closely interrelated. Any change in a subsystem will affect the whole system. For instance, attitudes, values, behaviors of work, life, entertainment, and so on changed a lot with appearance of personal computer and mobile.

Culture is coherent

Each culture, past or present, is coherent and complete within itself—an entire view of the universe. The pioneer researcher into the study of cultures, Edward Tylor, said in 1871 that culture is "the outward expression of a unifying and consistent vision brought by a particular community to its confrontation with such core issues as the origins of the cosmos, the harsh unpredictability of the natural environment, the nature of society and humankind's place in the order of things."

That different groups of human beings at different times in history could develop different visions is both a cause for wonder, and a cause of misunderstanding. The incredible richness of the variety of cultures fascinates historians, anthropologists, travelers, and nearly everybody.

Regardless of how peculiar a fragment of culture seems, when it is placed within the whole tapestry of the culture, it makes sense. The completeness of cultures also means members looking out from their own seamless view of the universe probably do not see anything lacking in their "unifying and consistent vision."

Culture is constantly changeable

Culture is subject to change over time. Culture loses some of its traits and gains new ones. Every culture changes in time although the rate of change of every culture varies. Some cultures are more open and accepting of change, others tend to resist it. The aspects of culture that change vary across societies. Cultures change in the process of transmission from generation to generation, group to group, and place to place. With the passage of time, new technologies emerge, new modes of work come up, social thinking undergoes transitions and so does culture. Four major mechanisms account for the change of cultures: technological invention, disasters (including natural and human calamities), cultural contact, and environmental factors.

Culture is learned and acquired

Culture is not instinctive. We all have to be taught our culture. Culture propagates through generations, which adopt their old customs and traditions as a part of their culture. The ideals they base their lives on is a part of their culture. Cultural values are imparted from one generation to another, thus resulting in a continual of traditions that are a part of culture. We begin to consciously and unconsciously acquire and learn our culture in our early life through senses and from experience, habits, skills, and knowledge. Interaction with family members and friends is the most common way for us to learn about our culture. Other sources for learning our culture are schools, churches, media, folk tales, and art. Culture is learned, understood and adopted by the younger generations of society. No individual is born with a sense of his/her culture. He/she has to learn it.

If culture is learned, then it is learnable. That means nobody has to remain for a life-time locked inside only one culture. If you want to understand other cultures, you can learn them—not just learn about them, but accurately get inside them and act according to what is expected in them. Many people have learned more than one culture and move comfortably within them. When circumstances dictate, they make the transition from one culture to another easily.

Culture is shared and transmitted

Every culture is shared by a group of people. Members of a society agree about the meanings of things and about the why. Depending on the region they live in, the climatic conditions they thrive in and their historical heritage, they form a set of values and beliefs. This set of principles of life shapes their culture. No culture belongs to an individual. It is rather shared among many people of a certain part of the world. Along with everyone from whom they have learned their culture—older family members, teachers, spiritual leaders, peers, and representatives of legal, political, and educational institutions—they have interpreted life experiences in ways that validate their own culture's views. Therefore, since they have little doubt about that validity, they all share the view that their interpretations are correct. Groups are motivated by common views, and these views are a dynamic force enabling groups to achieve societal goals— protecting economic sources from unscrupulous outsiders, for example.

Culture belongs to a single community. People in a given culture share symbols of that culture. The most obvious set of symbols is language. Culture also shares visual symbols. Company logos, icons, religious images, and national flags are examples of visual symbols.

Culture ranks what is important

What is of paramount importance to one group may be virtually meaningless to another. For instance, consider the amassing of wealth. In one Pacific Island culture, the Gururumba of New Guinea, a rich man is required to expend all his carefully amassed fortune—in this case, pigs—in the lavish entertainment of the members of his society. To be able to entertain this way is the real meaning of wealth because it means the giver is owed and therefore has great prestige. But explain that to a businessperson in the Unites States or China or Italy who has spent his or her life amassing wealth! Usually in these cultures resources are to be husbanded and increased, not depleted in one big blow-out. To be sure, businesspeople in these cultures often make generous charitable and philanthropic donations, but their cultures teach them to treat wealth with care and make it grow. Culture ranks what is important. In other words, culture teaches values of priorities. They enable us to evaluate what matters to us or to apply standards to our attitudes and beliefs. For example, a culture may put a high priority on honesty and a low priority on making a minimal effort. Priorities vary from culture to culture. When you understand the priorities people have, you can predict with some confidence how they will probably respond to a specific situation.

Culture furnishes attitudes

Attitude is a feeling about things, which is a tendency to respond the same way to the same object, situation or idea in the same culture. People from different cultures can have different attitudes toward the same things. In Mexican culture, a death of an aunt is an event that business associate are expected to view as significant to the family members; a boss is expected to have an understanding attitude toward an employee who is not able to get a report done by a deadline because of the funeral and family needs. In Britain, the attitude toward a business associate's loss of an aunt is that this is a private affair, regrettable and perhaps very sad, but something that should not affect work to a great extent. In fact, for a businessperson, handling the situation well means keeping it from having an impact on work. Reports should come in on time if possible.

Culture dictates how to behave

To continue the example of the previous discussion, a brief expression of sympathy by one businessperson to a bereaved work associate at their next meeting is appropriate British behavior. If the association is longstanding, perhaps a card is sent. In Mexico, on the other hand, much more than an expression of sympathy is appropriate behavior. Business associates may attend the funeral, send flowers, offer services such as transporting family members, and visit the family to show respect.

Behavior comes directly from attitudes about how significant something is—how it is valued. Values drive actions. Our life is mostly a composite of actions. Cultural priorities motivate our behavior. In intercultural contracts, cultural differences usually make themselves known first by behavior, which is related to attitudes and which springs from priorities (value) in the future.

Layers of Culture

There are many interpretations of culture. We look at culture from a special perspective. We like to compare culture with an onion. Culture, like an onion, consists of many layers. Stephan Dahl, a Spanish scholar, wrote a report of Communication and Culture Transformation—Cultural Diversity, Globalization and Cultural Convergence. In the report, the scholar pointed out that there were three layers in culture.

Surface layer: all kinds of behaviors a man conducts. It includes all the direct contents in the field of culture—language, clothes, foods, housing, all the products of arts and so on. This is the level of explicit culture.

Middle layer: criterion and sense of worth. Criterion and sense of worth lead to the recognition of being right and wrong. People's behaviors and ways of communication are affected by criterion and sense of worth. But they are not visible, despite their influence on what happens at the observable surface.

Deep layer: basic judgment. People have a basic judgment toward the questions: What is life? How to deal with the problems appearing in life? What is beauty? ... This is the deepest layer: the level of implicit culture. Understanding the core of the culture onion is the key to successfully work with other cultures. The core consists of basic assumptions, series of rules and methods to deal with the regular problems that it faces. These methods of problem-solving have become so basic that, like breathing, we no longer think about how we do it. For an outsider these basic assumptions are very difficult to recognize. Every culture has developed its own set of basic assumptions. These basic assumptions can be measured by dimensions. Each dimension is like a continuum. Cultures differ in how they deal with these dimensions, but they do not differ in needing to make some kind of response.

Dahl's Sketch Map of Layers of Culture

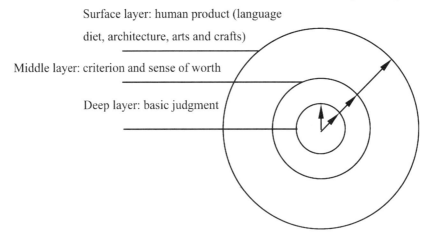

Surface layer: human product (language
diet, architecture, arts and crafts)

Middle layer: criterion and sense of worth

Deep layer: basic judgment

Culture Shock

Culture shock can be described as the feeling of confusion and disorientation that one experiences when facing with a large number of new and unfamiliar people and situations. Many things contribute to it—smells, sounds, flavors, the very feeling of the air one is breathing. Of course, the unfamiliar language and behavior of the native people contribute to it, too. People's responses to culture shock vary greatly, from excitement and energetic action to withdrawal, depression, physical illness, and hostility.

The notion of culture shock calls two useful points to mind. First, most people experience some degree of culture shock when they go to a new country, whether they admit it to themselves and others or not. Culture shock is more a product of the situation of being in a new culture than of the traveler's personal character. Second, culture shock, like other kinds of "shock", is normally transitory. It passes with time.

When an individual enters a strange culture, all or most of these familiar signs are removed. No matter how broadminded or full of goodwill you may be, a series of supports have been removed from you, followed by a feeling of frustration. When suffering from culture shock people first reject the environment which causes discomfort. The ways of the host country are bad because they make you feel bad. When foreigners in a strange land get together to complain about the host country and its people, you can be sure that they are suffering from culture shock.

Another phase of culture shock is regression. The home environment suddenly assumes tremendous importance. To the foreigner, everything becomes irrationally glorified. All the difficulties and problems are forgotten and only the good things back home are remembered. It usually takes a trip home to bring one back to reality.

Stages of Culture Shock

Culture shock is divided into five stages. Each stage can be long standing or appears only under certain conditions. Researchers have found that most people go through very similar stages during the process of adapting to a new culture. They have identified five distinct stages, called: honeymoon, rejection, adjustment, acceptance or adaptation, reentry. These five stages of culture shock may occur in different time; different person may have different reactions due to certain factors such as personality type, age, expectation, education background, health condition, and major. However, there are some effective ways to fight with the pressure caused by culture shock such as developing a hobby, making friends or contacting with family.

Stage 1: Honeymoon Stage

Like any new experience, the newcomer is usually excited to be in the new country. Everything is exciting and stimulating. People are friendly and the future is full of promise. This is where one will overlook minor problems and look forward to learning new things.

Step 2: Rejection Stage

Everything one is experiencing no longer feels new; in fact, it's starting to feel like a thick wall that's preventing you from experiencing things. During this stage, one starts refusing to accept the differences one encounters, and realizes that the familiar support systems are not easily accessible. One usually has some negative feelings such as lonely, difficult, depressed, lost or uncomfortable, even feel hostile to those around him/her. One dislikes the culture, the language, the food. One may even develop some prejudices towards the new culture. So one may long for food the way it is prepared in one's native country, may find the pace of life too fast or slow, may find the people's habits annoying, disgusting, and irritating, etc.

Step 3: Adjustment Stage

One is more familiar with the new environment and develops routines. He/she learns to accept the culture and to change his/her negative attitude to a positive one. One is adjusting during this period and begins to establish an objective, balanced, and impartial view of the whole situation. This is actually a pretty common reaction to anything new. Think back to when one started a new job or moved to a new house or a new city or when one moved in with someone. Any adjustment can cause one to look back in awe and wonder why one made the decision to change. One becomes concerned with basic living again, and things become more "normal." One starts to develop problem-solving skills to deal with the culture, and begins to accept the culture ways with a positive attitude. The culture begins to make sense, and negative reactions and responses to the culture are reduced.

Step 4: Acceptance Stage

One will feel at home and become involved in activities and may enjoy some of that country's customs. One starts to accept the differences and one can begin to live with natives. One feels more confident and is better able to cope with any problems that may arise. One no longer feels isolated and instead one is able to look at the world around him/her and appreciates where he/she is. One is now able to move into new situations with greater awareness of self and others. One demonstrates an increased competence and an ability to relax and enjoy the host culture.

Step 5: Reentry Stage

This is experienced upon returning to the home country and the return may follow with initial euphoria, crisis or disenchantment. It may be hard to readjust and may feel like he/she is not accepted. One feels different about the same thing from the original country when he/she returns. For instance, one feels the taste of food is different from that of used to be, which was more delicious in his/her memory even though his/her parents didn't agree with him/her. In addition, one feels the city where he/she had grown up is more crowded than before.

1.1.3　Case for Practice

Case 1

Try to put yourself in the shoes of Wang Ming. He has invited a foreign friend, Lisa, to his home for a meal. Unfortunately, as you read their conversation, the occasion gets off to a rather bumpy start.

(*Lisa; Wang—Wang Ming*)

Wang:　Hi, Lisa! Welcome! Come in, come in.

Lisa:　Thank you for your invitation. It's a lovely room and very warm here.

Wang:　My room is very small and untidy. Please sit down and have a cup of tea. You must be tired after the long walk here.

Lisa:　What a strange thing to say—your room is perfectly clean and tidy! And as for the walk, I'm very strong, you know. I usually walk for at least half an hour every day. Don't you think walking is a good way to keep fit?

Wang:　Yes, I do. Dinner is ready. Please sit at the table.

Lisa:　Wow! So many dishes—eight! They look very tasty.

Wang:　I'm sorry that I'm not a very good cook. Here are only a few cold dishes. Please try this fish, though I'm not very good at cooking, I'm afraid.

Lisa:　This is delicious.

Later on in the meal, just before they finish the cold dishes, eight hot dishes are placed on the table.

Lisa:　Another eight!

Wang:　You know the figure "eight" is a lucky number in China. So there are two sets of eight dishes for the most distinguished guests.

Lisa:　If I had known earlier, I would have left some room for the second eight. But I'm completely full. I'm terribly sorry, but I'm afraid I couldn't eat another mouthful.

(1) What remarks made by Wang shortly after Lisa's arrival seemed to surprise her? How did she react?

(2) Did Lisa think the meal unusual?

Case 2

David Li had just started working for the foreign owned company. He was sitting at his workstation but had not been given any assignment that he should be doing at this moment. He was relaxing and waiting and then thought he would take the opportunity to have a look around. He poked his head into several offices just to see what there was to be seen.

Suddenly Mr. Parker came up to him and angrily asked him what he was doing. David Li was embarrassed. He laughed and quickly started to move back toward his workstation. This did not seem to satisfy Mr. Parke who started to talk rapidly and angrily. Hoping to calm him down, Mr. Li smiled and apologized, trying to explain that he was trying to learn more about the department. However, Mr. Parker got even angrier. Finally, another worker came by and calmed him down, but as Mr. Parker left he still looked angry. Mr. Li sighed; he knew he had made a bad start, but still didn't understand why.

(1) Why Mr. Parker became even angrier while Mr. Li smiled and apologized?
(2) What suggestions can you give Mr. Li?

1.1.4　Further Reading

Passage 1

Individualism and Collectivism

According to cross-cultural theorists, individualism and collectivism are basic clusters of values and assumptions. To the extent that they accept their cultures' traditions, members of individualist cultures develop beliefs, attitudes, values, and behaviour quite different from those of people brought up in collectivist cultures.

Individualist cultures have been described as "I" cultures. That is to say, in cultures that score high on individualism, the basic social unit is the individual. In such cultures, the individual human being is seen as having intrinsic worth, and individuals tend to define themselves by the extent to which they are different from, rather than similar to others. Thus self-examination and self-disclosure are important activities that find expression in normal day-to-day communication practices. Members of cultures that score high on individualism learn to express their uniqueness: self-confidence and assertiveness. As a result, individualists do not fear actions that call attention to the self; in fact, they often seek the notice of others, for this notice affirms their uniqueness and thus their identities.

Cultures with collectivist orientations, in contrast, place little value on individual identity and great value on group identity. They have been labeled as "we" cultures because the basic unit is the in-group or collective. The survival of the group is more important than that of any individual member. Going one's own way is not thoughts or feelings, and the open discussion of disagreement is not valued forms of talk.

Passage 2

Culture and Context

Communication is not devoid of external influence—it does not take place in a void. All human interaction, therefore, is influenced to some degree by the cultural, social, and physical, settings in which it occurs. These settings are called the communication context.

Your culture to a very large degree prescribes your communicative behavior within a variety of social and physical contexts by prescribing rules that dictate appropriate behavior for specific communicative situations. When you communicate with members of your own culture, you and your cohorts rely on internalized cultural rules that prescribe appropriate behavior for the communication situation. You are able to communicate effectively with each other without having to think about those rules. But when you engage in intercultural communication, things can be different. Here you and your communication partners may be operating from sets of very different rules. Consequently, you must be aware of how diverse cultural rules influence the communication context.

Concepts of dress, time, language, manners, nonverbal behavior, and control of the communication ebb and flow can differ significantly among cultures. When doing business in China, for example, your Chinese colleagues will insist on paying for all the entertainment. Chinese hospitality is legendary and you will not be allowed to pay for even part of the meal. In the United States, the rules for business entertaining are very different. The cost of the meal or entertainment is often shared. Different cultures, different rules.

Both consciously and unconsciously, people expect that their interactions will follow culturally determined rules or shared forms of behavior. Communication rules prescribe proper behavior by establishing appropriate responses to communication stimuli for the various social contexts found within the larger culture. Social settings usually stipulate which rules govern a particular situation, but it is culture that makes the rules. In Iraq, for instance, a contextual rule prohibits women from having unfamiliar male guests visiting them in their homes. In the United States, however, this may not be socially inappropriate.

To be successful in intercultural communication, it is essential that you know not only your own cultural rules but also the cultural rules of the person with whom you are interacting. If you understand the rules, the other person's behavior will make greater sense to you and you will be able to control and modify your behavior to conform to his or her expectations. Consequently, you must be aware of how diverse cultural rules influence the communication context. Otherwise, you may encounter a variety of surprises—some of which could be embarrassing or unpleasant.

Notes

| culture shock | 文化冲击；文化休克 | disorientation | 迷茫 |
| layers of culture | 文化的层次 | criterion | (评判等的)标准；准则 |

Encounter Tips

◎ 一个民族的文化形态是可以变迁的，不同文化间的相互交流与传播必然导致文化的互化 (transculturation) 或涵化 (acculturation) 现象。其中互化指的是不同文化间的交互影响，涵化则是指对来自其他文明的文化成果的吸纳与消化。这两种方式都可能赋予某种既成的文化新的内容或形态。

◎ 西方文化强调人作为有理智、有尊严和自由意志的独立个体的地位，要求人对自己的命运负责。而中国文化则主要把人理解为类的存在物，重视人的社会价值，更多地把人看作群体的一分子，是他所属社会关系的派生物，他的价值因群体而存在并借此体现，因而会无条件地将自己的命运和利益都托付给所属的群体。这两种不同角度的人伦便带来了中西方文化不同的人格理想以及相应的社会政治结构。

◎ 群体本位与个体本位的不同原则不可避免地导致了中西方文化在民族性格和社会价值取向上的差异，即中国人注重节制，追求和谐与平稳，而西方人以鼓励竞争、追求功利、崇尚力量和进取为价值目标。

1.2 Understanding Intercultural Communication

1.2.1 Pre-reading

An American English teacher living in Thailand was glad to see her former student, who had just returned from a year's stay in the United States.

Teacher: Oh, Mr. Sittipunt, welcome back. How was your trip to the United States?

Mr. Sittipunt: Well, I'm glad to be home. In the Unites States, I saw old people trying to look young, and young people trying to look old. I found you Americans say "yes" when we would sometimes say "no." People said, "How are you?" And then they didn't even wait for an answer—they just continued on their way. I met unmarried couples living together, and married couples who are not living together. American women are as aggressive as the men. I'm really glad to be home. I just don't understand your American way of life. I had heard about the American dream, but take my word for it—it's no dream, but nightmare.

案例中的 Sittipunt 列举了他在美国期间遇到的许多不可思议的美国社会形态、生活模式等，这些社会现象有别于他从小建立起来的价值观，因此让他感到困惑和难以适应。在不同文化的交流中，若一方不懂对方的文化，可能会导致种种误解，小的误解会使人感到不舒服，就像例子中的 Sittipunt，大的误解会铸成大错。为了在不同文化的人际、群体间和国际交流时避免误会，进行有效交流，在人与人之间建立良好的关系，在群体间增进理解与合作，人们需要了解跨文化交流的知识，有意识地提高跨文化交流的能力。

1.2.2　What Is Intercultural Communication?

Intercultural communication looks at how people, from different cultural backgrounds, try to communicate. Intercultural communication tries to bring together such relatively unrelated areas as cultural anthropology and established areas of communication. Its core is to establish and understand how people from different cultures communicate with each other. Its charge is also to produce some guidelines under which people from different cultures can better communicate with each other. For example, how does a person from China communicate with a person from Turkey? Furthermore, what underlying mental constructs appear from both parties that allows for constructive communication?

Intercultural communication, as many scholarly fields, is a combination of many other fields. These fields include anthropology, cultural studies, psychology and communication. It is also frequently referred to as "cross-cultural communication."

Intercultural communication is the term first used by Edward T. Hall in 1959 and is simply defined as interpersonal communication between members of different cultures.

Intercultural communication can include international, interethnic, interracial, and inter-regional communication.

International communication

International communication takes place between nations and governments rather than individuals; it is quite formal and ritualized. The dialogue at the United Nations, for example, would be termed international communication. If Chinese President communicates with American President, we have international communication, because this is communication between two nations or countries.

Interethnic communication

Ethnic groups usually form their own communities in a country or culture. Interethnic communication refers to communication between people of the same race but different ethnic background. For example, in China, if a Tibetan communicates with a Han, we have interethnic communication, as they are from different ethnic groups.

Interracial communication

Interracial communication occurs when the source and the receiver exchanging messages are from different races which pertain to physical characteristic. For instance, if an Afro-American interacts with a white American, it's interracial communication. Interracial communication may or may not be intercultural.

Interregional communication

This term refers to the exchange of messages between members of the dominant culture within a country. If a northerner interacts with a southerner, we have what is called interregional communication. These are members of cultures who shared common messages and experiences over a long period of time, but who lived in different regions of the same country.

Intercultural communication as a phenomenon has the following features:

First of all, it is a universal phenomenon. Intercultural communication as a phenomenon is universal. It occurs everywhere in the world. When you talk with an American teacher, or send email to a foreigner, or even when you watch a foreign film or read an English novel, you are engaged in intercultural communication. As a result of this communication, whether being face-to-face, communicating over the Internet, watching a movie, or reading a book, if you are receiving messages from another culture, then you are involved in intercultural communication.

Secondly, the communication between cultures has been going on for thousands of years. The history of intercultural communication is almost as long as human history itself. It dates back to the time when primitive nomadic tribes started mingling with each other and needed to communicate with each other. It became necessary even more when sailors visited alien lands; and when thousands of "gold-diggers" from Asia and different European countries immigrated to North America in search of wealth, there was intercultural communication. During the Tang Dynasty in China, there was an example of the famous "Silk Road" in which people of Asia, Africa and Europe interacted and communicated with each other in order to conduct their business transactions.

Thirdly, intercultural communication is a common daily occurrence. The communication between cultures today is happening continuously, and taking place almost everyday. Today, you find thousands of Chinese students going abroad to study, while there are millions of foreign travelers coming to China to visit, foreign artists coming to China to give performances, and there are many joint venture enterprises doing business in many of our cities. These are all examples showing how prevalent intercultural communication is today.

Especially now during the 21st century the importance of intercultural communication has greatly increased. Why did an increasing number of people now recognize the importance of intercultural communication? Let's move on to the next point for the answer.

Elements Affecting Intercultural Communication

Intercultural communication is both difference-based and culture-based. Aspects of a culture are acted out whenever members of different cultures come together to share ideas and exchange information. As a discipline, intercultural communication studies problems that arise in the course of communicating across cultures.

Communication barriers are obstacles to affect communication. By understanding intercultural communication barriers, we can break them down and pave the way for mutual understanding and respect.

Condon highlighted three areas as most problematic in intercultural exchange: language barriers, different values, and different cultural patterns of behavior. As such, three main obstacles to intercultural communication are identified and accordingly expounded further below. It is noteworthy to the International Assignee the consequences if due care is not exercised when interacting with non-native English speakers.

Language

(1) Slang, Jargon

(2) Dialects, Pidgin

(3) Accents

The transfer of International Assignees across geographical borders perpetuates the use of the English language. That has never been as pervasive or as widely, although variations of the language and degree of fluency differ from country to country, individual to individual.

As it is, usage of slang and jargon-examples: sport, technical—is to be avoided unless the assignee is so sure that the local audience understands them well. Also, the presence of globally known brands, products and services does not mean that the locals possess the same level of mindset.

It is therefore imperative that the assignee be sensitive of both connotations and implications that may arise as a result of local usage; further influenced by the local languages where English is a second or third, or foreign language.

Modern technology

(1) Email

(2) SMS Text Messaging

(3) Video Conferencing/Teleconferencing

The advent of modern technology, especially the Internet, has made access easier and cheaper to people worldwide such that it helped speed up globalization. Similarly, the pervasive use of technological tools like Short Message Service (SMS) and email amongst locals does not mean that cultural mishaps will not occur.

The difficulty that comes with the aforesaid tools is gauging the recipients' expressions. Their responses could be not what the assignee expects or least anticipates. On the other hand, the ease of communicating electronically removes formality and business etiquette that can not only be misconstrued but also leads to a breakdown in communication.

Hence, it is pertinent on the assignee's part to convey himself as clearly and plainly as possible to avoid any misunderstandings that may arise.

Behavioral and mindset

(1) Anxiety

(2) Discomfort

(3) Fear of the "Unknown"

(4) Prejudice and Stereotyping

(5) Perceived Cultural Superiority or Ethnocentrism

(6) Discrimination = Racial, Sexual, Educational

Coming from a culture that upholds individualism, privacy and independence; the Assignee will certainly experience shock, resistance, and to a lesser degree, disgust towards the host culture that is perceived as inferior. As a result, he may withdraw himself seeking similar individuals, or refuse to adapt accordingly to his environment.

The assignee may also display anxiety and discomfort if he has not come across—or having little or rare opportunities to socialize with—people of other cultures before. He will lose sight on effectively communicating his ideas because he is afraid of being misunderstood.

Thus, it is to both the organization's long-term interest and the assignee's well-being that he has the ability to manage the conflicts well enough. Otherwise it is detrimental to his work performance which can affect the entire department's morale as a whole.

It is convenient to dismiss cultural differences as the major or sole reason for a breakdown in communication—which does not serve the International assignee well in the long run. Instead, he could be more proactive by confronting the issues that prevented him from working closely with his team.

By addressing the problem and then taking practical steps to remedy any unintentional misunderstanding caused; such actions will not only make him more motivated at work but his stay more pleasant too.

Just remember: Treat anyone regardless of ethnic, racial or cultural background the same way you would want to be treated.

Becoming Intercultural

To be communicative is to be open, responsive and non-judgemental. Here are the tips:

1. Know yourself

—Biases, attitudes, opinions—know likes and dislikes; identify and deal with them.

—Identify what kind of image you portray (communication style)—ask yourself:

—Do I smile? Am I tense or at ease?

—Do I give my undivided attention?

—Do I put others down?

—Do I interrupt?

2. Use shared "code"

—Omit slang, jargon, and acronyms.

—Use day-to-day vocabulary.

3. Take time

—Don't leap to conclusions—allow other person time to finish.

—Cultivate patience—allow other person time for pauses and silence.

—Relax—keep quiet—don't chatter or babble just to fill in silence.

4. Physical and human setting

—Timing—e.g. one doesn't usually talk business at funerals.

— Physical setting—e.g. one doesn't tell jokes in a Hindu temple.

—Custom and past practice—e.g. when to bow/shake hands/stand up.

5. Improve communication skills

—Interest—try not to bore people.

—Organization—make sense, don't ramble.

—Delivery—verbal and non-verbal (are you animated or sluggish; do you use your hands?)

—Message reception—be attentive.

—Concentrate on explicit/be sensitive to implicit.

— Be prepared to give feed-back.

6. Encourage feed-back

As a gauge of successful communication allowing for correction and adjustment of message:

—Comfortable atmosphere.

—Non-verbal sitting relaxed.

—Ask questions.

—Carefully read response—may find that emotional support is what is needed, rather than a solution to a problem (hidden agenda).

7. Develop empathy

Reduce one's own ethnocentrism; learn to appreciate the point of view and life orientation of others. Realize that even the most diverse cultures have some things in common. All people:

—Share the same planet.

—Desire to be free from external restraint.

—Seek to avoid stress and find some degree of happiness.

1.2.3　Case for Practice

Case 1

Melinda put down the pile of papers on the desk and confided to her colleagues, "I don't think that new person in the Accounting Department is going to fit in. He doesn't seem to be very sociable."

After a moment, her colleague, Tim, asked why. Then Melinda explained that she had met the new man in Accounting downstairs near the water cooler and that she had said the usual greeting and he had merely answered "hello" and walked off.

She went on to say that the following day, she had taken down some files to Accounting and had seen the new person and had smiled and said "hello" again as she stopped by his desk. To her question "How's everything?" he had responded "So-so." Then he had looked back at his work.

"I really had to work hard to try to get him talking. I thought he was shy at first but I don't think so. He just didn't want to talk. I've decided he's rude or there's something very wrong with his social skills." Melinda confided to Tim.

Tim tried to be understanding. "That's not the right way to treat someone who's a new person. Do you think he's really concentrating on doing a good job and making a good impression? Maybe he's worried about his new job."

Melinda considered this idea. "Well, even if that's so, he should know how to end a conversation politely. Just walking or looking away isn't acceptable. It gives the wrong message."

(1) Why was Melinda offended by the new person's behavior?

(2) What should the new person have done, even if he did not want to or have time to talk?

(3) Comment on Tim's conversation with Melinda. Is Tim giving the right message to his colleagues?

Case 2

Shao Bin, a Chinese student studying in Britain, was once invited by her British classmate Brain to his house to cook a Chinese meal. Her two Chinese friends were also invited. They busied themselves in the kitchen, making dumping while Brain did something in the garden and his wife sat on the sofa reading. Shao Bin felt a little upset for she thought that both the host and the hostess should offer to help with the kitchen work. The meal was great and everyone enjoyed themselves. The couple kept complimenting them on their cooking skills and asked for the recipe. But then after the meal, the couple just put down their chopsticks and started minding their own business, leaving the Chinese guests to clear the table and do the dishes. Shao Bin felt absolutely confused or even angry.

(1) How do you comment on this Chinese girls' experience?

(2) Will you feel confused if you are in such a situation?

(3) If you are the host or hostess, what do you do when you entertain guests at home?

1.2.4 Further Reading

Passage 1

Improving Intercultural Communication

Know Yourself

What you bring to the communication event greatly influences the success or failure of that event. Although the idea of knowing yourself is common, it is nevertheless crucial to improving intercultural communication. The novelist James Baldwin said it best when he wrote, "The questions which one asks oneself begin, at last, to illuminate the world, and become one's key to the experience of others." Baldwin's remarks serve as an ideal introduction for the portion of this book that urges you to begin your path to improvement with some self-analysis. As  with many of the suggestion we offer in this section, it is easier to state the advice than to practice it. We can write the words "know yourself" with just a few strokes on our keyboard, but it will take a great deal of effort for you to translate this assignment into practice. We believe that the application of introspection should take three directions: first, know your culture; second, know your perceptions; and third, know how you act on those perceptions. Although these three concepts work in tandem, it might be useful to examine them separately.

Know Your Culture

Your first step toward introspection should begin with your own culture, regardless of what that culture might be. Remember, we are products of our culture—and culture helps control communication. Steward and Bennett made a similar observation when they wrote "An awareness of American culture along with the example of contrasting culture contributes to the individual's understanding of oneself as a cultural being."

Know Your Attitudes

By exhorting you to examine your attitudes and perceptions, we are not referring to any mystical notions involving another reality, nor are we suggesting you engage in a deep psychological soul searching. Rather, we are asking you to identify those attitudes, prejudices, and opinions that we all carry around and that bias the way the word appears to us. If we hold a certain attitude toward gay men, and a man who is a gay talks to us, our precommunication attitude will color our response to what he says. Knowing our likes, dislikes, and degrees of personal ethnocentrism enables us to place them out in the open so that we can detect the ways in which these attitudes influence communication. Hidden personal premises, be they directed at ideas, people, or entire cultures, are often the cause of many of our difficulties.

Know Your Communication Style

The third step in knowing ourselves is somewhat more difficult than simply identifying our prejudices and predispositions. It involves discovering the kind of image we portray to the rest of the world. Ask yourself, "How do I communicate and how do others perceive me?" If you perceive yourself in one way, and the people with whom you interact perceive you in another way, serious problem can arise. We have all heard stories of how foreigners view Americans traveling abroad. The "Ugly American" example might be old and trite, but our experiences continue to reinforce its truth. If we are to improve our communication, we must, therefore, have some idea of how we present ourselves. If, for instance, you see yourself as patient and calm, but you appear rushed and anxious, you will have a hard time understanding why people respond to you as they do. As we have noted elsewhere, our most taken-for-granted behaviors are often hidden from consciousness.

Passage 2

World View and Intercultural Communication

A Nigerian student attending a major university spoke to his faculty advisor about a scene he had witnessed in his home country. Many onlookers, including the Nigerian student, observed a demonstration where one person allegedly brought a razor-sharp sword down upon the arm of another person wearing a special charm, but the person wearing the charm suffered no harm. The student then described the amulet and the secrets connected with this cultural phenomenon.

This student was reflecting on one of the most fundamental dimensions underlying a culture, called cultural world view. World view is a belief system about the nature of the universe, its perceived effect on human behavior, and one's place in the universe. World view is a fundamental core set of assumptions explaining cultural forces, the nature of humankind, the nature of good and evil, luck, fate, spirits, the power of significant others, the role of time, and the nature of our physical and natural resources. Because it is so fundamental, word view affects communication encounters and perceptions of difference.

A holistic interpretation of this definition implies a culture's belief regarding various forces associated with daily events and rituals. For instance, many tribal Kenyans believe that disease is the result of evil spirits. Some Latin Americans believe wealth comes from a pact with the devil or possibly luck in finding buried treasure. The Nigerian discussed previously believed in what is called "ju-ju" in West Africa. Voodoo and the evil eye are well-known belief systems in Caribbean cultures. In another example, a middle-school teacher working among a group of economically disadvantaged students faces examples of fatalism in communication with such language as "Why, try?" and "No one else will let me." Our interactions may be less than perfect for a number of reasons, but differences in world view intervene as one cause of misunderstanding in intercultural communication.

Elements of Cultural World View

By examining some of the typical concepts by which cultures influence their worlds, we have assembled a category system with which to assess some fundamental belief structures of a group of people. A knowledge of those belief structures can improve intercultural communication. These cultural world view continuums involve shame and guilt cultures, task and people cultures, spirit and secular cultures, the role of ancestors and the dead, nature of humankind, humans and nature, doing and being cultures, life cycle, fatalism, animism, and shamanism.

Personal World View Influencing Communication

Scholarly interest in recent years has turned toward how individuals internalize their beliefs about world-view-type issues and the influence of any personal application of world view has on communication. The term applied to this question is personal communication world view (or acronym PCWV), defined as how much control a person believes characterizes his or her communication encounter. The fundamental theory of PCWV posits that individuals organize a communication construct about themselves and others that reflects fundamental beliefs about perceived control within communication contexts. Consequently, one end of the PCWV continuum relates to helplessness, powerlessness, external locus of control, lack of initiative, and fatalism, while the opposite is true for the other end of the continuum.

The research connecting personal world view to intercultural communication holds far-reaching implications. First, this construct appears to influence values. Second, PCWV explains specific communication qualities such as openness, relationship initiative and assertiveness, innovativeness, high self-worth, organizational cooperation, cognitive complexity, and opinion leadership. Since these communication qualities are also associated with intercultural communication competencies, the concept appears very useful in understanding intercultural communication encounters.

Notes

intercultural communication	跨文化交际	international communication	跨国交流
interethnic communication	跨人种交流	interracial communication	跨种族交流
interregional communication	跨区域交流		

Encounter Tips

◎   交际的过程是人们运用语言知识和社会文化知识传递信息的过程，所以学习语言与了解语言所反映的文化背景知识是分不开的。了解英语文化知识，有助于交际畅通，反之，缺乏英语文化背景知识必然导致交际障碍、冲突和误解。

◎   在跨文化交际中，我们既不能用自卑的态度，也不能用自大的态度去面对异域文化，自卑会使彻底的文化开放呼声有市场，而自大会使文化保护主义有呼应。

◎ 中国哲学思维偏好运用直觉体验的方式去获取和传达涵盖力极强、极灵活、为认识主体留有极大领悟空间的认知成果。西方的哲学思维则希望通过严密的逻辑推理去获得和传递精确、可靠、稳定的知识，因而它注重规则的缜密，力求避免认识主体理解和阐释对象的任意性，重视认识的客观性与同一性。

1.3 Exercises

1.3.1 Exercise A

Decide whether the following statements are true or false.

(1) Culture shock is the term used to describe the strong reactions that many people undergo when spending an extended period of time in a culture that is very similar to their own.

(2) An awareness of one's own culture can help one to improve his/her intercultural communication.

(3) Culture can be learned through proverbs, folktales, legends, myths, mass media, and so on.

(4) Learning to understand people whose background is different from your own is an easy assignment.

(5) Culture strongly influences your beliefs, values, and world views. But it can't shape your relationships with your family and friends.

(6) Our own native language and culture are so much a part of us that we take them for granted.

(7) Everyone has a unique style of communication, but cultures determine a general style for their members.

(8) In fact people mean just the same things when they talk about the culture. All researchers agree that culture refers to beliefs, norms, and attitudes that are used to guide our behaviors and to solve human problems.

(9) Concepts of dress, time, language, manners, nonverbal behavior, and control of the communication ebb and flow can differ significantly among cultures.

(10) Culture is like an iceberg, and only some of the culture is visible.

1.3.2 Exercise B

We have learned some characteristics of culture. For example, culture is learned through proverbs. Discuss what value(s) the following proverbs represent.
Proverbs:

(1) A man's home is his castle.

(2) Time is money.

(3) Nothing is impossible to a willing heart.

(4) When in Rome, do as the Romans do.

(5) A bad workman quarrels with his tools.

(6) Haste makes waste.

(7) A bird is known by its note; and a man by his talk.

(8) Actions speak louder than words.

(9) The voice of one man is the voice of no one.

(10) Modesty makes you progress; conceitedness makes you lag behind.

(11) God helps those who help themselves.

(12) Sweet are the uses of adversity.

1.3.3 Exercise C

Discuss the following questions.

(1) Discuss the characteristics of the culture.

(2) Discuss the culture shock.

(3) Discuss elements affecting intercultural communication.

1.3.4 Exercise D

Read the following case and point out the mistakes Zhou actually made here.

When Zhou first started going to the supermarket nearby, he was pleased that he was finding his way around and being a little more independent. He often noticed, however, that people looked strangely at him, usually in annoyance. Sometimes people muttered words at him that he knew were not particularly nice.

He spoke to his friend Kim and asked her to go with him the next time and to see for herself what he was talking about.

At the end of the shopping, Kim suggested that they both go to have some tea at a nearby shop. With Zhou's shopping bags stacked up on the chair, Kim began to explain.

"There were some things, Zhou, which I did notice, caused some people to be annoyed," Kim looked kindly at Zhou.

"But what? I don't understand," responded Zhou. "I do everything that I do back home. Nothing is very different," Zhou said in exasperation.

"Well, I think that there are a few cultural differences that you have to get used to," Kim went on to explain.

"Such as?"

Kim began to gently tell Zhou the things that he had observed while they were shopping.

…

1.3.5 Exercise E

Read the following case, and discuss the questions.

Xin Yu had been studying at a large well-known university overseas for seven years. He had settled into a sound routine of hard work and spent almost all of his time revising, researching and improving his English writing.

In particular, he had a special effort with his first term essay. He had carefully researched the topic, finding several excellent books in the library. His first draft had been completed with great difficulty but he had preserved and re-written the essay, ensuring that the material was relevant and that the language was the best he could write. He asked a friend to revise it for him and was pleased that he had handed it in before time.

Upon receiving the essay back from lecturer, he was very disappointed not only with the C+ mark but with the marker's comments, "This is a satisfactory first attempt but it lacks originality. In fact it borders on repetition of the actual authors' work—in that sense it is close to plagiarism. Please see me as soon as possible."

Xin Yu was horrified and worried. So much effort, so many books, and now he was summoned to meet the lecturer. He could not understand what the problem was.

(1) What advice do you think the lecturer gave to Xin Yu?

(2) What points do you think Xin Yu talked about to his lecturer in regard to his essay?

Chapter 1 Keys

CHAPTER 2

Cultural Differences in Daily Interactivities

When in Rome, do as the Romans do.

—English Proverb

One man's meat is another man's poison.

—English Proverb

2.1　Greeting

2.1.1　Pre-reading

An American studying in China had an appointment at noon. As he was getting on his bicycle, a Chinese friend passed by. "吃了吗？" the young Chinese asked. This, of course, is a common Chinese greeting around meal time and the American merely nodded with a smile, waved goodbye and went off. Actually, another foreign student who had not been long in China once complained in broken Chinese "你们为什么老问我吃饭了没有？我有钱。" In his opinion, people were concerned that he was not getting his meals properly because of lack of money. Clearly, he was offended. There is a similar Chinese greeting, for example, "上哪儿去啊？" or "到哪儿去啦？" which if translated literally, would be "Where are you going?" or "Where have you been?" The natural reaction of most English-speaking people to this greeting would most likely be "It's none of your business!"

中国人见面打招呼时，喜欢问"你吃了吗？""你去哪呀？"而西方人对此都感到很奇怪。再如，汉语中的"上哪儿去啊？"和"到哪儿去啦？"这样打招呼的话直译成英语就是"Where are you going？"和"Where have you been？"用这两句英语来打招呼，大部分以英语为母语的人听了会不高兴，因为他认为你想打听他的隐私。隐私在

西方社会中受法律保护，任何人都无权干预或打听。而在这一点上中国文化正好与西方文化相反，见面时了解或询问个人或家庭情况是出于对对方的关心，也是增进人际关系最有效的沟通方式。在中国，同事、朋友之间，彼此相互了解各自的家庭、个人、学习及工作情况，见面时询问各自的家庭情况，以建立友谊、融洽关系。而在美国，同事、朋友之间互不了解，人们从不询问或打听他人的隐私，因为这是不礼貌的行为。

2.1.2　Greeting Carefully When in Different Cultures

Greeting is one of the important parts in our daily life. It is something polite or friendly that you say or do when you meet someone, in which human beings intentionally make their presence known to each other, to show attention to, and to suggest a type of relationship or social status between individuals or groups of people coming in contact with each other. They exist in all known human cultures.

Why people exchange greetings is roughly similar in different cultures. That is to establish or maintain the social relationship. So greetings have no function of transferring information. They only have phatic functions.

The words people use to greet each other are quite different from culture to culture. In English, "How are you?" "How are you doing?" "How are things?" "How are things going?" "How are things with you?" "How's everything?" "How's life?" are common greetings. They are not questions, but just greetings. So response is "Very well, thank you. And what about you?" And "Very well" can be replaced by "Fine/Fantastic/Terrific/Superb/Great." Other common greeting in English are, for instance, "Nice to meet you!" "Good morning/afternoon/evening!" "Pleased to meet/see you!" "Glad to meet/see you!" "My pleasure to meet/see you!" "My great honor to meet/see you!" "Hello!" "Hi!" For the above greeting, your responses can be the same, for example, "Nice to meet you, too!" "Good morning!"

Chinese, like all languages, has its own set of unique greetings which may be seemingly strange to learners from different cultures. This is particularly true if the two cultures are vastly different. In China when you meet someone for the first time, the most commonly used words are: "你好！" "很高兴认识你！" "幸会！" For greeting acquaintances, the words will be more informal and friendly like the following: "吃过了吗？" "上哪儿去？" "出去呀？" "干什么去呀？" "好久不见，近来怎么样？还好吧？" "忙什么呢？" "最近如何？" "最近身体怎么样？" "家人都好吧？" "上班去吗？" "最近工作顺利吗？" "出去了？" These greetings can't be understood according to their literalness. They are just phatic communion, not questions. So responses either "吃过了" or "还没呢" are just OK. It has no matter with the real fact whether the replier "has their meal" or not. Equally, ambiguous responses, for example, "没上哪儿" "就前面，" are suitable for "上哪儿去？" "去哪儿呀？" in Chinese. But the natural response of most Westerners to such kind of greetings would be: "It's none of your business!" or "That's my privacy!"

Greetings can be expressed both audibly and physically, and often involve a combination of the two. Along with words, many Western countries accept hugs and kisses as a popular form of greeting although a handshake is still the formal way of greeting people. In China, a handshake is considered to be the standard greeting. Instead of shaking hands very firmly, Chinese usually prefer to shake hands very lightly. Maybe in China the most useful form of greeting gesture is a nod or a slight bow. Additionally, you might also see Chinese people lowering their eyes a little when they meet people. This is considered a symbol of respect as staring into the eyes might make some people feel uncomfortable.

Greetings are often used just prior to a conversation, though not always. Topics after greetings will dominate whether communication goes well or not. Generally speaking, it is regarded as impolite and impertinent in Western culture to ask people about their age, salary, marital status, health status, religious faith, personal experience, and so on. These sensitive topics are counted as invasion of one's privacy. Western ideas of privacy are somewhat different from those of the Chinese. They have a very strong sense of privacy. They are easily offended by comments which seem to invade their personal life. So it is appropriate for Chinese to avoid questions like:

How old are you?

How tall are you?

Do you have a girlfriend/boyfriend?

Are you married?

How many children do you have?

Where is your husband or wife?

How much do you earn?

How much did you pay for…?

What is your religion?

Where are you going?

Where have you been?

Have you had your dinner?

Who are you going to vote for?

There are many topics that are acceptable to both Westerners and Chinese, such as the following:

Weather;

Hobbies;

Jobs;

Holidays;

Sports;

Travel;

Films/TV serial;

Books/magazines;

Local customs;

Local events.

2.1.3　Case for Practice

Case

You represent Guangzhou Light Industrial Product Import and Export Corporation, and you are assigned to meet an American business person—Ronald Vannburg, marketing manager of wholesaler, Vallery View Company—at the airport. You and Vannburg have never met each other before, so you say greetings, ask him how his flight was and show him to the car.

Now you act this out with another student in the class.

2.1.4　Further Reading

When I first arrived in my village in the Dominican Republic, I began to have a problem with my morning jogging routine. I used to jog every day when I was at home in the United States, so when I arrived in my village in the Dominican Republic, I set myself a goal to continue jogging two miles every morning.

I really liked the peaceful feeling of jogging alone as the sun came up. But this did not last for long. The people in my village simply couldn't understand why someone would want to run alone. Soon people began to appear at their doorways offering me a cup of coffee; others would invite me to stop in for a visit. Sometimes this would happen four or five times as I tried to continue jogging. They even began sending their children to run behind me so I wouldn't be lonely. They were unable to understand the American custom of exercising alone.

I was faced with a dilemma. I really enjoyed my early morning runs. However, I soon realized that it's considered impolite in Dominican villages not to accept a cup of coffee, or stop and chat, when you pass people who are sitting on their front steps. I didn't want to give up jogging. But, at the same time, I wanted to show respect for the customs of the Dominican Republic and not to be viewed as odd or strange.

The dilemma faced by the jogger is a classic case of how to balance personal preferences and the US-style individuality with the social expectations of local people in a strongly collectivist society. Although the jogger does not recount how the issue was finally resolved, the fact that some hard choices needed to be made involving seemingly diametrically opposed values and behaviors is a typical scenario and frequently encountered by students while abroad.

Another example would be an ill American student on a home stay in India wanting the privacy of staying in his or her own room with the door closed, while the family insists on putting him or her in the living room on a couch so the student will not feel "isolated" and everyone in the family can "help" him or her. What is meant to be kindness and a show of concern for the welfare of a guest on the part of the Indian family might be excruciatingly difficult for an American who wants nothing more than to be left alone in private.

Before one goes abroad, it is very useful to know not only how strongly a particular culture may stress collectivism, but also how strong your own preferences are for individualism or collectivism. If you have a marked preference for individualism, then going to a highly collectivist community may take some serious adjustment. If you tend to be more comfortable with collectivist values, you may fit easily into a culture that exhibits such behavior, but feel somewhat out-of-place in a society that is strongly individualistic.

This tendency to stress either individuality or a more collective response is one of the most widely distributed traits around the world. Not every culture is at one end or the other of the spectrum, but the majority tends to favor one over the other in everyday life. Knowing about the basis of this Collectivism versus Individualism construct will help you to recognize, understand, and anticipate attitudes in different types of cultures.

Individualist

The individual identifies primarily with self, with the needs of the individual being satisfied before those of the group. Looking after and taking care of oneself, being self-sufficient, guarantees the well-being of the group. Independence and self-reliance are greatly stressed and valued. In general, people tend to distance themselves psychologically and emotionally from each other. One may choose to join groups, but group membership is not essential to one's identity or success. Individualist characteristics are often associated with men and people in urban settings.

Collectivist

One's identity is, in large part, a function of one's membership and role in a group, e.g., the family or work team. The survival and success of the group ensures the well-being of the individual, so that by considering the needs and feelings of others, one protects oneself. Harmony and the interdependence of group members are stressed and valued. Group members are relatively close psychologically and emotionally, but distant toward non-group members. Collectivist characteristics are often associated with women and people in rural settings.

Notes

dilemma	两难的局面；困境	odd	奇怪；古怪
diametrically	完全地；全然地	scenario	电影剧本；剧情概要
excruciatingly	剧烈地；极其地	out-of-place	无所适从；格格不入
spectrum	光谱；领域；范围	rivalry	敌对；竞争
affiliation	加盟；入会；联营	consensus	一致；全体意见
potluck dinner	便饭		

Encounter Tips

◎　英美人士初次见面习惯谈论天气、运动、旅游、娱乐、食物、语言特点等。初次见面务必回避敏感话题如宗教、政治、财产、价格、年龄等，除非对话双方已认识很久。

◎　道别时，现在的欧美人士已经较少使用 Good-bye，因为在古英语里，这表示 "God be with you." 听起来像永别，所以现在的欧美人士常用的是 Bye, See ya, Catch ya later 等。Ya, 你，在现在的欧美口语里，是 You 的弱读，很流行，如将 "How are you doing？" 读为 "How are ya doing？"

◎　Howdy，你好，原来是美国西部牛仔 cowboy 的口头禅，现在美国很常用，尤其是现代年轻美国人，由 how do you do 变化而来。

2.2　Addressing

2.2.1　Pre-reading

Linda White taught English at a primary school in China. This is her first time to live in China. When she came into her office for the first time, she introduced herself,

"My name is Linda White. If you like, you can call me 'Linda'." Then one of her new colleagues introduced himself, "My name is Zhou Yang (周洋). Call me Zhou Yang." Linda looked confused. She didn't know which one the family name was, "Zhou" or "Yang," and she didn't know why she should use the whole name to call her new colleague.

在这个案例中 Zhou Yang 的名字让 Linda 感到困惑，原因一是在中国人和英语国家人的姓名里，姓和名的排列顺序不一样，中国人姓在前，名在后，英语国家的人刚好相反，如上述例子中的英语姓名 Linda White, Linda 是名，White 是姓，而中文名 Zhou Yang 里，Zhou 是姓，Yang 是名；原因二是从发音上看 Zhou 和 Yang 在中文里都可以用作姓，而且中国人取名没有固定模式，只要是字典里有的字基本都可以用作人名（除了忌讳、有明显贬义的字）；原因三是在英语国家里，人们通常可以直呼对方的名字，而在中国只有对同辈、小辈、职位比你低且较熟悉的人才可以直呼其名。

称谓是指人们在交际中以某种语言形式称呼对方，它既是一种语言现象，也是一种社会文化现象。在任何语言中，称谓语都担当着重要的社交礼仪作用。由于文化背景不同，中英称谓存在着种种差异，它们分别属于不同的称谓体系，具有不同的称谓习惯和泛化现象，更蕴含了不同的文化习俗。

2.2.2 Ways of Address

Address form is one of markers of politeness and is an indispensable part of communication. An appropriate address form promotes interpersonal communication smoothly. An address form is polite in one culture, but might be inappropriate in another culture. Address forms reflect the features of a language culture. People from different countries and cultures have specific ways of addressing and greeting others when making new acquaintances. Not knowing how to address someone properly can be a very embarrassing situation for both parties. Generally speaking, English address forms are less complicated than Chinese address terms. For instance, we can not translate Chinese forms Xiao Li and Lao Zhang literally into "Little Brown" and "Old Jones."

In recent years, the trend of many English-speaking people has been to address others by using the first name—Tom, Michael, Linda, Jane, etc. rather than calling the person Mr. Summers, Mrs. Howard or Miss Jones. This is especially common among Americans, even when people meet for the first time. This applies not only to people of roughly the same age, but also of different ages. It is not a sign of disrespect. It is not at all uncommon to hear a child calling a much older person— Joe, Ben, May, Helen, etc. This may even include the child's parents or grandparents. People of different social status do the same. For example, many college students call their professors by their first names. The professors do not regard this as a sign of disrespect or familiarity, but rather, as an indication that the professor is affable and has a sense of equality. This, of course, is quite opposite to Chinese custom. One can imagine the reactions of adults if a child were to call a grandparent by his or her first name, or a student did the same in calling a teacher, which will be considered impolite in Chinese culture.

In China, we usually address a stranger, even an acquaintance, with some titles, such as "大爷"(grandpa), "大妈"(grandma), "大叔"(uncle), "大婶"(aunty). The extension of kinship terms is a feature of Chinese culture. Terms such as uncle, aunt, grandpa, granny, sister, and brother are used as honorific titles for senior people or strangers. Native speakers of English would be puzzled if they are addressed in this way by people outside the immediate family. Literary translation of those terms may sound odd to English-speaking people. Even with relatives, English-speaking people tend to only use the first name and leave out the terms of relationship.

Some people may say that there is Brother Joseph or Sister Mary in English; however, these terms would commonly be understood as referring to persons belonging to a catholic group or some religious or professional society. In America, people usually use "Hi," or "Could you tell me…?" to address a stranger. And if there is a difference in status or age between two individuals, formal titles and last names are used unless the person of lower status is told to use the first name. For example:

Accountant (age 50): Hello, my name is Bob Thomas.

Clerk (age 20): It's nice to meet you, Mr. Thomas.

Accountant: Please, just call me Bob.

And also the kinship terms for both the paternal and maternal sides in Chinese culture are different. However, the English kinship terms, such as uncle, cousin, aunt, grandpa and grandma have no difference between paternal and maternal sides. As shown in the following examples:

Chinese Terms	English Terms
奶奶、姥姥	grandma
爷爷、外公	grandpa
公公、岳父	father-in-law
婆婆、岳母	mother-in-law
伯父、叔叔、舅舅	uncle
姑妈、姨妈、伯母、舅妈	aunt
堂兄弟（姊妹）、表兄弟（姊妹）	cousin
小叔子、小舅子	brother-in-low
小姑子、小姨子	sister-in-low
侄儿、外甥	nephew
侄女、外甥女	niece

In Chinese, address forms are oriented by generation, age, paternal and maternal relationship, and in-law relationship. In a Chinese family, a younger child should address the elder as elder brother（哥哥）or elder sister（姐姐）instead of names in English culture, otherwise, a younger child addressing old sisters' or brothers' names will be considered impolite and might be punished or scolded. In English-speaking culture, sisters and brothers address each other's name. People address their neighbors, friends, and colleagues by their name after the introduction was over.

It is also quite common for the Chinese to use position-linked or occupation-linked titles to address people, such as " 王经理 "(Manager Wang), " 张主任 "(Director Zhang), " 马组长 "(Director General Ma). In more formal situations, the title along with the last name is appropriate.

Americans have only a limited number of titles to be used before a person's last name—Doctor, Professor, Judge, President, Senator, Governor, Mayor, General, Colonel, Captain, Father, etc. Terms like teacher, manager and director are occupations or positions. In English, only a few occupations or titles would be used: Doctor Smith is common for those who have qualified in the medical profession, and Judge Smith for those authorized to try cases in law courts; Governor Smith and Mayor Smith may be used for those who hold such offices, although often without the name. The same with Professor Smith. However, there are very few others.

As a result, no wonder Americans are surprised to see that it is important to clearly indicate their positions in their company at a business meeting, because we Chinese always treat them differently according to their ranks and status!

English translations of Chinese works usually keep such forms as grandpa, auntie, sister-in-law, but they sound strange to the English ear. In English-language writings about China, such terms are used in order to keep or give a Chinese flavor to the story. Some of these terms, though, are especially troublesome. How to address a teacher has long been a problem. Should it be Teacher or Teacher Zhang? Neither of these is keeping with the English custom. Should we say Comrade or Comrade Li, which is not widely accepted in non-socialist countries? Or should we simply follow the English custom and call the teacher Mr. Zhang, Mrs. Yang? All of these would sound terrible to Chinese if school-age youngsters were to do so.

Other different terms are " 师傅 " " 警察叔叔 " " 解放军叔叔 ." If we translate the former one into "master," it would carry the meaning of a master-servant relationship. If we translate " 警察叔叔 " and " 解放军叔叔 " into "Uncle Policeman" and "Uncle P.L.A." respectively, they would sound very strange to the Westerners. There are two reasons. One reason is that many foreigners do not know, P.L.A. stands for " 中国人民解放军 "; the other reason is that the relationship between policeman, P.L.A. and people is closer in China than that in Western countries. The Westerners do not know why people call them uncles.

Interestingly, there is no general term in English for getting the attention of a stranger, or of a person whose name we may not know. In Chinese we have "同志" or "师傅 ," and now the fashionable " 小姐 " or " 先生 ," but what do people do in English if such a need arises? Depending on the situation, English customs might suggest using such expressions as "excuse me" "pardon me," or in England, "I say there." Expressions like "Hey," or "Hey you" or "You," are used, but are not considered polite. Often, people resort to a way that needs no language. They simply clear their throat loudly, or make some noise or gesture to attract the person's attention.

2.2.3　Case for Practice

Case

It was the first day that Linda White had her English class. At her class, she told her students, "My name is Linda White. If you like, you can call me 'Linda'. Now I'd like you to tell me your names. Let's start with you." Then the first student answered, "Yes, 'Teacher.' Let me introduce myself. My name is Zhang Nianci."

Linda told her student, "Well, please don't call me 'Teacher.' You can use 'Linda' or 'Ms. Jones.' " The student looked confused.

(1) Why did Linda White ask her students call her "Linda" or "Ms. Jones," but not "Teacher"?

(2) Why did Zhang Nianci look confused?

2.2.4　Further Reading

Difference in Power and Rank

Every society has hierarchy to some degree. In other words, some people have higher rank and more power than others, perhaps they are older, stronger, wealthier, or have some kind of official position. On the other hand, however, most modern societies also believe that equality is a virtue, at least to some extent. So each culture needs to find its own balance between hierarchy and equality.

While there are certainly differences in rank and power in the West, on the whole, individualist Western cultures tend to be relatively egalitarian. In other words, they try to minimize rank and power differences, and try to place limits on the power of people in authority. This can be seen in a variety of ways:

(1) Westerners generally have less respect for seniority—age, position, and so forth—than people in a collectivist culture do.

(2) Western societies often try to limit the power of government officials. One example of this is the structure of the US government, which was designed specifically to limit the power of each branch of government and prevent it from being too powerful.

(3) Westerners tend to have somewhat suspicious and even negative view of power and authority. This can be seen, for example, in the way Westerners view politicians and political leaders, who are often subject to a great deal of criticism and even outright insult from the people they govern. In English, the word "politician" even has somewhat negative connotation.

Furthermore, Western cultures try to de-emphasize differences in rank and power by creating as much appearance of equality as possible. For example, in American companies there are always differences in position and power, but the American cultural norm is trying to interact as much as possible as if there were no such differences. So, for example, the culture in many US organizations would be for people to address each other by first names, thus minimizing the appearance of rank differences. Also, a boss is generally more liked by employees if he or she acts like "one of the guys" and doesn't "pull rank" too often.

Some Western cultures emphasize egalitarianism more than others. For example, American culture tends to be more egalitarian than British culture. Likewise, Australian culture tends to be more egalitarian than American culture. Also, within any given country, some groups may be more egalitarian than others. For example, within American culture, belief in egalitarianism is stronger within the middle classes than it is in the upper (wealthier) classes.

It is also important to note that "equality" can mean different things in different Western countries. For example, in the US culture, "equality" almost always means "equality of opportunity", not equal wealth. Americans tend to believe that, as much as possible, all people should be given an equal chance, but then people deserve whatever rewards they work for. Americans thus tend to be willing to accept large differences in wealth between the poor and the rich as long as they believe these result from differences in effort and talent.

In contract, Western Europeans, especially Scandinavians, tend to feel that equality of opportunity alone will not guarantee social or material equality. They point out that some people naturally have advantages over others, for example, because they are born with healthy bodies or good minds, or because they grow up in a good environment. So these cultures place more emphasis on material equality, and their tax and social welfare systems are designed to ensure that the difference in wealth between citizens is not large.

Notes

roughly	大概；大约	social status	社会阶层
affable	和蔼可亲	minimize	最小化

Encounter Tips

◎ 称谓一般分为亲属称谓和社交称谓。亲属称谓是指对亲属成员的称呼。社交称谓是指对非亲属成员的称呼。在许多国家，部分亲属称谓又可用来称呼非亲属成员。

◎ 汉语社交称谓中有一个很大的特点就是"老"化称呼，如"老人家、老大爷、老先生、老大娘、老前辈、老伴、老公、老婆、老手、老板、老表、老师、张老、老李"，等等。连外国人也是"老外"，似乎"老"字称呼无处不在。而在英语文化中，则忌讳"老"字，因为"老"意味着"old, useless"，"保守、无用、失去活力和创造力"，等等。西方人不崇尚老，而是崇尚年轻活力。

◎ 在英语中，头衔性称谓对象一般只局限于皇族、政府上层、宗教界、军界或法律界人士，它可以是衔称＋姓氏，也可以是衔称＋教名，如 Queen Mary, President Bush, Father White, Colonel Quail, Judge Harley，等等。而且，这种称谓面称时还可以使用"Mr. 或 Madam ＋衔称"的形式，如 Mr. President, Mr. Judge, Mr. Ambassador，等等。

2.3　Visiting

2.3.1　Pre-reading

Alice has a English teacher named Ms. Merrick. Several times on campus, Alice has seen Ms. Merrick and chatted with her. At the end of conversations, Ms. Merrick often says "Come over and visit me sometime." So, one evening Alice decided to go and visit.

When Alice found Ms. Merrick's apartment, she knocked on the door. After a moment, Ms. Merrick opened the door, but she didn't look very happy to see Alice. Instead of inviting Alice in, she said, "Can I do something for you?"

案例中 Alice 交际失败的原因有两个：一是 Alice 未与 Ms. Merrick 约好，就贸然拜访，引起了 Ms. Merrick 的反感；二是 Alice 没有明白 Ms. Merrick 的邀请只是客套邀请 (polite invitation)，而不是正式邀请 (real invitation)，正式邀请一般要有内容、地点、时间、请求答复。例如，I would like to invite you over for my birthday party (内容) at my house (地点) at 7 next Saturday evening (时间). Can you come? (请求答复)

在日常生活中，人们为了增进感情或加强友谊，往往相互走访探望，因此拜访是人际交往中最常见的社交形式。由于文化背景不同，不同的国家、地区、民族之间的拜访礼节存在许多差异。

2.3.2　Different Countries Have Different Visiting Courtesy

Before visiting, the Westerners prefer to arrange the time in advance. Making an appointment in advance is the basic politeness rule in Western countries. Generally, the Westerners are accustomed to do one thing at a time and may be uncomfortable when an activity is interrupted. They are used to organizing and arranging their time. Visitors who "drop by" without prior notice may interrupt their host's personal time. Casual visiting is usually regarded as impolite. Thus, making an appointment before visiting him or her is generally preferred to a "dropping by." So to accommodate other people's schedules, the Westerners make business and social engagements several days or weeks in advance.

The language used to make a request of visiting should also be paid attention to. The following are some suitable expressions:

(1) Mr. White and I would like to come and visit you. Would it be convenient for us to come on next Friday evening?

(2) There's something I'd like to talk over with you. I wonder if it would be convenient to meet you this Friday afternoon.

(3) Shall we discuss the matter at 10 tomorrow morning? If not, please ring me to make another time—many thanks.

(4) Could we see each other for about an hour on Friday afternoon at three o'clock?

(5) I'm in town for a few days and would very much like to come and visit you at your house. Would it be convenient if I call on you this evening?

(6) I haven't seen you for a long time. I was wondering whether I could come round to visit you sometime.

After receiving an invitation, unequivocal reply should be given. The Western custom is much stricter than Chinese custom in the matter of replying to invitations. When you receive an invitation you should answer it immediately, saying definitely whether you are able to accept it or not. If the invitation is given by word of mouth, in conversation or at a chance meeting, you should answer at once whether you can come or not. If you cannot give an answer at that time, you may say, "May I let you know this evening?" or some such words. Reply, like "I'll try to come." will cause to be perplexed or confounded.

When visiting, the most important thing is punctuality. Visitors must arrive at the meeting place according to the given time. Otherwise, the Westerners may feel slighted and get unhappy. If someone is unable to keep the appointment or wants to change the appointment because of some reasons, he or she must notify the other party in advance and make an apology. Generally twenty four hours' notice is the absolute most polite time frame for cancellation of visiting without complaint.

During visiting, the Westerners often put things with them (such as out-door clothing, raingear) at the pointed place, sit down at the pointed sofa or chair. Then the host may offer something to drink like tea or coffee. They may take counsel with visitor like:

(1) How about a cup of tea?

(2) Would you like a cup of tea?

(3) Would you like some coffee?

(4) Would you like something to drink?

(5) Tea or coffee? Or something cold?

The responses can usually be "Yes, please." "Tea, please." "No. Thank you." The visitor is expected to answer honestly, and if they say no, the host will not offer them any. Generally, the host doesn't repeat the offer more than once. If the visitors accept, they will be given a cup and expected to drink it all. Westerners tend to relate the meal size more accurately to the people's appetites; both the quantity and variety of the meal are far less than that in China. According to Western custom, "seeing the bottom" of all plates is the ideal ending to a meal, for it means that the guest has thoroughly enjoyed the meal. In the Westerner's opinion, it is bad manners to leave drinks in one's own cup or to leave food in one's own plate, and it may offend the host.

Chinese hospitality is extremely different when involving food. Chinese host usually prepares a sumptuous meal. Moreover, every time the visitor had nearly finished a dish, they replenished it from the kitchen. In China "seeing the bottom" of a dish is a sign that the hosts have not prepared enough. They keep putting the best pieces of food on visitor's plate despite the fact the visitor may not like certain food, or they have had enough. This usually makes the Westerners feel very embarrassed. According to their culture they should finish eating all food on their plate. But the more they eat, the more they are given.

At the end of visiting, parting may be a difficult task in any culture. Two things often cause to be perplexed—"how long it is appropriate to stay" and "what it is appropriate to say."

After an hour or so of general chit-chat, it's probably time to head for the door. In Western culture, it is impolite to leave impulsively. Before leaving, visitors usually say something to imply preparing for leaving, but no immediate move to depart is actually made. At the same time the host may say something to urge the visitor to stay. Both continue their conversation or other shared activity for a while longer; this delay may last a couple of minutes.

The appropriate parting expressions in English like:

(1) We have to say good-bye now. We enjoyed the evening very much. Thanks a lot.

(2) I think I'd better be leaving now. It's very nice to have a talk with you.

(3) Well, it's been lovely to see you, but I must be going soon. I hope we'll be able to get together again before long.

(4) Thank you for a lovely afternoon, but I think it's time for me to leave now.

(5) I've very much enjoyed this afternoon. I'm afraid I must be going now.

The appropriate responses to parting expressions:

(1) Can't you stay any/a little/longer?

(2) Must you really be going?

(3) Do you really want to go?

(4) So soon? Can't you stay a little longer?

(5) Must you? It's still early.

To contrast to the Western culture, in China visitors often stand up suddenly and say, "得走了，我还有要紧的事" or "对不起，浪费您这么多时间，我该走了," which seems quite abrupt, even impolite to the Westerners. At the mention of parting expressions, Chinese have its unique ones like: "请留步""不要远送了." The host may say "请慢走""请走好""注意脚下""有空再来."All of these can't be translated into English literally. According to Chinese culture, the host and the visitor exit from the door together and continue walking some distance while continuing to converse. The distance to which the host accompanies a guest is an indication of the esteem in which he or she is held. It is not uncommon for a host to accompany the guest down several flights of stairs and out of the building, or even to the bus stop before saying the final good-bye. As a general rule, Chinese prefer not to go back until the visitor is out of sight.

2.3.4 Case for Practice

Case 1

Jane, an American teacher, had just started teaching English to a group of Japanese students in the US. She wanted to get to know the students more informally, so she invited them to her house for a party. The students arrived together at exactly 8:00 pm They seemed to enjoy the party: They danced, sang, and ate most of the food. At about 10:00 pm, one of the students said to the teacher, "I think it's time for me to leave. Thank you very much for the party." Then all the students stood up and left at the same time. Jane decided she would never invite them again.

(1) Why did the Japanese students leave together at the same time?

(2) How did the American teacher feel when all the students stood up and left at the same time?

(3) Why did Jane decide never to invite the students to her house again?

(4) What's the difference between the US and Japan in the notion of time?

Case 2

Tom, an American, went to a Chinese home for the first time. He was offered some tea. Just when the first cup was about to finish, more tea was added. He drank the second cup. Then the cup was filled the third time. Then he drank it, then… until he was quite full. Tom was totally confused by the way of entertaining.

(1) Why was Tom totally confused?

(2) What's the difference between America and China in entertainment?

(3) What reasons do you think caused the misunderstanding? Can you give any advice to help them avoid similar misunderstandings in the future?

2.3.5 Further Reading

Projected Cultural Similarity

One problem in intercultural communication is a phenomenon called "projected cultural similarity." This is the tendency to assume that people from other cultures basically think and feel more or less the same as we do. In other words, we sometimes assume that while foreigners may look different, dress differently, and speak different languages, inside we are all more or less the same.

Imagine, for example, the following situation:

Xiao Wang works for a Chinese company, and she has been given the responsibility of making arrangements to host Mr. Smith, a Westerner who will visit Xiao Wang's company for a week. As Xiao Wang makes plans to host Mr. Smith, she assumes she would treat him the same way she would want to be hosted. She knows if she were abroad, she would feel more welcomed if her host treated her to good meals. So she decides to arrange all the meals for Mr. Smith—and to make sure that there is plenty of food at every meal.

When Mr. Smith arrives, he enjoys the banquets, but after two days of banquets he starts getting annoyed. He likes to make decisions about what to eat, at least at some of the time, and doesn't like being served more food than he can eat at every meal. However, he assumes that Xiao Wang should be able to understand how he feels, so instead of asking her to change the meal arrangements, he just quietly becomes more annoyed at her. Meanwhile, Xiao Wang can tell that Mr. Smith is becoming much unhappier, but she doesn't understand why. She also feels that Mr. Smith should feel appreciative of all the efforts she has made for him, so she is unhappy because she thinks he is being ungrateful.

One reason why there are problems between Xiao Wang and Mr. Smith is that they make incorrect assumptions about each other. Xiao Wang mistakenly assumes that Mr. Smith would like having banquets every day. Mr. Smith mistakenly assumes that Xiao Wang should understand why he is not happy.

However, an even more important reason why there are communication problems is that Xiao Wang and Mr. Smith assume they understand each other instead of asking each other what they think. Because they each expect the other person to react more or less the same way they would, they don't check to see whether or not the other person actually has the same feelings and reactions they would. For this reason, the misunderstandings become worse over time rather than get better.

To become an effective intercultural communicator, you need to be aware of this tendency toward "projected cultural similarity." You should look for ways to find out whether or not a foreigner really views things the same way as you do, especially if it seems like there is some kind of miscommunication. When people don't check their assumptions, the result is often misunderstanding. When people are careful about checking their assumptions, many conflicts and misunderstandings can be avoided.

Notes

drop by	顺道拜访	unequivocal	不含糊的；明白的
similarity	类似；类似处	banquet	宴会
ungrateful	没良心的；不感恩的	assumption	假设

Encounter Tips

◎ 与美国人预约，最好提前一周，美国人性情开朗，个人计划较多，拜访前最好再用电话联系确定一下；德国人作风严谨，未经邀请的不速之客，有时会被他们拒之门外；日本人约会的规矩较多，事先联系、先约优先和严守时间是日本人约会的三条基本原则。

◎ 拜访的时间应以不妨碍对方为原则，一定要注意错过吃饭时间，午饭后或临睡前的时间都是不妥当的。一般说来，下午四五点或晚上七八点是最恰当的拜访时间。

◎ 按照英美国家的习惯，主人一般不主动给客人敬烟，并且即使客人自己想抽烟，也应事先征得主人的同意。

◎ 英美国家的人觉得，中国人到他们住处访问时，有时说走就走，给人的感觉是：前一刻还是热热闹闹，过一刻秋风扫过，冷冷清清。他们的习惯是当聊天聊到出现冷场时，客人先提出要走了，这时主人说些挽留客人的客套话，经过一阵"商议"式对话，客人才真正起身告辞。

2.4　Gift-giving

2.4.1　Pre-reading

Mark was in charge of a negotiation team sent to Japan. Upon learning the importance of gift-giving to a successful business relationship in this culture, prior to departure he asked his secretary to wrap these gifts: a clock with the company logo, a leather briefcase, a country ham, and a pen and pencil set marked "made in Japan." His secretary wrapped the gifts attractively in bright red paper and with matching bows and mailed them to his Japanese host. But the result was not as pleasant as he expected.

案例中的美方代表 Mark 对送礼的细节认识不周，以美国送礼的文化观来理解，而事实上两者存在着一定的差异，其结果必定适得其反。首先，从礼物的选择上来看，美国人用于公事上的礼品通常会选择一些价格低廉，且比较实用的小礼品，若礼品上标有受礼人青睐的商标或产地则更能体现送礼人的诚意；而日本人则比较喜欢舶来品，如进口香水、高档的小商品，以及一些名牌的礼品，如 Gucci、Tiffany, 或者是符合个人口味的音乐 CD，这些都会受到日本人的欢迎，日本人最忌讳的就是收到标有"日本制造"的办公文具，这有些不符合日本人的送礼习惯，也必定会引起对方的反感。另外，在礼品的包装上，送给日本人的礼物应有精美的外观包装。美国人喜欢在外包装上使用装饰性的彩带，日本人却不喜欢。

从以上分析中我们可以看出，美日两国文化在送礼这一小小环节上有非常大的差异，双方应学习和掌握对方文化中的一些禁忌和喜好，使送礼真正达到沟通情感、加深情谊的目的。

当然，每个国家都有各自的送礼文化，送礼前需要了解什么场合适合送礼，送什么礼，怎样送礼，送给谁，该说什么话，怎样接受或拒绝礼物，这些将对成功的跨文化交际有很大的帮助。

2.4.2　Gift-giving Etiquette

We can seldom go wrong when we give gifts to others. In general, people love to give and receive gifts. They are remainders of pleasant times and friendship. But each country has its seasons and occasions for giving gifts. Gift-giving in some cultures is an art and is considered as an integral part of building intercultural professional and social relationships. We'd like to pay attention to the careful selection, wrapping of a gift, and presenting it at the proper time and the proper place as well as with the proper manner.

To give the proper gift, one must understand the culture of the receiver. One man's meat can be another man's poison. Giving an inappropriate gift or one that is culturally insensitive can cause serious harm to a relationship—more harm than not giving any gift at all. However, one way to smooth out problems would be to learn about the intercultural gift-giving and gift-receiving rules.

When you're invited to someone's home or a social occasion, regardless of the culture, it is always appropriate to bring some sort of gift for the host or hostess. When giving your gift, you should know the specific superstitions and taboos in the culture. Be aware what gifts are appropriate. Generally speaking, it is better often to bestow several inexpensive, well-thought-out gifts instead of lavish expenditures. Often the best gift is one representative of your country, something crafted only where you are from.

Of course, there are various differences concerning selecting, wrapping and presenting the gifts in various countries. The following text names just some gift-giving etiquette of a few typical countries.

China

General guidelines

Chinese people have their own culture when it comes to giving friends or relatives gifts. It is important to know that giving someone gifts should not be a one-way business. Courtesy requires reciprocity. The person who receives the gift should find a chance in the future to return the same favor by returning a gift of similar value the next time you meet. You can do so simply by either paying a visit with a similar value gift or by inviting the friend out for a meal with you paying the meal. Don't do it right on the next day because it may appear awkward.

Foreigners may find it awkward when your friend says "You don't need to buy anything when you come here," or "Keep it to yourself. I have a lot of these." He may not mean it. What you need to do is to insist on him receiving the gift since Chinese people do not tend to receive the gift immediately.

Don't mind it if he doesn't open your present immediately too. Chinese people would think opening the present in front of you would be impolite and so they would tend to put it aside and only open it after you have left.

Appreciated gifts

When it is a new-born baby, usually jade or silver bracelet or necklace would be good, particularly ones which can make the clinging sound so it will make some sound when the baby moves. Alternatively, some children's clothes, shoes or gloves would be good, too. When it is an older child, some toys or stationary would be good.

When it comes to some old people, something practical should be considered. A walking-stick, some valuable food such as birds' nests or Chinese mushrooms would be highly welcome. For those who go to visit their prospective parents-in-law, something more valuable would be an option, such as some good wine or something meaningful. If it is a family, a vase, some dining sets or pictures would be ideal. It is not easy to think of something special for every occasion. So very often if it is not of any special visits, some fruits such as apples or oranges would be good enough.

Gifts to avoid

There are also some taboos to avoid in Chinese culture. Though modern Chinese don't seem to mind them so much, it is still necessary to know what would be suitable in an occasion. Books would not be welcome in places like Hong Kong or Macao because the pronunciation of "book" in Cantonese resembles the sound of "loss." Especially for those people who are frequent players in race course or Mark Six, they would definitely not welcome this idea.

Umbrellas would not be welcome in most places in China because the pronunciation of "umbrella" resembles separation. Of course nobody would like the idea of separation, particularly concerning your loved ones.

Clocks would not be welcome, particularly on someone's birthday because the pronunciation of "clock" resembles termination, which means death. No wonder people don't like receiving clocks as birthday gifts.

If you want to give your friends some fruits, remember to buy an even number of them because odd numbers would bring bad luck. So buy 10 apples instead of 9.

Japan

General guidelines

Gift-giving is an important part of Japanese business protocol. Moreover, gifts are exchanged among colleagues on July 15 and January 1 to commemorate midyear and the year's end respectively. It is a good policy to bring an assortment of gifts for your trip. This way, if you are unexpectedly presented with a gift, you will be able to reciprocate. The emphasis in Japanese business culture is on the ritual of gift-giving, rather than the gift itself. For this reason, you may receive a gift that seems too modest, or conversely, extravagant. An expensive gift will not be perceived as a bribe.

A wrapped gift is often carried inside a shopping bag to avoid ostentation and minimize any hint that a gift is about to be presented. The best time to present a gift is toward the end of your visit. You can discreetly approach the recipient, indicating that you have a small gift. Avoid giving a gift early in a relationship or at any conspicuous moment. A gift for an individual should be given in private. If you are presenting a gift to a group of people, have all of the intended recipients assembled. Present gifts with both hands. It is customary to comment that the gift you are presenting, even if it is extravagant, is "an uninteresting or dull thing." This statement is meant to convey, "Our relationship is more important than this trivial item."

It is a mistake to give the same gift to two or more Japanese of unequal rank. People will also take offense if you are in the presence of a group of people and give a gift to one person, but fail to give one to the others who are present. Gifts are opened in private, because if the gift turns out to be a poor choice, "loss of face" will result. Also, if several gifts are presented to people of different status, opening them privately prevents any possible comparisons.

Before accepting a gift, it is polite to modestly refuse at least once or twice before finally accepting. Ensure that your gifts are wrapped. It's the safest to leave this task to a store or hotel gift-wrapping service.

The safest gift-wrapping choices are pastel-colored papers, without bows. Avoid wrapping a gift with brightly covered papers or bows. If you are invited to a Japanese home, bring flowers (an uneven number), cakes or candy. If you receive a gift, be sure to reciprocate. Gifts in pairs are considered lucky.

Appreciated gifts

(1) Foreign, prestigious name-brand items.

(2) Imported scotch, cognac, bourbon, brandy or fine wines (top-quality brands only).

(3) Frozen steaks.

(4) Gourmet foodstuffs, fresh fruit.

(5) Electronic toys (if children are on your gift-list).

(6) Cuff links.

(7) Pen and pencil sets.

(8) Something that reflects the interests and tastes of the recipient.

(9) A simple commemorative photograph (i.e., taken from a gathering that the recipient attended).

Gifts to avoid

(1) Lilies, lotus blossoms, and camellias are associated with funerals. White flowers of any kind should be avoided. There is also a superstition that potted plants encourage sickness.

(2) Giving four or nine of anything is considered unlucky.

(3) Red Christmas cards should be avoided, since funeral notices are customarily printed in this color.

Germany

General guidelines

In Germany, a small gift is polite, especially when contacts are made for the first time. Substantial gifts are not usual, and certainly not before a deal has been reached if you don't want your intentions to be misinterpreted. Even small souvenir-style gifts to thank local staff for their assistance and hospitality during your stay at a company will not be expected but will always be appreciated. Avoid giving substantial gifts in private. The larger the gift is, the more official and public the giving should be.

Gifts are expected for social events, especially to express your thanks after you have been invited to a dinner party at a home. Avoid selecting anything obviously expensive, as this may make the other person feel "obligated" to your generosity. A lovely bouquet of flowers (though not red roses) for the lady of the house is a typical gift. When purchasing this at the flower shop, ask the florist to wrap it up as a gift. Upon returning home, remember to send a hand-written thank you card to your hosts for their invitation.

Appreciated gifts

For the company you are visiting, quality pens, tasteful office items with your company logo, or imported liquor are usually safe choices. Fine chocolates can also be an appropriate gift when you are invited to a home. If you decide to bring alcohol, good imported liquor is the safest choice. You can also bring a wine of excellent vintage from your home country or an exceptional imported red wine. A gift of German wine, however, should then be a more up market label. If you are staying with a family, good gift selections can include coffee table books about your home country, or anything that reflects the interests of your hosts and is representative of your country. An elegant, tasteful silk scarf can be an acceptable gift for the lady of the house. A local food speciality of your home country is usually a good idea for a gift, provided it is not too exotic. Keep in mind that German tastes are generally on the conservative side, so especially for older hosts, very unusual food gifts may well be under-appreciated.

Gifts to avoid

Red roses are for lovers; lilies are used at funerals. A general rule would be to avoid including heather in a bouquet as it is commonly planted in cemeteries. Clothing, perfumes, and other toiletries are considered far too personal to be appropriate gifts. Scarves, however, are acceptable gifts according to German business protocol. Avoid bringing beer as a gift, since many of the finest brands in the world are already produced and widely available here.

United States

Selecting and presenting an appropriate business gift is a thoughtful gesture, but it is not expected.

Business gifts are often presented after the deal is closed. In most situations, gifts are usually unwrapped immediately and shown to all assembled. In many cases, the best gifts are those that come from your country. You may not receive a gift in return right away.

During the holiday season (late November through the first week of January), gifts are exchanged. For your business associates, you can give gifts such as useful items for the office, liquor or wine. Choose gifts with no religious connotations (i.e. don't buy Christmas ornaments), unless you are certain of the religious background of your associates. While Christmas is the dominant celebration, and is widely commercialized during this period, people may be celebrating many other holidays during this period. Many stores and malls offer gift-wrapping services during the winter holidays.

When you visit a home, it is not necessary to bring a gift, although it is always appreciated. Flowers, a potted plant, or a bottle of wine are good gift choices. If you wish to give flowers, you can have them sent in advance to relieve your host or hostess from taking care of them when you arrive. If you stay in a US home for a few days, a gift is appropriate. You may also write a thank-you note.

Taking someone out for a meal or other entertainment is another popular gift.

Gifts for women such as perfume or clothing are usually inappropriate. They are considered too personal.

Gifts for children are often a thoughtful and appreciated gesture, but one should take into account the values of the parents. Many parents would object to your giving a toy gun or a violent video game to their child.

Saudi Arabia

Gifts should only be given to the most intimate friends. For a Saudi to receive a present from a lesser acquaintance is so embarrassing as to be offensive. It is not unheard of for an employee returning from leave to get the sack for the impertinence of bringing his boss a present from home. Even worse is expressing admiration for something belonging to another because it makes him feel obliged to make a gift of it. If one is confident enough and determined to give a gift, it must be the best affordable.

A carpet must, for example, be handmade even though most Saudis buy machine-made carpets for themselves. Never, however, buy gold jewellery or silk garments for men, as both are deemed effeminate in Islam. Platinum is most acceptable but, as it can be confused with white gold, silver is safer, provided it is properly hallmarked by a government authority (as opposed to merely bearing a maker's mark). As a gesture of respect, the recipient is likely to open and minutely examine the gift in the presence of the giver as well as any others who happen to be present. Nothing is worse than having him search in vain for a hallmark or, worse yet, turn a carpet over to find a loose weave or indistinct design on the reverse.

Owing to the extremely personal nature of giving gifts, traditional perfume is usually the most appreciated. Just as in Europe a man displays his status by his tailoring, so in Arabia he does so by his scent. The best quality costs well over £ 1,000 an ounce and the naive buyer can easily be deceived by synthetics which cheat him of his money and cause him to forfeit the esteem of the one to whom the scent is given. The same is true of incense, costing per kilogram roughly the same as an ounce of its extract. Before giving any scent, use it first and consider giving it only to those who express admiration for your taste.

2.4.3 Case for Practice

Case 1

Frank is a student in China who has just been granted a special scholarship to study at a university in the West. His English teacher, Ms. Kelsen, wrote a recommendation letter that was instrumental in his getting the scholarship. Frank feels very grateful to Ms. Kelsen, so he decides to buy her an expensive gift, a landscape painting, as a way of thanking her.

One day after class has ended and the other students have left, Frank presents the gift to Ms. Kelsen. Looking surprised, Ms. Kelsen says thank you, but says that she can't accept his gift. Frank offers the gift several more times but Ms. Kelsen insists on refusing.

Why do you think Ms. Kelsen won't accept the gift?

2.4.4 Further Reading

Interpreting What Foreigners Mean

A very important aspect of intercultural communication is interpretation, the process of deciding what foreigners' words and actions mean and why they do what they do. For example, when Frank tries to understand why Ms. Kelsen refused his gift, he is "interpreting" her behavior.

Interpretation is a part of all communication—including communication between people from the same culture. Imagine a Western friend greeting you by saying "How are you?" Even though his/her question seems very simple and easy to understand, you still need to interpret what he/she means:

(1) Perhaps "How are you?" is just a polite greeting, the same as "hello."

(2) Or perhaps he/she really wants to know how you are (and expects you to stop and chat with her).

(3) Or perhaps his/her question means he/she is worried about your health (maybe because she has heard that you were sick).

The words "How are you?" only convey part of the meaning of your friend's message, so you need to use other evidence—the setting, the expression on his/her face, the tone of his/her voice, your knowledge of Western culture, and so forth—to help you interpret what he/she means and decide how to respond.

When you interact with other Chinese people, especially Chinese people you know well, you can often understand their intentions quite accurately even if you interpret quickly without thinking about it very much. In fact, the interpretation process is so automatic that you are not aware that you have interpreted anything at all. Because it would be impossible for you to think carefully about everything other people say or do, you have to interpret very quickly, at least most of the time.

It is more difficult, however, when you try to interpret what foreigners mean, especially foreigners you don't know well. Your natural habit will be to interpret the words and actions of foreigners as quickly and automatically as you interpret the words and actions of the Chinese people. However, when you interpret the behavior of foreigners, you don't have so much background information to help you understand their behavior, so you have to guess and use your imagination much more. If you interpret their behavior quickly, without thinking carefully and getting as much information as possible, it is very likely that your interpretation will be at least partially wrong. In other words, that you will think the foreigners are worse (more rude, stupid, hostile, strange, dangerous, and so forth) than they actually are.

The way you interpret the words and actions of individual foreigners will shape how you evaluate those people. For example, if Frank decides that Ms. Kelsen refuses his gift because she wants something more expensive, he will also probably conclude that she is a greedy person. On the other hand, if he interprets her refusal as evidence that she doesn't want to appear like she is accepting a bribe, he will probably conclude that she has integrity. Often conclusions you draw about whether individual foreigners are nice or mean, intelligent or stupid, friendly or hostile, normal or strange, safe or dangerous, and so forth will influence how you evaluate other foreigners from that culture.

Effective intercultural communicators need to learn to how they interpret foreigners' saying and doing. The more aware you are of how you interpret, the more able you are to slow down and be careful, and the more likely you are to avoid misunderstandings.

Notes

birds' nests	燕窝	ostentation	夸耀；卖弄
extravagant	奢侈；奢华	integrity	正直；真诚

Encounter Tips

◎　一般来说，商务送礼应避免送现金。

◎　给阿拉伯人送礼，切忌送酒，因为在伊斯兰文化中，喝酒是非法的。

◎　在德国，送玫瑰和菊花都是不合适的，玫瑰是送给情人的，而菊花是葬礼上用的。

◎　在韩国，商务送礼一般在正式会谈之前进行，这与德国刚好相反。

◎　给拉美人送礼，忌讳送小刀和手帕，前者有绝交的含义，后者经常跟眼泪联系在一起。

◎　给日本人送礼，不要一次送4样或9样东西，因为"4"字在日文中与"死"谐音，而"9"则与"苦"字谐音。

2.5 Exercises

2.5.1 Exercise A

Decide whether the following statements are true or false.

(1) Many students call their professors by their given names in most English-speaking countries.

(2) We can address Roger Williams, who is an officer, as Officer Williams.

(3) The purpose of greetings is to establish or maintain the social relationship.

(4) Ranks in the armed forces like Captain, General, Major can be used as title in English.

(5) In Chinese there are no differences between paternal kinship terms and maternal kinship terms.

(6) Embracing is the traditional way of greeting in Northeast Asian countries like Korea and Japan.

(7) To give the proper gift, one must understand the culture of the receiver.

(8) It is accepted to give the same gift to two or more Japanese of unequal rank.

(9) For a Saudi to receive a present from a lesser acquaintance is so embarrassing as to be offensive.

(10) For an important guest, the Chinese host will see him or her to the building gate, or even to the bus stop.

2.5.2 Exercise B

Decide which of the followings are the polite invitations and which are the real invitations.

(1) It's good seeing you. I'll invite you to tea later.

(2) Why don't we get together one of these days?

(3) A：It was nice talking to you. I have to run to class.

　　B：OK, maybe we can meet sometime soon.

　　A：Yeah, love to. Why don't you drop by my house sometime?

　　B：Great. Gotta go, check you later.

(4) A：Before you leave for your vacation, can we get together and have lunch?

　　B：Sure, love to.

　　A：How about Friday ? Say about l2:30 at my place.

　　B：That sounds good. See you then.

2.5.3 Exercise C

Discuss the gift-giving culture in China.

One book that introduces Chinese culture to Westerners gives the following advice about gifts: "Our advice to anyone who lives or works with the Chinese is that they assiduously avoid giving or receiving highly expensive gifts, for an exchange of such items will probably involve an ongoing series of obligations that they will find burdensome if not downright troublesome." "Direct refusal of a gift is a fearful thing to do in any culture and perhaps especially so in Chinese culture where face-consciousness plays a major role. Nevertheless, expensive gifts must be refused."

(1) Interview a classmate to see what he/she thinks of this advice. Find out:

(a) Whether your classmate agrees or disagrees with the statement;

(b) Whether your classmate would modify it in some way.

Be ready to share your ideas with the class.

(2) Small group task: Should I open it now?

Imagine that a Westerner askes you why Chinese generally don't open the gift in the presence of the person who gives the gift. Discuss the question in groups and decide what reasons you would give for the custom.

2.5.4　Exercise D

Read the following case, and discuss in groups the possible alternatives.

Imagine that you are doing an MBA degree at a university in the USA as an international student. One of your teachers is a 40-year old woman named Maria Smith (Maria is her given name, Smith is her family name). She has a PhD degree/doctorate. In the first seminar she indicated that she had no particular preference as to how you address her.

How would you normally address her when you talk to her in class? Please rank the best three alternatives from 1 to 3 as shown in the following: Maria, Mrs. Smith, Professor Smith, Dr. Smith, Dr. Maria, Madam/Mrs. Professor, Teacher.

2.5.5　Exercise E

Read the following case, and discuss the question.

A Japanese businessman on his first visit to the United States was pleased to be invited to a US executive's home for cocktails. He arrived promptly at 7 pm. The host introduced him to a small group of people, then returned to the front door to greet others who were arriving, and the Japanese businessman apparently had nothing to contribute on the seemingly mindless topics that were discussed. After a few minutes, the others in the group wandered off to join other groups, and he was left alone. Since the host did not return to introduce him to others at the party, he left and returned to his hotel.

What, if any, rules of proper etiquette were breached in the case?

Chapter 2 Keys

CHAPTER 3

Cultural Differences in Social Value

Every man to his tastes.

—Sterne

Love makes the world go round.

—Dickens

3.1 Politeness

3.1.1 Pre-reading

A young Chinese woman in the US was complimented for the lovely dress that she was wearing. "It's exquisite. The colors are so beautiful!" She was pleased but somewhat embarrassed. In typical Chinese fashion, she replied, "Oh, it's just an ordinary dress that I bought in China."

At a reception in an American college, a newly arrived Chinese scholar was chatting with the hostess, who was an old friend. As an acquaintance of hers came up she said, "Ron, let me introduce Mr. Chen, an outstanding physicist and one of the nicest people I know." Mr. Chen offered his hand to the newcomer but looked at his hostess and said with a smile, "Should I blush, or should I tell him you don't really mean it?"

对于上述两个案例里中国人的回答，同是中国人的你是否听上去感到非常熟悉呢？答案是肯定的，因为我们在听到别人赞扬的时候，已经习惯了这样的表达方式，但是英语国家的人又期望听到怎样的回答呢？听到中国人谢绝赞美的回答，他们又会产生怎样的误解呢？

很显然，中西方对赞美有不同的回答方式。中国人虽然不吝啬给予别人赞美，但是听到对方赞美的时候就本能地回避，会感到不好意思和尴尬，通常会否定对方的赞美，一般会说自己不值得赞美。几千年来，中国人形成了自谦的传统美德，为了显示自己的谦虚，我们会贬低自己取得的成就，因而不由自主地否定别人赞美的真实性。相反，西方人喜欢赞扬他人，以增进彼此的了解，达到问候和感谢的目的，同时赞扬的目的还在于打开话题，拉近双方的距离，因此西方人以谢意接受他人的赞扬，这是对他人的尊重，通过接受赞扬和表示感谢，避免伤害对方的面子。

这些差异容易引起误解，从而导致跨文化交际失败。本节将从中英礼貌用语的语用差异出发，探讨中西方在礼貌上的跨文化差异。

3.1.2 Politeness

What is politeness? This sounds like a simple question. In daily life, we often make judgments about what is polite and what is not polite. For example, to offer your seat to the elderly on a bus is considered polite behavior, and to interrupt when someone is talking is considered impolite; to greet someone the first time you meet him in the morning is polite and to stand up to reach for the dish you want at a dinner table is impolite. So politeness can first of all be conceived as a phenomenon, an observable social phenomenon. Politeness is best expressed as the practical application of good manners or etiquette. It is a culturally defined phenomenon, and what is considered polite in one culture can often be quite rude or simply strange in another.

As an observable social phenomenon politeness is something superficial but to account for what is perceived at the surface we should delve into the depth where different cultural values are rooted.

Both Chinese and English have expressions for gratitude, apologies, remarks preceding a request; for example, there are " 谢谢，对不起，请 " "thank you, I'm sorry, excuse me." On the whole, they are quite similar and present no problem. However, even among these there are certain differences. So in this text, we look into the differences in various aspects of polite expressions and responses in every day life, basically praises, apologies, and thanks.

Compliments and Responses

Compliments and praises, part of verbal communication, are of important social functions because they help establish good relationship and contribute to the smooth process of communication.

Appropriate compliments can serve as effective supplementary means in interpersonal communication. Western and Chinese culture are at polar opposites about compliment.

We make compliments on other people's intelligence, talents, performance, manners, clothes, houses, furniture, cars, and good personal qualities. However, Chinese and Americans show some differences in responding to compliments. Chinese are very gracious people. In particular, Chinese frequently compliment foreign friends on their language skills, knowledge of Chinese culture, professional accomplishments, and personal health. Curious to Americans, however, Chinese are so embarrassed with a compliment as they are eager to give one, which is, to Chinese, a manifestation of the Chinese virtue of modesty. Chinese generally murmur some reply about not being worthy of the praise while Americans tend to accept the compliment gladly.

In the above two cases of pre-reading, the words of the Chinese conveyed a message quite different from what was intended. In the case of the Chinese woman, the reply could have meant that the one paying the compliment did not know what a really good dress is; otherwise, how could she get so excited about an ordinary dress? The implication was that the American woman's taste in clothing was questionable. In the second case, if Chen had not been smiling, his words could have been interpreted as meaning "You were just saying that to be polite; you didn't really mean that." So in the first case, the person had poor judgment. In the other, the latter case, the hostess was not sincere. What a gap between intention and message!

Certain remarks that might be fitting and proper in Chinese could lead to similar negative results.

A foreign visitor was looking at the host's potted flowers with obvious admiration. The plants were growing well and some were blooming profusely. The host remarked differently, "Growing flowers is my hobby, but I'm not much good at it."

A Canadian woman made the acquaintance of a Chinese art teacher and asked him to look over an article that she had written about Chinese painting. He agreed, but added that "I really know so little about the subject."

In both cases the Chinese would be suspected of fishing for a compliment, even though the remarks might have been quite sincere. In the first case, the foreign visitor was almost forced to say something like "But these flowers are beautiful." Or "I wish I could do as well!" And in the second case, the Canadian had to say, "Oh, come on, I know you're an expert on Chinese art." Or she could have said "Well, I certainly don't know anybody who knows more than you do in this subject!" Forced compliments like these can leave a bad taste in the mouth.

Who Can Be Complimented

Cultural differences also exist in who can be complimented. Chinese do not praise members of their own family in front of others. However, in Western culture, it would be natural for family members to praise each other. And the one who is praised usually feels pleased. For example, it would not be unusual to hear an American woman talking about how hard her husband works and how well he has done, and all the promotions and honors that he has received. She might do the same about a son or daughter of hers—how bright he or she is, what good

marks he or she makes in school, how active the child is in his or her stamp-collecting, etc.

Another example of a Chinese taboo is complimenting a man on his wife's looks. "You have a lovely wife" would be regarded as almost indecent by many Chinese, especially those beyond their youth. Yet the some compliment would be considered perfectly natural and even highly appreciated by Westerners.

Chinese speakers want to show modesty by denigrating ourselves, ignoring the factuality of the compliment paid to us. Over two thousand years, self-denigration has been at the core of the Chinese notion of politeness. In order to show modesty, we will go to such lengths as to underrate what we achieved and deny the truth of complimentary remarks. In contrast, Americans generally place sincerity above etiquette; genuine gratitude for the praise serves as a substitute for protestations of modesty. By accepting and showing appreciation of the compliment, they avoid hurting the positive face of the person who makes it.

A point to be remembered is that in both cultures compliments or praise should be natural, sincere, and appropriate, whatever other differences are.

Apologies and Responses

There is one word that is on the lips of Americans, day and night: "sorry." If you go to the movies and the tickets happen to be sold out, the ticket seller will say "Sorry, the tickets are sold out." Whenever one of your hopes goes unfulfilled, an American will say "sorry," as a sign of sympathy. Americans don't care much about who is responsible; if she is very busy, the secretary will say "sorry." If someone is troubled, a "sorry" is always necessary.

If wrong things are done, there must be apologies. As to how to offer apologies, both Western people and Chinese people may use "I am sorry…" "I apologize for…" and so on. But Chinese would like to apologize for the crowded state of their dwellings and for small numbers of dishes, although the room is big enough and there are many dishes. Chinese say these to express self-depreciation only out of courtesy, not having other implication. But the Westerners would wonder, since the room is so large and there are so many dishes, why do they say so. May be they do not welcome our visit, or they don't like us to eat more. When Chinese contact with Westerners, if they do not know these differences, it will lead to misunderstanding. The ways to respond to apologies are different, too.

A: Oh, I'm sorry. I forget it.

B: It doesn't matter.

C: That's all right.

C is Westerners, and B is a Chinese person. "It doesn't matter" is a translation of "没关系" from Chinese, which is a common pattern in Chinese to respond to apologies. If a Chinese uses this to respond to apologies, Westerners will think that he is a sharp person, who simply cannot forgive a very little wrong thing.

Thanks and Responses

"Thank you" is widely used in English to show gratitude in such cases as being invited, helped, given a gift, etc. Cultural differences exist between Chinese and Westerners in how to express thanks and responses. In fact, "thank you" is uttered in English for more than acknowledging favor or gratitude, and it is often a means to show politeness.

Saying "thank you" is very common in America, even between parents and children, husband and wife and for very small and most ordinary things. So they thank people all day long. For instance, they will thank the saleswoman after she has attended to them. They will say "thank you" to a student who has just answered the question. At home, the husband will thank his wife when she brings him a glass of water. The wife will thank her husband if he helps her with her chair.

For minor favors like borrowing a pencil, asking directions, requesting someone to pass on a message, calling a person to the telephone, etc., such polite expressions are often omitted by Chinese, especially among close friends and members of the family. The more frequent use of "thank you" and "please" by Westerners is often regarded as unnecessary and even tiresome by many Chinese. Excessive expressions of gratitude make us extremely uncomfortable and give a sense of empty thanks, a sense of formal or required kowtowing which does not indicate gratitude but insincerity.

Chinese students would always thank their teachers for the latter's help, but would seldom do so to their parents. Sometimes they might say something like "Do you feel tired?" or "Have a rest." to show their gratitude and concern. The traditional Chinese concept holds that it is the duty of the young and junior to do something for the elderly and the senior, so the latter don't have to say thanks. And traditional Chinese customs don't require people to express thanks for the small favors that others have done for them.

On the other hand, the Chinese attitude—that appreciation is understood and need not be expressed—is sometimes taken for rudeness or lack of consideration by Westerners. On many occasions, the English use this utterance while the Chinese may say "有劳您了." Or do not say a word at all but just smile or nod. Without using expressions of gratitude, misunderstandings may arise because the help seems to be taken for granted and is not appreciated. For Westerners, each person is an equal individual, whether he is a family member or not. In Chinese, "谢谢" is not frequently used between intimate friends and family members because it may imply a certain distance between the addresser and the addressee.

Native speakers may respond to "thank you" by saying "You are welcome." "It's my pleasure." "Not at all." "Don't mention it." "That's all right. While Chinese people may say "这是我应该做的," which may convey to Westerners the message that the Chinese did not really want to do it, or that he/she did it only because it was his/her duty. This message is quite different from what the Chinese speaker intended to express. Quite a different message is conveyed! A proper reply might be "I'm glad to be of help." or "It's my pleasure."

Other Differences in Politeness

The Chinese word "请" is usually regarded as equivalent to "please." However, in certain situations the English word "please" would not be used. When offering or urging another person to be first in going through a door or getting in a car, the expression is generally "After you." (not "You go first." as some people not well-acquainted with English are apt to say). At the meal table, "help yourself" is customary when urging someone to start eating, or to take more of the food.

Excuse me—this is a general term preceding a request or interruption. In Chinese, however, there are different terms: "劳驾" when asking a favor or requesting a person to do something; "借光" "请让一让" when asking a person to step aside or make room; "请问" when asking for information or making a query. Foreigners not knowing this distinction tend to use "对不起" for all such situations when they speak Chinese.

The Chinese term "辛苦了" is a good warm expression showing concern. Or it may be used in recognition of the fact that a person has put in considerable effort or gone through some hardship to achieve something. To put "辛苦了" into proper English, however, demands care; there is no equivalent that can fit all situations, to translate it simply as "You've had a hard time," or "You've gone through a lot of hardships," is hardly enough; in some circumstances it might even give the wrong impression. If used as a greeting to a person who has just completed a long trip, "辛苦了" could be expressed as "You must have had a tiring journey," or "You must be tired from such a long trip," or "Did you have a good trip?" When commending people who have finished a difficult task or are still working on it, one might say "Well done." That is "(You have got) a hard job." None of these English expressions, however, carries as much meaning or warm feeling as the Chinese one.

When a person sneezes, people nearby often make a remark. Some Chinese say something like "有人想你了" "有人说你," or humorously "谁在骂你了?" An American or Englishman would probably say "God bless you."

3.1.3　Case for Practice

Situation: Jonathan is a teacher in an adult school class in the United States. After class, he is speaking to Ann, one of his students from China.

Jonathan:　Ann, your English is improving. I am pleased with your work.

Ann:　(Looking down) Oh, no, my English is not very good.

Jonathan:　Why do you say that, Ann? You are doing very well in class.

Ann:　No, I am not a good student.

Jonathan:　You are making progress in this class. You should be proud of your English.

Ann:　It's not true. You are a good teacher, but I am not a good student.

Jonathan:　(He is surprised by her response and wonders why she thinks her English is so bad. He doesn't know what to say and wonders if he should stop giving her compliments.)

(1) What misunderstanding happened in the case?

(2) What's the difference in giving and accepting compliments between China and the US?

(3) Can you give some advice to help them avoid similar misunderstandings in the future?

3.1.4 Further Reading

Communication Style

There is a story below just explaining the differences between different cultures.

After an American woman was married and had lived in Japan for a while, her Japanese gradually improved to the point where she could take part in simple conversations with her husband, her husband's friends and family. And she began to notice that often, when she joined in, the others would look startled, and the conversation would come to a halt. After this happened several times, it became clear to her that she was doing something wrong. But for a long time, she didn't know what it was. Finally, after listening carefully to many Japanese conversations, she discovered what the problem was. Even though she was speaking Japanese, she was handling the conversation in a Western way.

Japanese-style conversations develop quite differently from Western-style conversations. And the differences aren't only in the languages. She realized that she kept trying to hold Western-style conversations even when she was speaking Japanese, so were her Japanese English students trying to hold Japanese-style conversations even when they were speaking English. They were unconsciously playing entirely different conversational ballgames.

A Western-style conversation between two people is like a game of tennis. If I am a Westerner, when I introduce a topic, a conversational ball, I expect you to hit back. If you agree with me, I don't expect you simply to agree and do nothing more. I expect you to add something—a reason for agreeing, another example, or a remark to carry the idea further. But I don't expect you always to agree. I am just as happy if you question me or challenge me, or completely disagree with me. Whether you agree or disagree, your response will return the ball to me. And then it is my turn again. I don't serve a new ball from my original starting line. I hit your ball back again from where it has bounced. I carry your idea further, answer your questions or objections, or challenge or question you. And so the ball goes back and forth. If there are more than two people in the conversation, then it is like doubles in tennis, or like volleyball. There's no waiting in line. Whoever is nearest and quickest hits the ball, and if you step back, someone else will hit it. No one stops the game to give you a turn. You're responsible for taking your own turn and no one person has the ball for very long.

A Japanese-style conversation, however, is not at all like tennis or volleyball, it's like bowling. You wait for your turn, and you always know your place in line. It depends on such things as whether you are older or younger, a close friend or a relative stranger to the previous speaker, in a senior or junior position, and so on. The first thing is to wait for your turn, patiently and politely. When your moment comes, you step up to the starting line with your bowling ball, and carefully bowl it. Everyone else stands back, making sounds of polite encouragement. Everyone waits until your ball has reached the end of the lane, and watches to see if it knocks down all the pins, or only some of them, or none of them. Then there is a pause, while everyone registers your score. Then, after everyone is sure that you are done, the next person in line steps up to the same starting line, with a different ball. He doesn't return your ball. There is no back and forth at all. And there is always a suitable pause between turns. There is no rush, and no impatience.

No wonder everyone looked startled when the American woman took part in Japanese conversations. She paid no attention to whose turn it was, and kept snatching the ball halfway down the alley and throwing it back at the bowler. Of course the conversation fell apart, and she was playing the wrong game.

This explains why it can be so difficult to get a Western-style discussion going with Japanese students of English. Whenever she serves a volleyball, everyone just stands back and watches it fall. No one hits it back. Everyone waits until she calls on someone to take a turn. And when that person speaks, he doesn't hit her ball back. He serves a new ball. Again everyone just watches it fall. So she calls on someone else. This person does not refer to what the previous speaker has said. He also serves a new ball. Everyone begins again from the same starting line, and all the balls run parallel. There is never any back and forth.

After finishing reading this story, you may know about the difference in the conversational ballgames. You may think that all your trouble is over. But if you have been trained all your life to play one game, it is no simple matter to switch to another, even if you know the rules. Tennis, after all, is different from bowling.

Notes

startle	震惊	bowling	保龄球
back and forth	来来回回地	switch	转换
rush	匆忙；赶紧	impatience	不耐烦

Encounter Tips

◎ 中国人一般不忌讳问别人的姓名、年纪、婚姻状况、薪水、家庭状况、体重、信仰等个人问题，并且以此表达关切，而西方人会认为这是侵犯个人隐私。

◎ 在西方文化中，邀请别人参加宴会或其他社交活动，必须注意提前预约并定好时间，尤其是在美国，邀请别人意味着借用他人的时间，因此非常尊重别人的时间，而在中国，不速之客也是受欢迎的，如果没有好好接待上门的客人，会被人认为是不好客。

◎ 美国人一般不会直接问对方姓名，而是先自我介绍，从而期待对方回答。在美国，跟陌生人交谈是相当普遍且容易被人接受的，不会觉得很唐突。

3.2　Friendship

3.2.1　Pre-reading

Why Was Edward So Indifferent?

Chou was puzzled by Edward's reaction and felt a little hurt. He thought Edward did not take him as a real friend. They had known each other for two years since they shared the same apartment. Chou thought they had become good friends and could talk everything. But when he asked Edward about his job and the salary, Edward did not answer but changed the topic to the football match. Chou could not understand. He had told Edward everything. Why was Edward so indifferent?

友谊是全人类所向往的。然而，由于文化背景的不同，对友谊的理解也不一样。自古以来中国人很看重朋友，认为好朋友之间应该无所不谈，没有秘密，所以 Chou 对 Edward 的反应不理解。但是 Edward 却不这样认为。因为西方国家如英美等国都是很重视个人隐私的，并不认为是朋友就可以分享自己的私人空间，所以，当 Chou 问及个人隐私问题时，他会避而不谈。本节将就中西方在友谊观方面的不同做简单介绍。

3.2.2　Different Friendship Attitudes

Hospitality vs. Privacy

All people in the world like to make friends. "A friend in need is a friend indeed." However, because of the different cultural background and social values, the attitude toward friendship is quite different. If these differences are ignored during intercultural communication, many misunderstandings would be caused, even between friends.

One of the obvious differences is the attitude hospitality and privacy. In china, there is no word like "privacy" in traditional Chinese culture, and it is always considered as a courtesy and consideration to ask about other's personal information, especially among friends. The questions, "Are you married?" "How much do you earn a month?" and so on are regarded as common topics, because most Chinese think these questions show friendly feelings, care and consideration to others. However, in many Western countries such as the UK and the USA, such questions are not appropriate to ask. Privacy is an important part of human rights. People do not like to talk much about themselves, even among friends. The above-listed questions may cause embarrassment and effect the communication carrying on unsmoothly. Even among the Westerns, people from different countries share different attitudes toward hospitality and privacy.

For the British, they do not like to talk much about their family, job, and earnings, except that they begin these topics themselves. Even in all other Europeans' mind, the British are the most suspicious and unfriendly people. The characteristic of prudence makes the British more cautious in making friends. However, the friendship of an Englishman once gained is more strong and true than any other. Compared with the British's caution, the Americans are more open and active. They may talk friendly with others, and will talk about their families, jobs, and other private affairs. Then, if you meet a British and an American at the same time, you may find that the American is more talkative and friendly than the British and easier to make friends.

The different attitude toward hospitality and privacy between China and the West, especially America, are mainly caused by the fact that they have quite different culture values. Chinese value highly collectivism and Americans value highly individualism. China has been an agricultural country for a long time. Most people live in countryside and few people live in cities. Many families live in the courtyard houses and it's easy for them to meet each other and talk about everything about each other. There are few things that can be hidden and become secrets. On the contrary, the Americans have lived in cities and freestanding house since early times. There's a saying going like this: "Good fences make good neighbors." So privacy is taken as a necessary part of their life.

Hospitality vs. Distance

Although the Americans are much warmer and easier to get in touch with, they just walk on the surface. Living in a fast changing society, Americans have to change their job and living places often. This means that they can not have enough time to cultivate the long-lasting friendship, so they are used to getting in touch with strangers at different places. They may be friendly to people around them, but they are not very serious about that. For example, if you hear your American friends saying "Let's get together another day." just after you finished a meal together, you'd better not take it seriously, because they maybe forget it themselves.

Americans make friends in different circles, i.e., the friends do not share the same circles. The friendships are usually tied to specific circumstances or activities. When a person changes circumstances and activities, he or she changes friends. For example, a person may have friends for fishing, friends for excising, and work friends, neighborhood friends, etc. In different circles, the friends are different. This is because friendships in the West are based on equality. Friends should exchange similar activities and give similar things to one another. However, in China, friends are like brothers or sisters. They usually stay together, no matter in what circumstances. The following is a story about the different attitude towards friendship between Americans and the Chinese people.

Tom and Wong first met in their chemistry class at an American university. Wong came from China and he wanted to learn more about American culture and to be a good friend of Tom. At first, Tom was very friendly. He always greeted warmly before class and sometimes offered to study with Wong. He even invited Wong to dine together with him. But after the semester was over, Tom seemed more distant. The two former classmates didn't see each other very much at school. One day, Wong decided to call Tom, but it seemed that Tom was not very interested in talking to him. Wong was hurt because he thought friends were friends forever.

As a foreigner, Wong does not understand the way Americans view friendship. Americans use the word "friend" in a very general way. They may call both casual acquaintances and close companions "friends." These friendships are based on common interests. When the shared activity ends, the friendship may fade. Now as Tom and Wong are no longer classmates, their "friendship" has changed. In China, friendship means a strong life-long bond between two people, then the friendship develop slowly, since they are built to last. American society is change rapidly. Studies show that one of five American families moves every year. American friendships develop quickly, and they may change just as quickly. People from the United States may at first seem friendly, and they may change just as quickly. People from the United States may at first seem friendly because they often chat easily with strangers. Their friendliness is not always an offer of true friendship. After an experience like Wong's, people who have been in this country for only a few months may consider Americans to be fickle. Learning how American view friendship can help non-Americans avoid misunderstandings. It can also help them make friends in the American way.

There is another point that should be noticed between the American friendship and Chinese friendship. Friends in China share too much privacy and more obligations among them. For example, no matter how busy a person is, if her friend wants to go shopping, she will put her work aside and go shopping with her friend. Chinese people often expect more help from their friends. They often share their social connections. A Chinese friend will help friends get something hard to obtain such as a job, commodities in short supply, an appointment with a good doctor, education chances for kids in good school, an easier path through an official procedure, or an introduction to another person who might also be able to give concrete help. This is rarely part of Western friendships, because the Westerners usually expect friendship to be more independent. Just like other things in the West, people prefer independence to dependence. If they obtain more help from others they will feel uncomfortable. Westerners' friendship is mostly a matter of providing emotional support and spending time together.

However, the British may be different in Americans' eyes, because they pay more attention to their social connections. Living in a society in which social class is still very important, people in the UK pay more attention to building their social connection net and, of course, benefit a lot from such a social net for their life, such as education chance and job.

Chinese people should also pay attention to the physical distance with their Western friends. For the British and Americans, people of the same sex do not walk hand in hand, arm in arm, or with one's hand on the other's shoulder. The same happens with the friends of the same sex. In China, such behaviors are very common. Then when staying with friends from the UK or America, Chinese people should avoid such close behaviors.

Besides these differences, business people should keep in mind another difference when doing business with Western friends. Because friends in Western countries do not share much obligation among them, they usually draw a clear distinction between friendship and business. They would not like to give up their benefit only because of friendship. Friendship is friendship. Business is business.

A Few Tips on Making Friends with Americans

(1) Visit some places often that are favorable for Americans: parties, churches, Western restaurants, parks, and sports clubs.

(2) Be willing to take the first step. Don't wait for them to approach you. Americans in China may not know if you can speak English. They may be embarrassed if they can't speak your language.

(3) Use small talk to open a conversation. Ask them where they're from, why they came to China, etc. Remember: be careful to avoid personal questions about age, salary, marital status and appearance.

(4) Show an interest in their culture, their country or their job (Americans like to talk about themselves).

(5) Invite them to join you for dinner or just for coffee or tea. Try to set a specific time. Americans sometimes make general invitations like "Let's get together sometimes." Often this is just a way to be friendly. It is not always a real invitation.

(6) Don't expect too much at first. Maybe they're just being friendly. Or maybe they do want to be your good friends. It will take time to tell.

3.2.3　Case for Practice

Case 1

What is True Friendship?

Yang Ruifang worked as a secretary in an Australian company in Melbourne. She became friendly with one of the Australian secretaries, a woman named Cathy Lane. The two usually ate lunch together and Yang Ruifang often asked Cathy for advice on problems she faced adjusting to Australian society. Cathy gave her a lot of advice and helped her move from one apartment to another. Cathy went with Yang Ruifang to the Immigration Bureau several times to help sort out some problems. Yang Ruifang visited Cathy several times at home but did not invite Cathy to her apartment because she shared it with four other people. If they did not see each other over the weekend, they usually talked on the telephone. As Yang Ruifang was also preparing to take an English test, she was able to get a lot of help with English in this way.

However, something seemed to be going wrong. Cathy seemed to be getting impatient, even a little cold. She started going out by herself at lunchtime instead of eating with Yang, and seemed reluctant to answer questions. Yang Ruifang was puzzled. She couldn't imagine what the problem was.

(1) Why did Yang Ruifang think the relationship was developing well?

(2) From this case what do you think Australians and other Westerners expect from their friends?

(3) Give advice to Cathy and to Yang Ruifang to help them restore their friendship.

3.2.4　Further Reading

Passage 1

Chinese Hospitality

"How happy to have friends from far away!" this old saying has been carried on for more than 2000 years in China and shows that Chinese are proud to have many guests on celebrating occasions. With the 2010 World Expo holding in Shanghai, the city is ready to greet friends from all over the world. This is also a good chance for the world to experience the Chinese hospitality.

One of the typical ways for Chinese people to show their hospitality is banquets. Chinese people like to serve guests with the best food they have. A Chinese banquet may be made up of scores of dishes, including cold dishes, hot fried dishes, salted dishes, sweet preserved fruit and fresh fruit. The famous Complete Manchu-Han Banquet (满汉全席) even includes 108 dishes and 44 courses of dim sum. It takes three days and nights to finish the banquet. Even in the countryside, if a man marries, his parents will invite the whole village to a banquet for several days.

This kind of hospitality has much to do with countryside culture and tradition. It is also a Chinese way of making friends. Chinese people like making friends and they cultivate their friendship carefully. For them, friendship is a life-long issue, and it should be formed on the basis of faith and trust. A lot of examples can be found in action films on the Chinese attitude towards friends. In these movies, a good Chinese man is ready to do anything to help his friends. He is faithful as well as smart.

There is another Chinese proverb: "The friendship between noble gentlemen is as pure as water." This shows the spiritual side of Chinese friendship, which is making friends on the basis of mutual interests and a good personality.

Passage 2

Personal Network

Throughout much of Chinese history, the fundamental glue that has held society together is the concept of guanxi (关系), or relationships between people. It has been and remains a deep seated concept that lies at the core of Chinese society. It is very important for the Chinese to have good relationships. They often regard good social relations as a symbol of personal ability and influence. Someone who has no connections would be despised and is only half-Chinese. An established network of quality contacts can help accomplish almost anything, and thus having good relationships is a very powerful asset.

In China, there is another important vehicle in social exchange, that is, renqing (人情), which is literally translated as human sentiment or human emotion. A Western scholar once defines it as "covers not only sentiment but also its social expressions such as the offering of congratulations, or condolences or the making of gifts on appropriate occasions." In fact, renqing follows Confucian notion of reciprocity .

Such situation can also be found in Britain. Britain is a society in which social class is still very important. In Britain, the accent people speak with, the clothes people wear, and the schools children attend are all markers that identify their social class. The education opportunity plays an important part in children's future life, thus the school tie has been a clear marker of social class. If a child goes to a famous public school or a well-known university, he will have more chances to know some "useful" persons who would give help in his future life. In Britain, there is a group of people called "the old boys network," which means the group of men who went to school and university together. Such group of people not only dominates government, but also is very influential in banking, media, arts, and education.

Notes			
freestanding house	独立式的	walk on the surface	维持表面关系
dominates	支配；控制	influential	有影响力的

Encounter Tips

◎   美国人给人的第一印象是很友好的，他们常随意与陌生人交谈。因此，他们的友谊建立得非常快。不过，美国人的友好并不总是真正友情的表现。而英国人相对来说要谨慎得多，也似乎冷淡得多。但是一旦获得了英国人的友谊，就比任何人的友谊更牢靠、更真挚。

◎   美国人对 friend 一词的使用非常广泛。他们可能把一般的朋友和亲密的伙伴都称为 friend。这些友谊都是基于共同的兴趣、共同的活动，当这些活动不复存在时，友谊也随之淡化。

3.3　Family Relationship

3.3.1　Pre-reading

Emma felt worried these days. She lived with her parents-in-law in China. A year ago, she married Chen and came to China from America with her husband. They loved each other very much and she thought she would have a good relationship with her parents-in-law. However, she found it was becoming difficult now. Her mother-in-law had given too much advice on her matters. She often had to give up her own idea to obey, or her mother-in-law would feel unhappy. This also influenced the relationship between her husband and her. She wanted him to stand on her side, but he did not.

　　该案例体现了中西文化，尤其是中美文化观念中很重要的一个不同之处：家庭观念的不同。生长在美国的 Emma 是很难理解和接受中国的大家庭观念以及中国的家人观念。家庭是社会生活的重心，也是最能反映文化差异的地方。中国传统以大家庭为主，讲究的是长幼有序、尊老爱幼，而且强调长辈的绝对权威。对孩子的教育，也是强调对长辈的礼让和服从。然而，在西方国家，尤其在美国，一般都是以核心家庭为主，做长辈的在自己孩子成家之后就不再干涉孩子的事情。这时，父母的家庭与孩子的家庭已经像两个完全独立的个体，而非有血缘关系的家人。有时连孩子帮助父母做点家务事都要付费，因为美国更多强调的是父母对孩子的责任，而非孩子对父母的义务。说到家庭，总会不可避免地提及爱情和婚姻。爱情无国界，但不同的择偶观却能体现社会文化的不同。本节将就中西方在家庭、婚姻和爱情方面的一些不同之处作简单介绍。

3.3.2　Family and Marriage

Extended or Nuclear Families

　　Family is where people get their start in life. It is among the oldest and most fundamental of all human institutions. It gives children knowledge about their historical background information regarding the permanent nature of their culture, and specific behaviors, customs, traditions, and language associated with their ethnic or culture group. Different countries cultivate different
family values. China and the United States, these two leading countries in the world, have shown much difference in family structure and family values.

　　In China, the traditional families are the extended families, which include grandparents, aunts, uncles, cousins, nephews, nieces and in-laws. Such big families are becoming less and less. More and more families usually include grandparents, parents and children. Although there are many changes to the traditional families in China, the basic family values do not change. The authority of the elder in a family and not disputing with parents are the basic values for people to follow and to teach children. For many parents are still living with their children after their children have got married, they often interfere in the young couple's affairs and sometimes even change the couple's decision. Of course, this sometimes causes conflicts between the two generations.

In the United States the nuclear family is considered as the family, which usually consists of the father, the mother, and the children. This nuclear family has its own separate residence and is economically independent of other family members. The parents of the nuclear family are heads of households and the relationships between them and other relatives are not as strong as those in the extended family.

A point can be easily noticed between these two types of families is the relationship between parents and children after the children get married. In China, parents always live with children even after their children get married, and they live as a single family. They live together and spend money together. However, children in America live separately after they get married, not only in residence but also in economy. For example, a professor in America has two daughters who have got married. One day, one of his sons-in-law helped him fix a fence, and the professor paid him for his work because they had discussed payment before the work was to be done.

Such things are unbelievable in a Chinese family, because it is considered the responsibility of the young members to help the older members. It is the obligation, not only for parents to raise children, but also for children to help or take care of parents. Parents give birth to children and raise children up. When they get old, children should take care of them, no matter they are healthy or not. In this way both young and old members feel the warmth of the family. This family value has carried on throughout Chinese history. However, it is different in America. The American parents have the obligation to raise their children but their children have no obligation to take care of their parents. Of course, this doesn't mean that children pay no attention to their parents after they grow up. There are many chances for them to stay with the old members, such as vacations and family get-togethers. It is believed in America that it is the parents who decide to have baby or not and the babies do not have the chance to choose their birth, so it is the parents' obligation to raise their children and get children educated. Children do not have the obligation to take care of their parents after they grow up. It is the country's burden.

Love and Marriage

Family is always built on love. A man and a woman who are in love with each other would decide to build their family and face the future together. Love is always the same, no matter in which country, but people in different countries may hold different views toward marriage.

Here is a personal advertisement in a newspaper:

Male, 31, 175cm, manager in a bank, having a residence in downtown and a car; seeks female, attractive, 25—28, warm-hearted and good at housework.

From this advertisement it can be seen that the purpose of personal advertisment in China is to look for a life-partner or a person to get married. And men pay more attention to the appearance and moral values and the ability of dealing with housework when they look for a spouse, while women pay more attention to the wealth and career, or the ability to earn money of their future husbands. This may reflect the traditional Chinese family value that men determine the affairs outside and women take charge of the matters inside. This is quite different from the situation in the Western countries. Please read the following advertisement:

Male, 25, 5'9", slim built, likes pubs, clubs, sports, seeks female, 18—30, to share the good things in life.

There is nothing related to the man's career or wealth in this advertisement, because women in the west prefer to know about men's physical situation and hobbies than know about men's income. The men who are strong in figure and gentle in mental and good at sports are more attractive. On the other hand, a man would like to look for a woman who may share life together. They hope that both of them may share the same hobbies, the same life experience or something romantic together. They prefer their spiritual world. This is different from the purpose of Chinese personal ad. Not all of the personal ads in the Western countries are about looking for a spouse. Some of them are just for partners or friends. For example,

Female, 31, single, medium-build, looking for male, 30—40, for friendship & possibly more. Call me on 09069 553917.

When a woman accepts a man's courtship, they will arrange their engagement and marriage. It is said that wedding is one of the most holy moments in people's life. Because of the different cultures and customs, weddings show many differences between China and America. The first is the color. Americans prefer white while Chinese people like red, so in America, the bride usually wears a beautiful, long white wedding dress and the groom wears a formal suit or tuxedo. A new couple in China usually decorates their new home with red "Xi" paper characters (meaning "happiness") and some red decorations. Their quilt on bed is red, too. On the wedding, the bride usually wears a red dress. Sometimes the modern brides in cities may wear a long white wedding dress at the wedding, but they would change the dress for a red one during the wedding time.

The usual place in America for a wedding is in a church. The ceremony begins with the groom, his attendants and the minister standing and facing the entrance where the beautiful bride will appear when the music begins. Then the young couple repeats their vows and gives each other a gold ring. Finally the minister announces the big moment, "I now pronounce you man and wife. You may kiss your bride!" At the wedding reception, the couple cut the wedding cake and feed each other a bite. Guests mingle while enjoying cake, punch and other treats. When the reception is over, the newlyweds run to their car, which is "decorated" with tissue paper, tin cans and a "Just Married" sign, and speed off to take a honeymoon.

In China, the traditional marriage usually involves six necessary procedures: match-making, engagement, betrothal presents, meeting the bride, three bows, and drinking wedlock wine, but now most of them have been simplified, except some distant countryside. Most people like to choose a holiday or special Chinese festival for their wedding, but a few others, especially those in the countryside, would ask a fortune-teller for a lucky date (usually an even number) so that their marriage would have "double happiness." The wedding in the countryside is usually held at home, with the attendance of most relatives and friends, who gave their help to organize the wedding, and the wedding banquet usually lasts several days. People live in cities prefer hotels to homes to hold the banquet. At the wedding ceremony, some favorite treats would be prepared, such as red dates, lotus seeds, and peanuts, which give the hope that the new couple would have a baby soon.

3.3.3　Case for Practice

Case

An American young man loved a Chinese girl. They married soon. At last the Chinese girl resigned her desirable position, and went to America with the American young man.

"I gave up a good job, and went far away from my hometown. I do all of these just because of you. This is my contribution," said the Chinese girl. But the American young man argued, "Oh, no. I don't think this is one kind of contribution. In my opinion, this is just a choice. If you feel happy, and think your choice is correct, everything is all right."

Shortly after that, the Chinese girl said to her husband once more, "I had an excellent major before, but now I should spent so much time in studying a new major. I wasted so much time. Is it one kind of contribution?"

Beyond her expectation, the American husband said, "Oh, no. Don't always mention contribution. Everyone should be responsible for her choice. Now that you think your choice is valuable, this choice is correct, and you'll feel happy about it."

(1) Can you explain the misunderstanding between this young couple?

(2) In your opinion, the Chinese girl's action is one kind of contribution, or just a choice?

(3) Everyone should be responsible for his or her choice. How do you think about

this? Why do American people think everyone should responsible for his or her choice?

(4) When you make a choice, do you realize that you yourself should be responsible for it?

3.3.4　Further Reading

Passage 1

Collectivism and the Family

There is an Indian proverb that states "An individual could not be more separated from the family than a finger from the hand." We see the proverb being acted out when Wolpert tells us that in India, "people share property, all material possessions, food, work and love, perform religious rituals together, and often live under the same roof." This collective view of family is very different from the ideas just examined when we looked at the United States. One might say, "I will achieve mainly because of my ability and initiative"; the emphasis in Mexico on the extended family, close attachments, and tight bonds leads the Mexican to say, "I will achieve mainly because of my family, and for my family, rather than myself." We find the same attitude in Costa Rico, where "kinship ties guide and control individual behavior". According to Asselin and Mastron, France also sees the extended family as a major influence in the individual's life. They note, "The extended family serves as an active support network. Relatives, including godparents, are resources for finding jobs, an apartment, a car, and any kinds of products and services."

Directly linked to collectivism in the family is the notion of dominance—who controls the child? In the Arab world, children learn that God controls them and must be listened to. In the United States, children learn to answer mainly to themselves or their parents. Among the Maasai of Africa, many people share in raising the child. A Maasai proverb says, "The child has no owner"— all members of the tribe are responsible for the socialization process.

While learning such characteristics as self-reliance and responsibility, the child, through the extended family, is also being taught the parameters of loyalty. In the Bedouin tribes of Saudi Arabia, intense feelings of loyalty and dependence are fostered and preserved by the family. You find much the same attitude toward loyalty in the extended families of Africa. Richmond and Gestrin note, "The African extended family is extended indeed. Among its members are parents and children, grandparents, uncles and aunts, in-laws, cousins of varying degrees, as well as persons not related by blood." There are large networks of loyalty in other cultures. Mexicans are also "intensely loyal to their families and pride themselves on their willingness to put their families first." So important is this value toward family loyalty that even Mexicans living in the United States, as Valenzulz tells us, have a "strong sense of loyalty."

The Japanese also "hold loyalty in the highest esteem." This means that children are brought up "to seek fulfillment with others rather than individually". The Chinese family also takes this approach to loyalty. For historical and geographical reasons, most Chinese have always felt detached from their central government. Hence, family loyalty comes first for them, as this Chinese proverb makes clear: "Heaven is high and the Emperor is far away." Chu and Ju make much the same point, "An important Chinese cultural value is filial piety. Traditionally Chinese children felt a lifelong obligation to their parents, ideally exemplified by an unreserved devotion to please them in every possible way." You can also observe the value of collectivism influencing loyalty in the Arab family. As Nydell notes, for Arabs, "Family loyalty and obligations take precedence over loyalty to friends or the demands of the job."

Passage 2

The British live longer, marry later, have fewer children and are more likely to get divorced than ever before. Young people leave home earlier, though not necessarily to get married. More women now go out to work and more people, especially the old, live alone. The nuclear family (parents and perhaps two children) has largely replaced the extended family where several generations lived together.

Although patterns are changing, most people in Britain still get married and have children and stay together until the end of their lives. People are marrying later: the average woman gets married at 24 to a man who is just over two years older (although it is estimated that 40 percent of couples live together before getting married). Mrs. Average now has her first child at the age of 27, but she will have only one or two children: only one mother in four has more. Nine out of ten married women will have children at some points in their lives. And despite the changes in working habits it is usually the woman who has overall responsibility for domestic life: The traditional division of family responsibilities still persists.

Britain has one of the highest divorce rates in Western Europe: Approximately one in three marriages ends in divorce, half of them in the first ten years of marriage. As a result more people are getting remarried and there are now over a million single parents looking after 1.6 million children.

Notes

son-in-law	女婿	courtship	求爱
tuxedo	男士无尾半正式晚礼服	mingle	(使)混合
fortune-teller	算命者	kinship	血族关系；亲戚关系
parameter	参数；参量		

Encounter Tips

◎ 美国人来自世界各地，婚礼形式也就迥然各异。有热闹非凡的教堂婚礼，也有根本没有宗教仪式的世俗婚礼，甚至还有宾客在山顶上光着脚举行的婚礼。不过，这些婚礼中仍然包含着一些传统习俗，如交换戒指，往新娘、新郎身上洒生米等。

◎ 在教养孩子的过程中，人们的行为都受文化的影响。对于美国人，教养的目标在于帮助孩子们自力更生。他们将孩子视为个体，但同时，他们也认为处罚是训诫孩子时必要的一部分。

◎ 美国中产阶级的教育理念之一是培养孩子的阅读兴趣。多半中产阶级家庭的孩子，从抱在手上开始，就被抱进了图书馆。有的年龄太小，根本不是在看书，只是把书抓在手上，翻来覆去地摆弄。在图书馆的地上爬得久了，孩子们很容易就把读书视为生活的一部分。美国不少孩子真是从会吃饭起就会读书。这些孩子们上小学的时候，好多已经会煞有介事地查资料写论文了。

3.4　Education

3.4.1　Pre-reading

Professor Li was on a hotpot these days. He had difficulty in communicating with his son. Professor Li had stayed in America for more than 10 years and just came back to China with his family. His son was 14 years old, and recently Professor Li found his son always locked himself in his room and said nothing about what he was doing. Professor told his friend his problem, and his friend asked why he did not open the room's door to see what happened. Professor said he couldn't because that was his son's room, so he could not open the door without his son's permission.

李教授的这种想法对于大部分的中国父母来说是很难理解的。在中国人的传统思维里，孩子是父母的。在孩子的成长过程中，父母有权知道孩子的一切。而对于已经受美国文化感染的李教授来说，孩子是一个独立的个人，应该有自己的空间，父母也应该尊重孩子自己的独立性。其实这也是中美文化在家庭教育方面的差异。中国父母希望的是孩子将来能成为父母所希望的人才，实现父母未能实现的愿望。从某种方面来说，孩子的人生轨迹是父母人生轨迹的延续。而在美国，父母更多的是培养孩子的独立性和自主性。孩子有权选择自己的一切，父母给予的是建议、理解和支持。与家庭教育相似，中美两国在学校教育方面对孩子的培养也有显著的不同之处。本节将就中美两国在家庭教育和学校教育这两方面的特点做简单的介绍。

3.4.2　Family Cultivation and School Education

Family Influence

Children are the hope of a nation, and family education is the elementary education for children. There are many types of family education in the world and each of them shows distinctive features and is closely responsive to its culture. There are great differences on cultivating children's independence, interests, creativity, psychological health, fame, and the relationship with their parents between American family education and Chinese family education.

Have you ever felt annoyed by your parents' orders? Maybe most of Chinese children would say "Yes." That's right. Chinese parents give too much orders and tough advice during their children's growth. Since as babies, children have been told by their parents something like "You should do this. You shouldn't do that." Such advice would even last till the death of the parents in some traditional families, no matter the children have grown up or not. Maybe it seems difficult to understand in modern society, but this is the truth. Most Chinese parents, especially those in traditional big families, think that it is they who give lives to children, so they have the right to know about everything about their children and it is right to "help" their children no matter in what kind of situation. Chinese parents always hold the view that parents are older than children and their decisions are definitely wiser than children's, because they have more life experience than their children. In Chinese parents' mind, children are children and cannot be independent, so most children in China depend much on their parents and family during their growing time.

Such things seldom happen in America. American parents are comparatively more democratic than Chinese parents. American parents of course tell their children what can be done and what cannot be done, but most of such advice is about morals and social values. For example, American parents may tell their children to save water, not to make noise in public places or something like this. They seldom shout at children "Don't make friends with that bad child!" or "You should learn playing piano!" They leave the chances for their children to decide to do or not. American parents take their children as individuals, that is, in their mind, children are independent individuals. Individualism is the core value in American families. Parents leave their children in an individual room since the children are born. Children have independent space not only physically but also mentally. Parents do not involve too much in their children's individual space, but that does not mean they pay no attention to their children. They always take care of them and give their hands to children whenever children need help.

There is another obvious difference between Chinese family and American family in raising children. That is the attitude toward responsibility. For example, if a boy broke a neighbor's window when he played football, who would pay for the repairs? In most

Chinese families, the parents would do it, but in American families, the parents would ask the boy to pay for it himself! In Chinese parents' mind, children are always children, and children do not have the ability to share such responsibility. However, for American parents, children are individuals and children should take responsibility for what they do. If their children do something wrong, they should apologize for that and if something has to be repaired, they have to get the money by doing some part-time jobs. Thus American children seem more independent than Chinese children during their growing time.

School Education

School education witnesses many differences between China and America. Generally speaking, Chinese education pays more attention to the basic knowledge and speculative knowledge. Since primary school, students have to spend a lot of time in classroom to listen to teachers and have a lot of homework to finish out of class everyday. Under the pressure of passing exams, students have to learn much knowledge by heart. The main aim for children to go to school is getting knowledge. There is less free time for them to develop their interests. This is much different from America. In America, students have much time to do what they like. In primary schools, children do not have to spend a lot of time in classroom to listen to their teachers. They only have about 5 hours of classes to finish and then they may do anything they like. Comparatively speaking, American schools pay more attention to developing students' creative ability. Students may choose some handwork courses or something else they like, or they may do nothing, just play in their spare time. They do not have to face a-small-hill-like homework, which is very common in Chinese schools. So it is always thought that Chinese students have better basic knowledge than American students while American students do better than Chinese students in creative ability.

Another difference between American education and Chinese education is what teachers teach in class. Once a Chinese girl went to America and entered a secondary school to go on with her study, but several days later, she complained with her father that she did not know what the teacher said in class. It seemed that the teacher said less about their textbook, and what the teacher said seemed disordered. And then several years later, she came back to China and went on study in a high school, and then several days later, she complained with her father again that the teacher taught nothing but the knowledge in the textbook. This is the difference. Teachers in America focus more on the knowledge out of class and it is students' task to read the textbook, while Chinese teachers focus on textbooks while teaching. They reorganize the content in the textbook and then teach students to get the main ideas. So American students are more active in study textbooks than Chinese students if they are interested in the course, but Chinese students are more hardworking than American students in the whole study.

Another point should be noticed for education is what the purpose is for children or students to study hard at school. Generally speaking, what students learned at school in China, especially at college, determines what kind of jobs they will get after graduation. If a student majors in computer, the first choice for his job is something related to computer. However, in America, what students learn at college has less relationship with their future jobs. For example, a student who majors in camera may do a job of repairing bicycles. Of course, what they learn at school is the base for them to find a job, but it is not the decisive factor.

3.4.3　Case for Practice

Case

　　Xiao Li came to America three weeks ago. She was in Grade 3 in a senior middle school in Beijing before she came to America. And now she goes on with her study in America because she wants to enter a good university, but what makes her confused is which grade she is exactly in at this American school. When she arrived at this school, she was asked to pass an exam for each course to see which grade she could study in. However, the result puzzled her a lot. The marks of English and Math allowed her to study in Grade 12, Chemistry and Physics in Grade 11 while History in Grade 10! Thus she has to study with students from three different grades! This is unbelievable in China! But, study is study. She has no choice but to follow the courses in three different grades.

　　(1) What do you think is the main difference between American school education and Chinese school education?
　　(2) Which education mode do you prefer, the American one or the Chinese one?

3.4.4　Further Reading

Passage 1

　　Boston is called a "college town" because there are 68 colleges and universities in the city (most famous are Harvard and MIT). Because there are thousands of college students in Boston, there are lots of things for young people to do.

　　In the fall, students can watch Boston's baseball team, the Red Sox, play at Fenway Park (America's oldest ballpark, built in 1912). People in Boston love the Red Sox. The team won the World Series last year.

　　The lovely Charles River is in Boston. Students can ride a bike, play rollerblade, or run on the beautiful winding path next to the river. Many college and university rowing teams also practice on the Charles and all the city's students watch the world's biggest boat race, Head of the Charles Regatta every year in October.

　　Students also play Frisbee in the city's largest park, the Boston Commons. The Commons has a large pond. In the winter, lots of young people go ice skating.

Students also eat the city's famous seafood restaurants or go shopping. Boston also has wonderful art museums and the Boston public library.

At night, students can dance at the popular clubs and bars of Lansdowne Street.

Most importantly, Boston is a walking city, so people can go everywhere on foot or on the "T" (the subway). Just be careful during a snowstorm!

Passage 2

China's education system is composed of 4 components. They are basic education, occupational/polytechnic education, common higher education, and adult education. Basic education includes pre-school education, primary education (6 years), junior high school education (3 years), and senior high school education (3 years). Since the issuing of the Compulsory Education Law of the PRC in 1986, governments at all levels have actively promoted nine-year compulsory education, and made remarkable achievements. Occupational education is mainly composed of medium-level professional schools, polytechnic schools, occupational middle schools  as well as short-term occupational and technical training programs of various forms. Common higher education comprises of junior college, bachelor, master and doctoral degree programs. Adult education is comprised of schooling education, anti-illiteracy education, and other programs oriented to adult groups.

Although Chinese education has developed a lot during these years, there are still a lot of problems left to be solved. Scholars and officials classify these outstanding problems into three aspects. The first main aspect lies in the difficulties in entering school. The most prominent issue is whether the national and local governments can provide enough opportunities for education and whether students can afford schooling. The second main aspect is the quality of education. This is one of the significant core issues. With the economic and social development of China, the demand for education at a higher level and of better quality is greater than ever. The third problem is post-graduation employment. A deep concern for ordinary people is whether or not school education can better enable students to find jobs so as to promote economic and social development and to meet the demands of the general public for higher living standard.

Encounter Tips

◎　美国没有全国性的课程标准，但各州、县甚至学区都可以自行编订课程标准。从总体上看，美国的课程设置相当灵活，主要包括必修课和选修课两大类。

◎　中国的基础教育是重知识，"学多悟少"，而美国的基础教育是培养创新能力的教育，"学少悟多"；中国的基础教育重视扎实性，而美国的基础教育重视多元化；中国的基础教育注重深度，而美国的基础教育则注重广度。

◎　美国教育小时管得严，美国父母会立下许多规矩，比如小孩子不能在公共场所大声喧哗之类，而孩子越大管得越松，家长在孩子高中以后就放手让他们自己去闯荡；中国父母则恰恰相反，孩子小时候对其约束少，而长大后则多有限制，甚至连大学专业、恋爱等也都要参与意见。

3.5　Exercises

3.5.1　Exercises A

Decide whether the following statements are true or false.

(1) Politeness is a culturally defined phenomenon, and what is considered polite in one culture can often be quite rude or simply strange in another.

(2) In Western culture, it would be natural for family members to praise each other.

(3) Chinese really mean it when they apologize for the crowded state of their dwellings and for small numbers of dishes, although the room is big enough and there are many dishes.

(4) "Thank you" is uttered in English for more than acknowledging favor or gratitude, and it is often a means to show politeness.

(5) Generally speaking, American children are more independent than Chinese children.

(6) It is impossible for a Chinese and an American to be true friends because they hold different views towards friendship.

(7) Americans make friends in different circumstances or activities.

(8) In China, friendship means a strong life-long bond between two people.

(9) Generally speaking, basic education of China seems "intensive" while basic education of America seems "extensive."

(10) American children have to remember too much knowledge by heart in primary school.

3.5.2　Exercise B

The following are three dialogues, read carefully and tell the difference. There are three choices A, B, and C, choose one for each scene.

A. Between two Chinese.

B. Between two Americans.

C. Between Chinese and American.

Scene 1

A: We're going to New Orleans this weekend.

B: What fun! I wish we were going with you. (If she wants a ride, she will ask.)

A: Three days. By the way, we may need a ride to the airport. Do you think you can take us?

B: Sure. What time?

A: 10:30 p.m. this coming Saturday.

Scene 2

A: We're going to New Orleans this weekend.

B: What fun! I wish we were going with you. How long are you going to be there?

A: Three days. (I hope she'll offer me a ride to the airport.)

B: (She may want me to give her a ride.) Do you need a ride to the airport? I'll take you.

A: Are you sure it's not too much trouble?

B: It's no trouble at all.

Scene 3

A: We're going to New Orleans this weekend.

B: What fun! I wish we were going with you. How long are you going to be there?

A: Three days. (I hope she'll offer me a ride to the airport.)

B: (If she wants a ride, she will ask me.) Have a great time.

A: (If she had wanted to give me a ride, she would have offered it. I'd better ask somebody else.) Thanks. I'll see you when I get back.

3.5.3 Exercise C

Decide which of the following sentences are suitable for you to talk about when you want to make American friends.

(1) Is this the first time you come to China?

(2) What are your hobbies?

(3) What's your favorite sport?

(4) How much do you earn a month?

(5) Can you help me find a position in your company?

(6) How much do you pay for your new computer?

3.5.4 Exercise D

Imagine what the following people would probably do if seeing a friend in a poor situation.

(1) The Americans.

(2) The Chinese.

(3) The Jews.

3.5.5 Exercise E

Read the following case and discuss the questions. There may be more than one possible answer.

A very distinguished 75-year old Chinese scholar and statesman were being honored by a university in the eastern United States. He and his wife had just made the 21-hour flight from Beijing and they were met at the airport by some friends who exclaimed, "You must be tired!" His response was "可以 ," which means "It's OK."

(1) As a Chinese, how do you interpret the scholar's response?

(2) Why the scholar gave such kind of reply?

(3) In this encounter, what misunderstanding may probably arise?

(4) Suppose the situation in reverse, an American traveler to Beijing gets off the plane after 24 hours of continuous travel, and what kind of response would he/she give to the same comment "You must be tired!"

Chapter 3 Keys

CHAPTER 4

Cultural Differences in Connotative Meanings

No one when he uses a word has in mind exactly the same thing that another has, and the difference, however tiny, sends its tremors throughout language.

—Wilhelm von Humboldt

The limits of my language are the limits of my world.

—Ludwig Wittgenstein

4.1 Color

4.1.1 Pre-reading

The world is a colorful place, but many of us may not realize that many factors affect how people feel about colors. Studies have been done to establish that colors do have a psychological influence on each of us. Studies also indicate that we do not have the same responses to the same color. Our ethnic background affects the associations we may make to a color. We need to recognize that not only does each color have many shades, but each also has varied shades of meaning. A glance at the chart below provides an insight to why a Chinese bride would prefer a red dress to a white dress. The meanings listed on the chart are not absolutes; they merely reflect possibilities.

Different Cultures Have Different Symbols for Similar Colors

Color	In Chinese Culture	In English Culture
Red	luck, happiness, prosperousness	aggression, blood, violence, danger
White	bloodless , lifeless, death, ill omen	purity, peace, non-malice
Black	evil, reactionary, illegality, crime	darkness, death, wickedness, sadness
Green	freshness, life, vigor	vigor, freshness, envy, immatureness
Yellow	glory, prosperity, pornography	timidity, derogatory meanings
Blue	calmness, imagination, patience	gloom, depression, nobility, eroticism
Purple	power, dignity, mystery	royalty, power, wealth

颜色是人们对客观世界的一种感知，无论是在大自然还是在社会生活中，都存在着各种各样的颜色。所谓"绚丽世界""五彩人生"，都说明人们的实际生活与颜色密切相关，人们生活在色彩之中。

颜色是一种视觉效果，由于人类具有相同的生理机制和视觉神经，颜色词产生的物质因素也有相似之处。在人类语言里，存在着大量记录颜色的符号——颜色词。这些词语在语言中经常被使用，蕴涵着深厚的民族文化心态和感情色彩。

颜色词多数具有丰富的象征意义。一般认为颜色词的象征意义是通过客观事物的色彩联想而生发出来的，即人们常说的看到某种颜色就会产生某种联想。由于民族心理、历史传统、宗教信仰、情感色彩、地理环境等文化背景的差异，人们对颜色词的感受和表达不尽相同，对颜色产生的联想意义和语用意义各不相同，有些特点甚至构成了人们经过引申、转义以后对颜色的崇尚和禁忌。这种不同文化之间颜色象征意义的差异是在社会的发展、历史的沉淀中约定俗成的，是一种永久性的文化现象。如果说人类本能的生理色觉感知形成了最初的颜色概念，那么不同的民族文化是最终造成两种语言词库中颜色词语差异的决定因素。

4.1.2 Same Color in Different Cultures

Color is a very important area of people's world knowledge, and it is concerned with people's life closely, carrying basic attributes of physics and rich cultural connotations. Color is seen at all time and in every corner. It's a really powerful tool. There are six kinds of colors on the flag of the International Olympic Games. The bottom is white and it implies the pure friendship and fair competition. In the center, five colored rings were linked together mutually, namely, blue, yellow, black, green, and red. The blue stands for the Europe, the yellow the Asia, the black the Africa, the green the Oceania, and the red the America.

Man has a common feeling about colors, because color words can not only express the natural gorgeous colors, but also reflect the view of value and aesthetic standard of a people. Human beings have the same physical mechanism and optic nervous system. There are no differences in the feelings of colors in theory: sensory organs such as eyes, ears, and nose to sense the environment, and the sensations received by them are routed through our nervous system to our brains, where they are interpreted and recorded. Therefore, the reflections in our minds of the objective world are the same. However, due to the differences of national psychology, historical tradition, religious beliefs, habits and customs, emotion of the color in different nationality, some colors have already been the obstructions in cross-cultural communication, and different color words have different meanings in different backgrounds of national culture.

The National Psychology

As we know, the world does not only consist of the physical world, but also the psychological world. And the latter really influences cross-cultural communication. Chinese and Western people's psychological factors are somewhat different. Different color words may be used to describe the external features of the same things. "Tea" in Chinese is translated into cha, but " 红茶 " in Chinese is "black tea" in English. The reason is that the speakers of Chinese and English perceive the physical world differently. The Chinese people pay more attention to the red color of the water, whereas the Englishmen put their eyes on the black color of the tea when it is dry.

Black is often seen as the "color" of death in Western culture. Black represents darkness and the unknown, and death is associated with the extinguishing of light. The association of white with death in Eastern cultures could come from the white cloth used to enshroud corpses (as in Egyptian mummys), the pale skin of a  dead person, or the stark whiteness of bones and skeletons. Many Eastern cultures also view death as the passage into a higher state of being (Buddhism, Hinduism), and thus could view white as a positive color association for death.

The West relatively pays attention to the analysis things with rational science from the beginning. So, the symbolic meaning of colors is often more direct in Western culture. For example, red in Western culture mainly refers to the color of blood, and in minds of the Westerners, blood is the liquid of the life. So the Westerners always associate red with violence and danger, such as red hands, red revenge, and a red battle.

Color intension and symbolic meaning are very abundant in Chinese culture. In Chinese culture, the thought that the color expresses has strong mystery flavor. For example, the red in Chinese culture comes from the sun. Our ancestor has a kind of instinctive attachment and worships to the sunshine. It is a tradition for Chinese people to use red to express happiness, luck, and prosperousness. Red is a color that always appears in festive circumstances. For example, people use red paper to write spring festival scrolls. On wedding ceremony, red is the main color. People use red xi zi (囍), and wear red clothes and shoes. On a serious welcome occasion, Chinese use "红灯高挂" "披红戴绿" to describe it. In addition, people use "红红火火" to describe someone's career is great .

White, opposite to red, is a taboo color in Chinese culture. It is said that in the initial stage of mankind, our ancestor is small and weak, which makes them completely exposed in broad daylight, and face the attack of the beast without any shelter, and therefore the color white has a kind of instinctive frightened sense. In Chinese, people like using "white" to describe unhappiness and death. At a funeral, Chinese people often wear white clothes. For example, there are " 穿白衣 " " 戴白帽 " " 贴白纸 " " 白事 ." However, white in Western culture is considered pure. White is the traditional color for the brides at weddings. As white is the color of the snow, there is a white Christmas and a white winter. White stands for honesty and integrity, such as a white spirit, white man, and white hand. It is obvious that the symbolic meaning of the color demonstrates the human psychological characteristics.

Historical Tradition

A lot of color words are produced in special historical background, most of which are called "culture limited word." If we don't understand these words and the social custom and culture background of them, it is even harder for us to communicate with each other. Therefore, it is of great importance to grasp the difference between the literal meaning and amplifying meaning.

In the Qing Dynasty, the book that was authorized by the emperor is called "red book." It is different from the "red book" in English-speaking countries which means the book with a red cover.

In ancient China, according to Han's traditional mind, yellow is the most respectable color in all colors. Yellow River is the mother of all rivers and the mother river of the Chinese nation. It flows through Shan and Gan Plateau and Central China of Jin and Yu, which are the origin of Chinese civilization. Because the earth there is yellow, ancient Chinese lay stress on yellow at that time. Also, yellow symbolizes supreme power, position, and emperor's rights. So from the Tang Dynasty, yellow has been the special color to royal families. When a person became an emperor, he must wear the special yellow clothes. The Architectural color for royal families alone is also yellow. Ministers and common people are not allowed to use yellow for any use.

In the same way, in English culture, blue and purple are also connected with royal families. For example, having blue blood means a person belonging to the royal family. Blue Book is the report from English royal administration.

Religious Beliefs

Religion is also one of the most important factors affecting the culture and cross-cultural communication. Religion has endeavored to explain those motions about life that otherwise could not be understood or resolved.

Religion deals with the life and death in nature, the creation of the universe, the origin of groups in the society, the relationship with each other, and the relation of human beings to nature. The usages of colors in religion exert great influence on the meaning of the color terms.

In English there is a phrase "black Friday." In religion, black means grief, despair and death. Friday refers to the Friday before Easter day. Jesus was suffering at that day. Based on the nation's culture background and traditional custom, people in English countries use black Friday to symbolize the disaster.

Emotion of Colors

Colors that can remind us of a time or place can evoke an emotion related to that experience. When someone asks you what your favorite color is, you can be certain that there are some color experiences that you like better than others.

Language has certain emotion. In various languages, it is not uncommon that the word contains a different emotion, and the color word is no exception. For example, blue may stand for the pessimistic feeling: "the blues" indicates depressed and unhappy feelings, which can be shown in the expressions "in blue," "sing the blues," and "cry the blues." In Chinese, on the contrary, the color of blue stands for calmness and hope, which has nothing to do with the depressed or sad feelings.

Environment

Culture is defined and generated on the three-fold reality of culture, society and people. The evolution of a culture is the result of the interaction between the subject and the object, which we can call "environment." Geographical position is a part of it. For instance, because of the geographical position in European countries, Europeans can always see snow—the color of white, which makes them have a strong feeling of white. So they think white is the color of purity and brightness. In ancient China, people can always see earth—the color of yellow. So they think yellow is the center of everything.

Yellow is the color for emperors. Yellow often decorates royal palaces, altars and temples. For example, there are " 黄袍加身 " " 黄马褂 ."

4.1.3　Case for Practice

Case

Translate the following short passage into Chinese.

Mr. Smith, a very white man, but a very yellow one. He was very red with anger when he found himself cheated by his close friend, but, he said nothing. Last Friday, a black letter day, he had a car accident. He was looking rather green and feeling blue lately. When I saw him, he was in a brown study. I hope he'll soon be in the pink again.

Color Idioms: Definitions

(1) Many people feared that the new millennium would cause black-outs because of problems with electricity production.

(2) What a beautiful car! I'm green with envy.

(3) Don't rely on him under pressure in battle. He's yellow.

(4) She was such a difficult child that her family always treated her like a black sheep.

(5) Mr. Jackson is very important to the success of this program. Make sure to roll out the red carpet when he arrives.

(6) We're looking for a new home in the green belt.

(7) It's not quite as black and white as you think.

(8) Try to cheer Susan up. She is feeling rather blue these days.

(9) Jack gave me the green light on the project.

4.1.4　Further Reading

Passage 1

Color Words in Economy

In economy life, the color words are also vastly used. There are a great number of phrases and fixed usages which are related to colors in economy glossary. The followings are some combined meanings of color words and some economy words which formed by it.

(1) In economy, the word "red" is always related to debt or bankruptcy. When the net income on reckoning is negative, people use a red pen to register. Therefore there are phrases like "red figure, red ink, in the red, red-ink entry, red balance." In addition, usages like red cent, red gold, red tip on stock market are also used frequently.

(2) In English-speaking countries, when people talk about "black," it is always

related with "bad, evil, and wicked." For example, "black money" means the money with wrong source; "black market" means exchanging things which the government forbids or doing illegal speculated marketing. Except this, "black" can also mean payoff. Like red, black is also a kind of color when people keep accounts, such as black figure, in the black, black figure nation, and interest in the black.

(3) "Blue" in English means unhappiness and gloom. It can also be used to describe the nobles on the upper class; for example, he is a real blue blood. Another phrase "blue-eyed boys" means the employees on which the management dotes. In economy glossary, blue has many meanings, such as blue book, blue-sky market, blue-collar workers, and blue chip. "Blue button" means the broker who has the right to enter the stock exchanging. "Blue return" is a kind of table that can only be used by honest taxpayers. "Blue-chip rate" is British favorable credit interest rate. "Blue law" is a kind of laws in America which forbid people from doing commercial exchange on Sunday. "Blue-sky law" refers to the law which used to manage the stocks. "Blue sky bargaining" means that the agreement cannot be made because of unpractical request during the negotiation.

(4) In common English "green" always means freshness or envy, but in economy English "green back" is equal to American dollars for the reverse side of the dollar is green. "Green power" means consortium. "Green meat" means fresh meat. "Green stamp" means the ticket for helping poor people. "Green sheet" is the comparative table of government budget.

(5) White makes one think of immaculacy in English; for example, white war is the war without smoke, which always refers to the economy competition. "White goods" refer to the family electric equipments which are big and expensive. Others like white money, white coal, white elephant, white sale, the white way are all useful phrase.

(6) There are still other color words in economy life. "Grey market" means half-black market. "Grey area" means the area where many people lose job. "Pink slip" is the requisition that sends away workers. "Yellow pages" means the classify telephone book.

Passage 2

Colors in Chinese and English Cultures

On the basic color words, there is not so much difference in English and in Chinese. In Chinese, there are "赤，橙，黄，绿，青，蓝，紫，" while in English there are red, white, black, green, yellow, blue, and purple. Owing to the different historic cultural backgrounds of the two cultures, the same color words have different symbolic meanings.

Red

Red in the Chinese culture is a basic esteem color. It is a tradition for the Chinese people to use red to express happiness, luck, and prosperousness. Red is a color that always appears in festive circumstances. For example, people use red paper to write spring festival scrolls. On wedding ceremonies, people use red xi zi.

Red in Western culture mainly refers to color of blood, and in minds of the Westerners, blood is the liquid of the life. So the Westerners always associate red with violence and danger, such as red hands, red revenge, and a red battle.

White

White, opposite to red, is a basic taboo color in Chinese traditional culture. It is an exhausted, bloodless, and lifeless, expression, and stands for death and ill omen. When a relative dies, the family members wear white clothing in order to show grief. In Chinese feudal society, the common people were forbidden to dress in any other colors except white. From the Han Dynasty to the Tang Dynasty, "white clothing" means the ordinary people.

White in Western culture is usually an esteem color. White is considered pure. White is the traditional color for the brides at weddings. As white is the color of the snow, there is a white Christmas and a white winter. White stands for honesty and uprightness, such as a white spirit, white man, and white hand. White also stands for luck, for example, one of the white days in somebody's life, white magic, and white hope is a person who is expected to bring success to a team. White stands for legality and non-malice, such as white market and white list.

Black

In Chinese traditional culture, black and white both belong to the Five Colors. At Chinese funerals, people usually wear a black armband to show their mourns to the death. On one hand, black stands for solemness and justice, such as Baozheng; on the other hand, it stands for evil and reactionary. Black also stands for illegality and crime.

In the West, black is a taboo color, which stands for darkness. It means death and sinister, such as Black Mass, to wear black for her mother, black words, a black letter day, and Black Friday. Black symbolizes wicked and guilty, such as black man, a black deed, black guard, black-hand, and black-hearted. And it means disgrace, such as a black mark, a black eye, and a black sheep. Besides that, it also means depression and resentment, such as black dog, black future, a black look, and black thoughts.

However, black also stands for solemnity and dignity. Black suit is the Westerners' favorite traditional dress. On solemn occasions, officials and celebrities would prefer to dress in black.

Yellow

In Chinese traditional culture, yellow is located in the center of the Five Colors. So far, yellow is still the symbol of ancient China. "黄袍" is the emperor's dress, and "黄榜" is the proclamation published by the emperor. "黄道吉日" means an auspicious day. However, yellow in modern China has negative meanings, such as "黄色书刊" or "黄色录像." Here yellow has an extended meaning of obscenity and pornography, while in

English there are similar expressions like the blue video and the blue talk.

Yellow in the West mostly has derogatory meanings. In English, yellow has some particular meanings in certain texts that have no relationship with sentiment. For example, the yellow page is the telephone dictionary, and yellow boy is the golden coins.

Green

In the Chinese traditional culture, green ranks the first in the Five Colors, signifying everything grows. In the feudal society, the dress of the government official on a lower level was regularized to be green, so it also symbolizes humble. "青衫绿袍" is a symbol of low position in the official career.

In English there is a term green-eyed or green with envy, both of which mean jealous and envious. However, in Chinese "眼红" describes the same meaning.

No matter in English or in Chinese, this symbolic meaning of green is identical. Green in Western culture is mainly related to the color of the plants, and is the symbol of vigor and energy; for example, a green old age is associated with an old but vigorous man or woman. And to remain green forever means to keep fresh and vigorous forever; green also means fresh, such as keep a memory green, a green wound, and green meat; and it means immature, inexperienced and easily fooled, such as a green hand, a green horn which refers to a raw, simple and inexperienced person, easily fooled or parted from his money. In some certain phrases, green has different meanings. For example, green-light means giving permission to go ahead with.

Purple

In China, purple is more often adopted by feudal emperors and Taoists. They called the auspicious air "紫气," and the Taoist books "紫书." The place which the Deity lives in is "紫台" and the emperors' palace is "紫禁城"(the Forbidden City).

In English, purple shares the same connotation as in Chinese. In the eye of Westerners, purple is the symbol of emperor and power. "To be born in the purple" means to be born in a royal family; "to be raised to the purple" means to be promoted to the position as a pope; "purple passages" means too florid words, etc. In Chinese, "红得发紫" means popular.

Blue

It seems that blue is a favorable word to Chinese. The blue sky, for instance, can arouse us to yearn for a better future.

In Western culture, however, blue does not associate with happiness and imagination, but gloom and depression. He is in a blue mood means he is sad or gloomy.

Blue is also often associated with high social status or being aristocratic. "He is a real blue blood" means he is from an aristocratic family. In addition, in the US, a book with the names of famous figures, especially top government officials, is called blue book. "Blue film" means erotic film while in Chinese we call it "黄色电影."

Notes

architectural	建筑	mourning	哀痛；悲伤
exert	发挥	grief	忧伤
evoke	激起	pessimistic	悲观的
interaction	相互作用		

Encounter Tips

◎　"红茶"译为 black tea，"红糖"译为 brown sugar，"红豆"译为 love pea，"红白喜事"译为 wedding and funerals；"brown bread"译为黑面包，"brown paper"译为牛皮纸，"black cloth"译为青布，"blue pepper steak"是指胡椒牛排煮得极嫩。

◎　美国有些城市的出租车上标有"yellow"（而不是"taxi"）字样，因为那里的出租车为黄颜色。

4.2　Number

4.2.1　Pre-reading

Here is an excerpt from a letter by an American to his friend on number that causes cross-cultural misunderstanding:

I bought a phone number in Beijing several days ago. It was surprising that they were differently priced depending on whether a certain number was included. The one including "four" costed 40 yuan, and those without "four" was much higher. It was said that "four" was an unlucky number in China.

But I bought the cheapest one including "four" because I didn't believe in that. However, misfortune came one after another since I got this phone number. My purse lost; my cell phone broke; my bike was stolen. Did my phone number including "four" bring me bad luck?

Well, I began to rethink about the number "four"!!!

　　这个案例中的美国朋友不太理解中国文化中数字"4"的谐音联想，电话号码中有"4"的价格比没有"4"的要低得多。在中国"4"被视为一个不吉祥的数字，在古代人们对于"4"并无特别的忌讳，这主要是因为随着科技的发展，人们生活中越来越多地使用到数字，如门牌号、手机号码、车牌号等。而因为"4"的发音与"死"谐音，所以车牌号码、电话号码等尾数有"4"的就不受欢迎。

　　数字是语言科学中的一个特殊领域，是随着人类文明的产生和发展而产生和发展的。语言中数字是反映客观物质世界的规模、大小的数和量，是表示数量或

顺序的词类。人们的生活离不开数字，数字作为计算功能的意义是一致的。数字本无好坏、褒贬、吉凶之分。但随着语言和文化的发展，人们却不断地丰富其内涵，增添其色彩。由于受民族心理、宗教信仰、神话传说等文化差异的影响，汉英语数字泛化的内涵和外延，虽有共同的规律，但也存在着较大的差异。对不同或相同的数字，汉英有着不同的崇尚或禁忌习俗，以及不同的联想和意义，并由此孕育出各自独特的数字文化。

4.2.2　Numbers Penetrate into Every Aspect of Human Life

A number is a word or symbol that represents an amount or a quantity. Numbers play an important role in daily life. Numbers are used widely in every aspect of life. Without numbers, nothing can get along well in the world.

All human beings use numbers so that the culture of numbers has come into being. Numbers penetrate into every aspect of human life. There are numerous Chinese idioms and idiomatic usages with numbers, such as "说一不二""五湖四海""三十六计，走为上计""三句话不离本行""八九不离十""百战不殆""九九归一""十万火急."

In English-related culture, there are also a large quantity of idioms or idiomatic usages with numbers, such as "three sheets in the wind" (大醉), "the upper ten" (上流社会), "second to none" (最好的), "two-by-four" (小的，微不足道的), "two-left feet" (极笨拙的).

Numbers are created from the interaction of humans' social and cultural behavior with their abilities to conceptualize the outside world. So a number is not only used as a counting and calculation tool, but also carries profound connotations, reflecting the unique culture of a country.

Due to the influences of national psychology, religious belief, mythology, and so on, there exist different cultural connotations and extensions between Chinese and English numbers.

The National Psychology

Numbers came into use about 3,000 years ago in China. From one, ten to hundred, thousand, ten thousand, the number system was complete as early as in the Shang Dynasty and the decimal system also dated back to that time.

In Chinese culture, heaven and earth produce everything by the interaction of two existential and powerful forces of the universe, yin and yang. In China, the mystery of numbers has been much influenced by the concept of yin and yang. Ancients divide the ten numbers into two groups: the odd numbers are yang, implying "the heaven, the male," while the even numbers are yin, implying "the Earth, the female."

"Nine," as the largest single digit, symbolized the supreme sovereignty of the emperor who was "the Son of Heaven." And the number "nine" (or its multiples) is often employed in the Chinese ancient architecture, particularly imperial buildings. Take the Forbidden City for example, which is located in the center of Beijing. It has a total of 9,999 bays. The Chinese people show preference to number "nine," not only in the construction of buildings, but also in other fields, for example, a division of ancient feudal government officials was "nine level." By and by, the number "nine" became exclusively reserved and adorned by the Chinese people, even today.

Generally speaking, in Chinese culture, even numbers are regarded to be lucky and propitious symbols, which can bring people good luck and fortune. As a rule in day-to-day life in China, it is customary to regard even numbers as being more auspicious than odd numbers. In China, traditionally gifts are given as a party of the celebration for all occasions. Thus, guests will always give even-numbered presents. As the number two, usually suggests germination and harmony, at wedding celebrations, decorations are invariably set out in pairs: a pair of red candles, a pair of pillows, and couplets hung on two sides of the hall. "Six," pronounced as liu, conveys indirectly its homophony's meaning—do everything smoothly.

The number "four" in Chinese has a bad and unlucky association and connotation, for it has a similar sound with the Chinese character si, representing death. So a large number of people make every effort to avoid it. In contrast, the number "eight" is fortunate because it sounds like fa, namely, making a fortune. When it comes to the cases like telephone numbers, vehicle license numbers, door numbers, people show special preference to number "eight" or something associated with number "eight," such as 168 (to make a fortune all the way) and 518 (I want to make a fortune).

But as far as the English people are concerned, when celebrating or sending flowers to friends or relatives, people should take one, three, five, or even more (excluding 13), whereas, people send two or four, six flowers or its multiple when condoling with deceased persons. English people worship number "four," which is the symbol of justice, righteousness, power, the fountain of creation, and the key of everything in the world. For instance, to the ancient people, the cosmos is made up of four elements: earth, air, water, and fire.

Religious Belief

Religion influences people's conception of culture without doubt, because of its dominant role in most countries. For ancient Chinese, "three" stands for the three parts of the universe: heaven, earth, and human. And it is said that there are three creators of the universe, governing the earth and the fairyland. Lao Zi expressed that one produces two, two produce three, and three produce everything. Therefore, in Chinese there arise many idiomatic phrases about "three," like " 三人行必有我师焉 " and " 一日不见，如隔三秋 ." The number "three" indicates perfection and completeness. The idiom " 三生有幸 " expresses that a person is fortunate all his life. Here " 三生 " refers to the previous life, present life, and next life.

The Han People worship yi (一) since ancient times. They hold the belief that all things on earth come from yi, because yi has the similar meaning with yuan (元), shi (姓), chu (初), meaning "the source" (源头). The Taoist believes that "one makes two, and two make three, and three make everything on earth". Yi sometimes means complete. For example, "all the thing." Yi often goes together with other words expressing "quantity," but means "whole or complete," such as " 一身泥土 " (with mud all over the body) and " 一生穷困 " (lead a poor life the whole lifetime).

Christianity has a strong influence in the cultural connotation of numbers in Western countries. The religious tradition of the Christian Trinity, which is, Father, Son, and Holy Spirit, has endowed a mysterious number "three" with divinity and perfection. The widespread interest of number "three" still remains in Westerners' minds or thinking today.

Similarly, number "seven," a number with strong religious color, is used frequently in the *Bible*, indicating that God spent seven days in Creation. At times it has reference to bringing a work toward completion, or it can refer to the complete cycle of things as established or allowed by God. There are plenty of idioms or idiomatic usages with "seven" in English culture, such as, the Seven Virtues, including Faith, Hope, Charity, Justice, Fortitude, Prudence, Temperance, the seven days of creation, and the Seventh Heaven.

Number "thirteen" is regarded as an evil number, standing for misfortune. According to the Scripture, Judah, the thirteenth comer during the last supper, betrayed Jesus. Hence, people in Western countries avoid "13" in many aspects of life. People avoid a room numbered 13, a seat in the 13th row of an airplane or renting a flat on the 13th floor.

The belief that Friday is an unlucky day is one of the most widely known superstitions in Britain today. Some say Friday's bad reputation goes all the way back to the Garden of Eden. It was on a Friday, supposedly, that Eve tempted Adam with the forbidden fruit. Adam bit, as we all learned in Sunday School, and they were both ejected from Paradise. And, of course, Friday was the day of the week on which Christ was crucified. It is therefore a day of penance for Christians.

Today, the 13th floor is often missing in Chinese hotels, which is proof that the Western superstition of regarding the number 13 as a bringer of bad luck has been added to the list of numbers or number combinations with fortunate or unfortunate connotations in China. But when you get on an elevator in a Chinese hotel, you will not find yourself on the 14th floor, but on the 15th floor once you pass the 12th floor due to the inauspiciousness of the number 14. Fourteen is by far the most feared number in Chinese superstition. The combination of the words, shí = ten and sì = four, can mean "accidents" or, when both numbers are read separately, yāo sì, means "will die." Add a five in front, and the death wish is made even more personal, as the string 514, wǔ yāo sì, is pronounced the same way as "I will die." Not the best combination for anyone with a tendency to believe in superstitions!

This demonstrates clearly how the Chinese have adopted Western mindsets while keeping a tight grasp of their own traditional beliefs.

Mythology

Mythology associated with numbers in both Chinese and English culture has deeply influenced the cultural connotations of numbers. In Chinese, the cultural connotations of numbers have connection with the ancient myth. For instance, four character words "三头六臂" originated from Chinese myth, narrating a supernatural being. Nezha, who takes charge of the justice, has three heads and six arms. He has vastly magic power to transform himself into three at random. Accordingly, number "three" is endowed with cultural connotations of magic and power.

And, English culture has been more strongly affected by the Greek and Roman mythology, whose gods resemble the character of humans with feelings and desires, happiness and sadness. In Roman myth, god Jupiter, whose power stems from his trident or three-pronged thunder-stick in his hand, governs the others. Neptune, the god of the sea, relies on his three-pronged spear, and Pluto is a dog with three heads. Thus number "three" is lodged with extension of power and divinity.

4.2.3　Case for Practice

Case

Do "Lucky Numbers" Really Bring Good Luck?

Some people believe that lucky numbers bring good luck. In China, out of the ten numerals from 0 to 9, 3, 6, 8, and 9 are considered to be the lucky ones. A good case in point is the number "eight" in China. In Chinese "eight" has the similar pronunciation to the Chinese character fa, which means to be rich. So, more and more people prefer "eight." They believe they can be richer and richer with this number. Thus some people are willing or even eager to spend money on telephone numbers or car numbers with "eight" at the end of them. Those who believe in "lucky numbers" want to be connected with them as many as possible in their daily lives. For example, if a person's phone number is 3366 8899, he or she is considered to be very lucky, for he or she will have backup, success, fortune and longevity.

Other people do not believe in "lucky numbers." Numbers are just a tool for counting. They think numbers have nothing to do with good luck or happiness. They believe good luck belongs to those who are diligent and persistent enough to create it.

(1) Do you believe in "lucky numbers"? Why?

(2) What do you think is the key to success?

4.2.4   Further Reading

Craving Lucky Numbers in Daily Life

Call it an obsession, infatuation or whatever you will. But for any newcomer to China it won't take long to find out how madly in love the people are with lucky numbers.

From the day they are born to the day they move into the realm of the afterlife, for many Chinese, gathering auspicious numbers is a way of life.

The unflinching faith in "lucky" numbers can be found everywhere: From gift money given on birthdays and red packets distributed every Spring Festival (in sets of two for a stronger effect), to the apartment, floor and even street numbers where people live, to the amount of "thank you" money paid by the groom to his fiancee's bridesmaids on their wedding day.

People are mostly interested in plates that have the numbers six or eight because they believe these numbers will bring them good fortune.

The highest price paid at the two-day auction was for plate number AW6666, which was bought for 272,000 yuan (US$34,000) by an anonymous bidder on behalf of a motorcycle dealership in Zengcheng, Guangzhou.

Hong Kong tycoon Albert Yeung Sau Shing is still the all-time champion, though. He paid a whopping HK$13 million (US$1.67 million) for the number 9 for his licence plate in 1994.

That's not all. The craze for lucky numbers even extends to phone numbers.

The Chinese mainland's 11-digit mobile phone numbers make grasping luck a little more difficult. Although some view multiple eights or nines as a must, to others it's all just a game.

"I don't believe in these kinds of things," said Penny Guo, who works as a trader for a large import & export company in Dongguan, Guangdong Province.

Guo, who says her friends are also practical, and believes lucky numbers are for the old and rich or for very young girls. Even my parents don't believe in such things.

Paying extra for a lucky number is a waste (of money), and I do not believe numbers will bring luck. I am happy if I can get an eight or nine in my phone number, but I don't care if I don't. People think 888 or 999 at the end of the (phone) number will bring luck, but I will not pay for it.

"What I get does not depend on any number. It depends on my effort."

For Feng Xie, who lives and works in Shenzhen, it's more important to avoid unlucky numbers than to chase good ones.

Feng, a 26-year-old professional, says that although she doesn't have any faith in numbers specifically, she still avoids anything to do with the number four, and would not feel comfortable with that number in her mobile phone number or address. Most Chinese regard it unlucky because "four" sounds too close to "death" in Chinese.

"Whether it is Chinese New Year, on wedding days, or any important event, there are numbers and dates that are important," said William Tan, a well-known fashion designer and one of the city's best-known cultural gurus.

The amount of money given on New Year or as a gift from a couple should always be even and distributed in pairs, he said.

On a couple's wedding day, the husband should give "sisters' money" to the sisters and bridesmaids of the bride, when he goes to pick the bride up. The amount given should be a multiple of three or eight, such as HK$8,888, he said.

For major events, such as graduation, moving houses or opening up a new business, Tan suggests using the Tung Shing or "lucky almanac" to see which date is suitable for the occasion. "Lucky dates will include three, six, eight or nine," said Tan.

Notes

propitious	吉利	omen	预兆
connotation	内涵	inexhaustible	无穷无尽的
worship	崇拜	cosmos	宇宙
endow	赋予	pronged	尖端分叉的
divinity	神		

Encounter Tips

◎ 在中国文化中有"七日来复""正月初七为人日""山中方七日，世上已千年"之说。不过，"七"在汉语中却是人们常常忌讳的数字。给人送礼时忌七件或七样，饭桌上的菜绝不能是七盘。人们在挑选吉日良辰时不挑七、十七或二十七。其原因，一是与中国人崇尚偶数的心理有关，二是与中国祭奠死者的传统有关。

◎ 在西方"seven"却是个神圣的数字。西方人讲究七种美德，七次圣餐，人生有七个时期。这是因为它与神圣有关。例如，上帝用六天创造了世界，第七天为休息日；耶稣劝告人们原谅别人要七七四十九次之多；圣母玛丽亚有七件快乐的事、七件悲哀的事；主祷文共有七部分；圣灵有七件礼物。

◎ 在中国"六"是一个时空谐和数，我们常说"眼观六路，耳听八方"，六路即前、后、左、右、上、下，或天地四方，亦即三维空间的六个方向。"六"在中国人看来是个最吉祥不过的数字。俗语"六六大顺"即是最好的印证。英语中的 "six" 却不是一个受欢迎的数字，人们视 6 为大凶数或野兽数，这从以下习语中可见一斑。如：at sixes and sevens（乱七八糟的），hit sb. for six/knock sb. six（给敌人／某人以毁灭性打击），six penny（不值钱），six of one and half a dozen of the other（半斤八两）等。

4.3 Associative Target

4.3.1 Pre-reading

Mr. Johnson is a sales representative of an American electronic company. He has worked for the company for many years, and has built up some loyal clients who have helped him a lot. Among those clients there is a Mr. Han from Hangzhou, China. Mr. Johnson was assigned by the company to Hangzhou to resolve some technical problems. The first idea that came to his mind was that he should go and see Mr. Han. From what his American colleagues have told him before, Mr. John learned that in China it would be better to bring some gifts if you visit someone. He decided to bring a very special gift to Mr. Han—a new model of electronic clock, which is the new product of the company and sells very well in America. He was very proud of himself for this great idea. But to his surprise, Mr. Han looked offended when he saw the clock. He simply refused to accept it with no explanation. Mr. Johnson was very embarrassed and puzzled.

在这个案例里，Johnson 先生由于不懂中西文化差异闹了个不愉快。在英美人看来，朋友双方送些书、闹钟之类的东西既实用又贴心，但他们不知道，在中国，送钟给别人会让人有 "送终" 的不愉快的联想，别人当然不接受这个礼物了。语言是文化的载体，同时又是文化的一个重要组成部分。在语言的各要素中，词汇是基本要素，因而文化差异在词汇上必然有所体现。不同的民族由于在地理、民俗、宗教及价值观念等方面存在着差异，表达同一理性概念的词，在各自独特的文化传统作用下必然会产生附加在词汇本身概念之上的不同的联想意义。这种联想意义与词义本身没有必然联系，而是在说者和听者的文化知识基础上，在特定的语境中，对于一个词所产生的某种特定感受。不了解这种联想意义的差别，就不能完全接受一个词所承载的全部语言信息量。尤其是在跨文化交际中，对于词汇联想意义的理解有助于人们更恰当地了解和掌握所学语言的文化，从而达到真正交际的目的。

4.3.2 Different Connotations

Language is the carrier of culture. Words are the building blocks of a language. Thus differences in Chinese and English cultures are reflected in the words. It is not unusual for the same word to have different connotations.

Different Connotations of Animals

Dragon

The Chinese people regard themselves as the descendants of dragon. The dragon is a sacred symbol of power and charity. The image of dragon enjoys high prestige among Chinese people and its cultural implication is taken for granted. In the West, dragon is described as a monster with wings and claws, which is evil and can breathe fire. Many English legends, like Beowulf, usually ended up in the victory that the national heroes killed the dragons. Many Chinese parents " 望子成龙 "(literally, which means expecting one's son to become a dragon), which would sound ridiculous to the English-speaking people.

Phoenix

In Western myths, phoenix has the connotation of rebirth. According to the Greek myths, phoenix can live a very long life—some say 500 years. After this period, phoenix would build itself a nest and burn itself. When everything goes to ash, a new phoenix would fly from it. So when someone just suffered a fire, people would wish the building would rise like a phoenix from the relics.

In traditional Chinese myths, the phoenix is the head of all birds. In feudal society, it symbolizes the imperial power and auspice. So the character " 凤 " could be found in many Chinese girls' names. Phoenix could also be used to refer to rare or precious people or things, such as " 凤毛麟角 ."

Owl

In English, there is a phrase "as wise as an owl." So owls are the symbol of wisdom. In children's literature, owls are always intelligent and serious. When there are disputes among the animals, they would ask for the owl's judgment. In the English nursery rhythm Mother Goose's Fairy Tales, owls are like this:

A wise old owl lived in an oak.

The more he saw the less he spoke.

The less he spoke the more he heard.

Why can't we all be like that wise old bird?

However, in Chinese, owl is thought as a symbol of omen because it always flies around graveyard at night, sending out sad voice. In the old legend, it is said that someone would die if the owl rest on his house. Owl is related to bad luck and death. So when people hear the cry of an owl, they would worry that something bad will happen. Amazingly sometimes owls in English also have bad connotations. For example, in Shakespeare's *Macbeth*, when Macbeth murdered Duncan, there is a conversation between him and his wife:

Macbeth: I have done the deed. Didn't you hear a noise?

Lady Macbeth: I heard the owl scream and the crickets cry.

Whale

A whale is a huge animal, so in English it is a symbol of valuable things. The following examples prove it—"a whale of a chance"(一个极好的机会), "whale on skating"(滑冰高手), "a whale at tennis"(善打网球的人). However, in China, people pay little attention to its value but to its huge appetite. " 蚕食鲸吞 " means that a small country is embezzled by others like a silkworm eating little by little or like a whale swallowing.

Cat

In Chinese, the cat is a symbol of loveliness and shrewdness. Chinese people love cat because it is a lovely companion and it is a master in catching mice. Some ancient poets wrote poems to prize cats. But in English, the cat is the embodiment of devil. People detest cats, especially the black cat.

Dog

The dog is universally acknowledged as men's best friend for the sake of their faithfulness among the English-speaking people in the Western world. Nowadays, more and more Chinese are inclined to choose dogs as their pets for the same reason. Dogs stand for the image of faithfulness and friendship in both Chinese and
English. This is reflected in sayings like "love me, love my dog" in English and " 打狗 也要看主人 " in Chinese. In most cases, the dog is a neutral term in its image-making in English. It is preferable to call a person as a lucky dog, a top dog, etc. in English. "To let sleeping dogs lie" means not to make trouble or disturb others. "Every dog has its day" means every person will succeed or become fortunate some day. All the phrases do not contain derogatory connotations. But most Chinese phrases with " 狗 " are associated with negative implications, such as " 狗仗人势 " " 狼心狗肺 ". So dogs are given more affirmative attitudes in English.

Magpie

In Chinese, the magpie is an auspicious bird which brings unexpected good news. It is said that its voice brings good news as the following saying shows " 今朝闻鹊喜， 家信必有归 ." What's more, its voice is the forecast of fine weather, such as " 鹊声宣 日出 ." It is proved that magpies can bring us good luck, whereas in English, it refers to wordy people. For example, "She kept muttering like a magpie." It is said that people in English-speaking countries feel disgusted towards its voice. Besides, it stands for chaos and disorder, such as "a magpie collection."

There is an interesting custom of counting magpies in Britain and Ireland. People believe magpies may represent good or bad luck of various forms in a complex manner, depending on the number of magpies present, according to various traditional rhymes. One of them goes like this: One for sorrow, two for joy, three for girl, four for boy, five for silver, six for gold, seven for a secret never told, eight for heaven, nine for hell, and ten for the devil's own self.

Cricket

In Chinese culture, crickets give the connotation of loneliness and dreariness. Many famous poets used the image of crickets in their works to invoke such feelings. For example, "昨夜寒蛩不住鸣，惊回千里梦，已三更 ."

While in English, crickets are merry and joyous. English people think that those who can hear the singing of crickets on Christmas Eve are the luckiest.

Bat

In English there are such phrases as "as blind as a bat" "have bats in the belfry"(异想天开). Bats will cause bad connotations in the Westerners because they think bats are ugly, ferocious. In the myths bats are always connected with "vampires"(吸血鬼).

But in Chinese culture, bats symbolize auspice, health, and happiness because the Chinese character of "bat"(蝠) has the assonance of " 福 " which means happiness.

Chicken

In English the chicken has the connotation of "coward"(胆小). They would say, "You chicken!" (你这个胆小鬼). But in Chinese, there is no such connotation.

Fox

The fox, in both English and Chinese, refers to a common wild animal with a cunning nature. When used in comparison, it is a synonym of slyness, trickiness, and deceitfulness. On this point, the similarity of cultural connotation of the animal word is beyond our minds. People are very familiar with a series of English and Chinese idioms, such as, as cunning as a fox, as sly as a fox, a sly old fox, and " 露出了狐狸尾巴 ."

Meanwhile, foxes have different connotations in the two respective cultures. For example, in Chinese, the coquettish women are blasphemed as " 狐狸精 "; a group of evil people who accompany each other are called " 狐 朋 狗 友 "; the behavior that a person bullies others by evil authority is referred to " 狐 假 虎 威 "; flattering is known as " 狐媚 ." In English, the fox does not have a derogatory meaning to such an extent. It refers to deceitfulness while it also refers to a good-looking or shrewd person. For example, in America, "a fox" is used to refer to a sexy, charming or smart girl; "crazy like a fox" refers to a shrewd person who is not easy to be cheated. Even some people take fox as their name, from which people's favoritism towards the animal is obviously understood.

Peacock

In English, a peacock always has a derogatory meaning. Webster's Third New International Dictionary of the English Language explains it as following: One making a proud or arrogant display of himself. Collins Cobuild English Language Dictionary explains that "if you describe someone, especially, a man as a peacock, you mean that he is rather proud of himself and likes wearing attractive clothes and looking good." It shows that a peacock usually has a derogatory sense in English. Therefore, "as proud as a peacock" could be heard in their daily life. In Chinese, the peacock is said to be vain, conceited. For example, " 孔雀开屏，自作多情 ." On the other hand, the peacock is a symbol of good luck. People say that it is auspicious to see peacocks open the wings. People of the Dai Minority living in the south of Yunnan Province show their hope by peacock dance, whereas, in English, peacocks' prettiness is ignored while their vanity is taken notice of.

Tortoise

Chinese people believe that the tortoise can live for hundreds of years. So it is a symbol of a long life in Chinese culture. It is the reason for that there are many carvings about tortoise on ancient palaces, temples, and other buildings in China. On the other hand, the tortoise has a very derogatory meaning. It is a terrible insult for somebody to be called " 王八 ." In English there are no such connotations and a tortoise is only a tardy animal.

Buffalo

The buffalo has no connotative meanings in Chinese, whereas, in American English, there is an idiom "to buffalo." How it originated has something to do with "west movement." At that time, people in the west part of America hunted a great number of buffaloes for the skin then they could get much money from leather trading. However, they found that it was not an easy job to hunt buffaloes, so some people complained, "We are buffaloed." It means that they felt helpless. Then it evolves into threaten and menace.

Petrel

The petrel in Chinese culture is a bird to be eulogized. The mental image that the term evokes is a small lonely bird winging over the vast ocean, braving storms and flying with stamina and courage. Many young people in their moment of fantasy compare themselves to petrels, struggling to get ahead in the vast world of humanity, braving hardship and adversity, advancing with perseverance and courage. What a blow it is to discover how little respect Westerners have for the bird! A stormy petrel is "a person regarded as a herald of trouble, strife or violence or someone who delights in such trouble, etc."

In English there are also some other animals with connotations which Chinese doesn't have. A goat in English refers to a person who always does sexual harassment towards women. "Duck" can be used to refer to a lovely person apart from the denotative meaning. A unicorn, looking like horse but having only one horn, exists in the Western legend. It refers to something existing in name only.

Different Connotations of Names about People and Place

Every object has a name, but names of Chinese people and places do not contain the same connotations as those of the English-speaking people and places.

A score of figures in literary works claim their unique images among the native readers generation after generation. "孔乙己" under the pen of Lu Xun is taken for granted as a poor scholar who was shabby, miserable, and pedantic. No such image can be linked with the image when the English-speaking people come cross "孔乙己" unless they have read or heard about him before. On the contrary, the Chinese people might not be familiar with the connotative image of the name Grandet (葛朗台), one of the most notorious misers, unless they have known something about Balzac's work.

New York is a metropolis in the USA and the city is well known all over the world. But few Chinese people can connect the term "Big Apple" with New York. Shaoxing is not a common city for Chinese people because a great number of famous persons came from Shaoxing in history such as Qiu Jin, Lu Xun, Cai Yuanpei. The  Western people who know little about the history of Shaoxing may not place the city in the center of cultural background with its long history and many celebrities.

Different Connotations of Natural Phenomena

Britain faces the sea in the west of Europe, whose climate is conditioned by the sea for its sake. The summer in Britain is as mild as gentle spring breeze due to its location influenced by the maritime climate. That is the reason why in Shakespeare's poem such a line is frequently quoted "Shall I compare thee to a summer's day." Summer in Britain has the connotation of the whole mild climate, which stimulates the English without any hesitation to have a number of sound associative images linked with love. On the contrary, summer in China is too hot for people to endure because the country is mainly influenced by the continental climate. The image of the summer only spurs the Chinese to think about the burning sun high in the sky and people are sweating under it.

From where is the wind blowing? In the history of English literature, a great number of poems sang high praises of the west wind including Shelley's Ode to the West Wind. As west wind blows in Britain, the temperature is mild and animating. On the contrary, in China west wind blows in the season of the freezing winter and is always associated with something shabby or sorrowful while "东风" seems like the "west wind" in English.

Different Connotations of Plants

Plants are symbols of the natural world and the representative of the beautiful natural surroundings and they are closely related to human existence. There are occasions when one plant word is rich in connotation in one culture while deficient in another. For example, in Chinese culture, the plants "pine, bamboo, and plum" remind people of the spirit of  being vigorous, tall and straight, the symbol of long life and exemplary conduct and nobility of character and branches and flowers that withstand the frost and defy the snow while English doesn't possess such connotations.

The potato is so favored by the people in Western countries that it has entered into many English idioms with different connotations. For example, "A couch potato" is someone who spends most of his time watching television and does not exercise or has any other hobbies; "a small potato" is an insignificant figure; "a clean potato" refers to a decent man; In English, you can refer to a difficult subject that people disagree on as "a hot potato." Such potato-related instances are extremely common in English. In Chinese, however, such phrases and idioms are seldom seen.

Daffodils, or yellow narcissuses, are merely a sort of flowers in Chinese. While in English they are a symbol of spring and happiness. We can see it in many literature works, especially William Wordsworth's masterpiece I Wandered Lonely as a Cloud.

The oak has long been considered sacred by many European civilizations. In the *Bible*, the oak tree at Shechem is the site where Jacob buries the foreign gods of his people. In addition, Joshua erects a stone under an oak tree as the first covenant of the Lord. In classical mythology the oak was a symbol of Zeus and his sacred tree. According to legend, King Arthur's round table was made from one huge slice of an ancient oak tree. The oak is a common symbol of strength and endurance and has been chosen as the national tree of England, the United States, and many other countries. Many famous poets wrote about oaks in their works. While in Chinese literature, the images of the oak are hard to find.

The willow is a famous subject of Chinese culture, particularly painting (pen and ink). When ancient Chinese were seeing their friends off, they would present them with wigs of willow showing that they wanted their friends to stay longer. In English folklore, a willow tree is believed to be quite sinister, capable of uprooting itself and stalking travelers. The ancient Celts believed that the spirit of the dead would rise up into the trees planted above, which would grow and retain the essence of the departed one. Throughout Britain many cemeteries, particularly those situated near rivers, lakes or marshes are often to be found lined with willow trees to protect the spirits in place.

4.3.3 Case for Discussion

Case

Insulting a Dragon in China Is No Laughing Matter

Nike's newest ad. showing the NBA star LeBron James battling a cartoon Kungfu Master and dragons has invoked great controversy in China.

It shows James, the Cleveland Cavaliers' rookie of the year, defeating Kungfu Masters, two women in traditional Chinese attire and a pair of dragons. All the traditional Chinese figures in the commercial are depicted as impediments to James and are defeated in five different rooms in a basketball game with James. In the commercial the Feitian—

a Chinese sacred woman who flies through the sky—is shown as a vicious woman who tries to seduce James.

"China banned the ad., describing them as an insult to the country's national dignity. The commercial, titled "Chamber of Fear" was broadcast on local TV stations and CCTV 5, the national television sports channel, before being pulled last month.

The ad. was also available for downloading online and topped all flash animations and movies in popularity.

"The advertisement violates China's regulations on ads. and commercials which mandate that all advertisements and commercials in China should uphold national dignity and interests and respect the motherland's culture," the State Administration for Radio, Film and Television said on its official website. "It also goes against rules that require ads. not to contain content that blasphemes national practices and cultures." The statement also said, "The ad has received an indignant response from Chinese viewers." "We respect and comply with the Chinese Government's laws and regulations," he said.

"The ad. shocked me when I saw LeBron James beating Chinese dragons and the sacred Feitian symbols," said Yang Xiling, a NBA fan who saw the commercial during the break period of the NBA game. "I felt I was being defeated too, along with the whole Chinese people," said Yang.

Heated discussion about the commercial has choked up online forums.

"The ad. leaves me with the impression that American culture wins against Chinese culture. Most of my friends share this impression. I know Nike does not mean to insult us, but the commercial has been a real torment for me," said Zhang He, a Shanghaiese working in a foreign-invested company.

Nike made the ad. for James' Air Zoom LeBron II sneakers. The ad. was based on films featuring martial arts icon Bruce Lee. James is a big fan of Lee. "It was not intended to hurt anybody or any culture or anything like that," James told the Associated Press after practice in Cleveland on December 6. "We put the ad. together basically for kids." James said he was disappointed that the ad. was pulled, since this will prevent some of his fans from seeing him. "That's big. I need as many fans as I can get," he said. James, who signed a seven-year deal with Nike, hoped to have things patched up with his Chinese fans in time for the 2008 Beijing Olympics. "I'll be there in 2008, so maybe they'll love me a little more when I get there," said James, who played for the US Olympic team this summer in Athens but failed to win a gold medal.

Culture Conflict

"This commercial was always likely to provoke dispute in China," said Yao Ming in an after-game interview on December 9. "So it didn't surprise me when I heard it had been banned and widely criticized by the Chinese people, especially youngsters."

"It is a cultural conflict. In China, the dragon is the symbol of China and Chinese culture and the Feitian—the flying woman—is regarded as sacred and holy. They are not respectfully treated in the Nike commercial," said Yao.

Yao clearly understands how cultural conflict can have a great impact. The NBA

All-Star centre himself had the experience of adjusting to American culture when he arrived in the US to play in the NBA. "My modesty is often regarded as cowardice. But Chinese tradition has taught me not to be aggressive. Yet aggression is valued on the basketball court of the NBA," said Yao.

"Conflict will occur when you are ignorant about another culture and things will be even worse if you take too much for granted," said Professor Gu Donghui, a sociology expert at Fudan University. "For example, many foreign Chinese calligraphy-lovers like to wear shirts bearing Chinese characters. I once saw a foreign girl wearing a T-shirt with the Chinese character Ji on it. She knew Ji meant chicken in Chinese, but she did not know it also means prostitute," said Gu.

"I saw that some NBA players like to have Chinese characters tattooed on their bodies. But most of them mean nothing. Kenyon Martin's tattoo means passiveness and silly-sally," said Yao.

(Excerpted from: Nike's Dragon-insulting Ad. Sparks Controversy)

(1) Do you think the ad. should be banned? Why? Why not?

(2) What do you think insulting the traditional Chinese figures in China is no laughing matter?

(3) What do you think we should do to avoid culture conflicts?

4.3.4 Further Reading

Science Gets the Last Laugh on Ethnic Jokes

Study shows that real personalities don't match national stereotypes.

By Kathleen Wren

WASHINGTON—"Heaven is where the police are English, the cooks are French, the mechanics are German, the lovers are Italian, and everything is organized by the Swiss. Hell is where the police are German, the cooks are English, the mechanics are French, the lovers are Swiss, and everything is organized by the Italians."

Obviously the national stereotypes in this old joke are generalizations, but such stereotypes are often said to "exist for a reason." Is there actually a sliver of truth in them? Not likely, an international research team now says.

The study, which compares "typical" personalities in many cultures with the personalities of real individuals from those cultures, appears in Friday's issue of the journal Science, published by AAAS, the nonprofit science society.

Generalizations about cultures or nationalities can be a source of identity, pride, and bad jokes. But they can also cause a great deal of harm. Both history and current events are full of examples in which unfavorable stereotypes contribute to prejudice, discrimination, persecution or even genocide.

"National and cultural stereotypes do play an important role in how people perceive themselves and others, and being aware that these are not trustworthy is a useful thing," said Robert McCrae of the National Institute on Aging.

The new findings also call into question other stereotypes, such as age stereotypes, according to McCrae.

The researchers tested the possibility that cultural stereotypes might be based, at least partly, on real experiences that people have interacting with each other. If this were true, then such stereotypes would reflect the average personality of real members of that culture.

But, McCrae and his colleagues studied real and perceived personalities in roughly 50 countries and found that this wasn't the case.

"These are in fact unfounded stereotypes. They don't come from looking around you and doing your own averaging of people's personality traits," McCrae said.

How stereotypes are born?

If national stereotypes aren't rooted in real experiences, then where do they come from?

One possibility is that they reflect national values, which may emerge from historical events. For example, many historians have argued that the spirit of American individualism has its origins in the experiences of the pioneers in the Old West.

Social scientists such as psychologist Richard Robins have proposed several other possible explanations for stereotypes and why they may be inaccurate. In a commentary that accompanies the science study, Robins notes that some stereotypes may have been accurate at one point in history and then persisted while the culture changed. Or they may have grown out of historical conflicts between cultural groups.

Yet another possibility is that some very specific components of a stereotype may be accurate—for example, Italians may gesture with their hands a lot—but that they don't necessarily tell us anything more generally about personality.

We may be "hard-wired" to some extent, to maintain inaccurate stereotypes, since we are less likely to notice and remember information that violates our stereotypes. Generally, according to Robins, when we encounter people who contradict prevailing generalizations, we perceive them as unique individuals rather than representatives of their national or cultural groups.

Notes

connotation	联想；隐含意义	descendant	后代
feudal	封建的	affirmative	肯定的
wordy	啰嗦的	cunning	狡猾的
vain	虚荣的	conceited	自负的
herald	使者	strife	冲突
sexual harassment	性骚扰	filthy	肮脏的
miser	吝啬鬼	celebrity	名人
maritime climate	海洋性气候		

Encounter Tips

◎   出国访问、考察或旅游，有时为表示感谢主人的盛情，送些鲜花以致谢意，但不能乱送，否则会犯忌，因为不同的花在不同的国家表示不同的感情。

◎   百合花在英国人和加拿大人眼中代表着死亡，绝不能送。德国人视郁金香为"无情之花"，送此花给他们代表绝交。在意大利、西班牙、德国、法国、比利时等国，菊花象征着悲哀和痛苦，绝不能作为礼物相送。

4.4   Taboo

4.4.1   Pre-reading

> Kevin and Lanlan were colleagues. One day, Lanlan delivered a new textbook to Kevin who lived in a room in the foreign guest house. Kevin thanked her, and after a few exchanges, he asked her whether she would like to go in and talk for a while. Lanlan agreed. She followed Kevin into his room and left the door slightly open.
>
> When Kevin found the door open, he went to close it. Lanlan wanted to say something but did not know how to say it. Nonetheless, her discomfort grew until she could stand it no longer. She made up an excuse and left.

在这个案例中，兰兰和 Kevin 是老同事，但分别成长于不同的文化背景，中国人忌讳孤男寡女共处一室，所以当兰兰走进 Kevin 房间的时候故意把门虚掩着，当 Kevin 把门关上后，兰兰就感到很不自在，而 Kevin 却没有意识到他关上门这件事有违于中国传统文化的人际交往礼节，也就导致了交际失败。

人们在交际中，出于某种原因，不能、不敢或者不愿说出某些词语，这些词语有的被认为危险、神圣、神气，有的被认为令人难堪，还有的被认为不堪入耳，人们甚至相信语言本身能够给人们带来幸福或灾难，认为语言是祸福的根源。谁亵渎它，就会得到惩罚；谁讨好它，就会得到它的保佑和庇护。因此有些词语往往只限于某些人或某些场合使用，这就是"语言禁忌"，英语叫做 linguistic taboo，这类词语称为禁忌语，英语为 taboo word，也可以简称为 taboos。禁忌像一种无形的戒律束缚着人们的语言和行为，禁忌几乎无处不在，充斥着我们日常生活的方方面面。世界上的每一种文化都包含有禁忌，禁忌因民族、社会、文化、地区、情景、场合等因素而异，某一文化所崇尚和赞赏的行为很可能是另一文化所讳忌和回避的举止。由于这一点，禁忌就为跨文化交际活动和交流设置了一个障碍，我们必须要对其他文化的禁忌有所了解，否则可能就会犯了人家的忌讳而却毫不知情，交际效果则必然会大受影响。

4.4.2   Taboo Words: East vs. West

A taboo is a strong social prohibition (or ban) against words, objects, actions, or discussions that are considered undesirable or offensive by a group, culture, society, or community. Breaking a taboo is usually considered objectionable or abhorrent. Some taboo activities or customs are prohibited by law and violations may lead to severe punishments. Other taboos result in embarrassment, shame, and rudeness.

There are two aspects of taboo: One is that objects, being respected, can not be used freely, the other is that objects, being despised, can not be touched freely. In a broader sense, taboo exists in all known cultures, referring to certain acts, objects or relationship which the society wishes to avoid and the language used to talk about them. In other words, taboo consists of behavioral taboo and verbal taboo. Generally speaking, behavioral taboo causes verbal taboo.

Naming Taboo

The naming taboo is a cultural taboo against speaking or writing the given names of noble persons in China and neighboring nations in the ancient Chinese cultural sphere.

There are several kinds of naming taboos. The naming taboo of the "state" (国讳) discouraged the use of the emperor's given name and those of his ancestors. For example, during the Qin Dynasty, Qin Shi Huang's given name Zheng (政) was avoided, and the first month of the year Zheng Yue (政月 :the administrative month) was rewritten into Zheng Yue (正月 : the upright month) and furthermore renamed as Duan Yue (端月 : the proper/upright month). The character 正 was also pronounced instead of to avoid any similarity. Generally, ancestor names going back to seven generations were avoided. The strength of this taboo was reinforced by law. The violation of the law would result in the violator and his family's executions and confiscation of their property. The naming taboo of the "clan"(家讳) discouraged the use of the names of one's own ancestors. In diplomatic documents and letters between clans, each clan's naming taboos were observed. The naming taboo of the "holiness"(圣人讳) discouraged the use of the names of respected people. For example, writing Confucius' name was a taboo during the Jin Dynasty.

Basically in English there is no such thing as naming taboos of the state or the clan. People could call each other's given names directly to show equality, intimacy, and friendliness.

In English, taboos on the names of gods include taboos on the name of God, of Jesus Christ, of Saint Mary, of Satan, and of some other gods, such as fairies and goblins. Taboos on the names of gods are very strict. For the people who believe in Christianity, God exists everywhere, and the name of God and other words connected with the religion can only be used in the religious situations. In other situations, those words are taboos. So usually people use gosh, golly or gawd to refer to God, and Gee, Jeepers (Ceepers), Jiming Cricket, Criminey instead of Jesus. Besides, they also avoid speaking of the name of St. Mary. Besides, the English people also have taboos on the name of Satan who is an evil and the opponent of God. They do not refer to the name of Satan directly, because they think "Speaking of the devil, it is sure to appear." People usually call him "the Evil one" "the Tempter" "the Common Enemy," and so on.

Taboo Words on Death and Illness

Death and illness are main disasters for man, while health is a great bliss which man hopes to achieve all the time. Taboos on death and illness are universal. But there is something special in Chinese taboo on death. For death is all man's destiny, Chinese people just hope for longevity, and death that follows longevity is also a blessing. For example, people will say "驾鹤，仙逝，圆寂" (for the Buddhist monks) instead of die.

Chinese taboo on illness has much to do with Chinese tradition. The Chinese people seldom speak of illness directly. They do this partly because illness itself is unpleasant, and partly because they think mentioning one's own illness would appear self-centered by paying too much attention to oneself and by giving burden to the hearer. They don't mention other's illness partly because they do not intend to increase other's worries and partly because they want to express their wish for the patient to recover soon.

Western people rarely talk openly about death. Even in hospital, if somebody's death is announced directly to him or her, hospitals will receive complaints for doing so. It seems that people still prefer the traditional practice of telling the truth mildly, because it seems to show more human concern and consideration. When people have to talk about it they usually use euphemisms. People will use "pass away" "pass out" "close one's days" "fall asleep forever" "join great majority" "pay the debt of nature" "be no more" "depart to God" "go to a better world" "be with God" "depart from the world forever" "breath one's last" "be in heaven" "go the way of all flesh" "be done for" "disease," etc. to substitute for death. All the phrases or expressions above show positive or at least neutral feelings towards the deceased person. Some of them reflect different attitudes towards death. For example, one expression generally used by a person speaking of himself or herself is "I will be seeing Mark anyway in a few years." However, expressions like "kick the bucket" or "be done for" are highly informal and are slang terms. The expression like "pay the debt of nature" carries strong religious sense because of the influence of Christian doctrine. Christian doctrines think human is born of sin, so human has to return to earth and thus can pay the debt of nature.

One reason why people refuse to discuss illness in English is superstition. Another reason for taboo on illness originates from people's feeling of shame for illness. When seeing a doctor, the English people used to say, "I'm sorry to bother you, Doctor."

Taboos on death and illness in English do not distinguish different people, which is quite common in Chinese. If we say that Chinese taboos on death and illness are for the purpose of showing modesty of oneself and showing respect for others, we find little hue of caring for each other in English taboos on death and illness. In English, taboos on death and illness reflect the concept that death and illness are equal to everybody, noble or humble, rich or poor, others or self. We can only find the bitterness and horror of death and illness from strict taboos on them.

Taboo Words on Vulgarities

The word vulgarity refers to the language used by the common people, or the under-educated. Generally speaking, vulgarities often include rude expressions of certain body part, of physical phenomenon like excretion, menstruation and pregnancy, some expressions of toilet and so on. All nations in the world have vulgarities.

The English-speaking peoples have always had an especially strong fear of words for the organs of sex and excretion.

Although in Western countries, sex education has been a long history and sex problems are no longer something novel, words or phrases concerning sex still remain to be verbal taboos in English. Sex is a sensitive topic in English and most people will feel embarrassed when mentioning words or phrases concerning sex, sex organs or sexual activities whether in ancient or modern time. These words are confined to be used between bosom friends or in medical field. In most conversations, especially in mixed groups with women and men, you should never mention those so-called four letter words, e.g. piss, fuck, shit, cunt, tits. Here we should pay attention to some words which have something to do with sex because of lexical change. These words include ass, gay, cock, rubber, etc. which are originally not taboo words. For instance, the original meaning of gay is cheerful, happy, and full of fun, but later it has the connection with homosexuality, so nowadays people rarely use it to express their happiness to avoid misunderstanding.

Taboo on vulgarities has a long history in English and reaches a very high degree even belly and leg were both once the victims of verbal prudery. In English, taboos and euphemisms of vulgarities have always been considered as the symbol of a developed civilization. A variety of words used by the common people are regarded as vulgarities while the so-called upper class uses genteel language. For example, the words below are considered as taboos: belly, leg, arm, buttock, the genitals, the breasts; women's shirt, the garments that lay next to legs, belly, buttocks and breast (such as breeches, trousers, corset), piss, shit, excretion, defecate, urinate, vomit, menstruation, and pregnancy.

We could see that both Chinese and English consider these things to be not clean, so they try to avoid these things in language on one hand, but on the other hand, Chinese taboos on vulgarities have something to do with Chinese traditional values about life and death, shame and ethics, which are ultimately shaped and formed by Chinese traditional cultural mode—the harmony between men and nature, and which are reflected in Confucian values.

Confucianism puts emphasis on the inner values of men. As we have mentioned above, the harmony between men and nature is considered as the basic belief in Chinese traditional culture. The ideal living state of men is to reach a harmonious relationship between men and nature. The life and death of men is shown in and determined by the omens of nature.

So in ancient China, in order not to offend the way of nature, people pay much attention to their behaviors, especially those behaviors connected with excretion and reproduction of men, because they are closely related to men's existence. When regulations are made for these behaviors, taboos on them are created.

English speakers take much notice of the elegance of language and many words referring to things that they consider indecent fall into vulgarities. In English, we can tell a person's breeding and social status by the choice of vulgarities or euphemisms (elegant language) he or she makes. So it is important for us to pay attention to the English taboos on vulgarities and euphemisms of these vulgarities in the process of communication.

Taboo Words on Discrimination

In modern English, language tends to show more and more equality than before. Although they are not taboos in the traditional sense, a lot of words that may cause discrimination and prejudice against certain group of people now become taboos to some extent in English. In fact, a lot of them are still used by many people. But for more people, they begin to choose more neutral words consciously. As a result, a lot of neutral words come into being in English.

First, in English, racial taboo is always an important subject, especially in American English. The African-American were discriminated in the American history. In English, white means innocence, purity, cleanness, charity, and so on, which are active words. While black is related with evil, sin, dirty, and so on, such as blackguard, blacklist, black mark, and black sheep. The kind lie is called white lie, while the black lie means the vicious lie.

At present, the words discriminating blacks become very sensitive and are regarded as taboos. For example, nigger is a taboo word with strong discriminative meaning. Negro is also a taboo word. In the twentieth century, a tendency to place screens of euphemisms round the terminology of race began to emerge. Other words that may show prejudice against those who are thought to be in a disadvantaged position in society are also replaced by more beautiful sounding words. These people include people of low professions such as bill collectors, garbage collector, garbage man, ashman, dustman, floor-walker, street sweeper, barber, hair dresser, table waste cleaner, dishwashers, junkman, iceman, porter or red cap, janitor, gardener, rat-catcher, grocer, bedding manufacturer, window dresser, gravediggers, and person who prepares dead bodies for burial or cremation and so on.

Second, with Women's Movement in the 1960s and the criticism on the prejudice in language, a lot of traditional words that may show prejudice against women are now replaced by new created words for the females. The words showing prejudice against the females are considered to be taboos like chairman, postman, fireman, policeman, statesman, congressman, and sportsman.

Third, in the English-speaking people's opinion, old and poor means useless and stupid. The words of this kind are also taboos in the presence of somebody, such as old, wrinkle, old age, and old age pensioners.

In a word, the appearance of these taboos, on the one hand, shows the changes of social attitudes towards people of low positions in society, and on the other hand, taboos on the terms of discrimination aim to evade social conflicts among different classes by resorting to the magic of language. The demand for equality in language is a result of demand for equality in social status. The English always pursue equality and the individual's influence. This tendency to emphasize the importance and values of individual, whether he is noble or humble is quite different from the Chinese traditional way of valuing modesty. In Chinese traditional culture, as we have discussed above, the character of modesty is the merit of earth. And man has to follow this merit to reach harmony between men and nature. What's more, by cultivating the character of modesty, man can change his fate and maintain his existence. This modesty tends to ignore the values of individual. However, the English have long developed the tradition of valuing the individuals. This tradition also gets its source from the distinguishing of men from nature.

In English, taboo words connected with discrimination are a very important branch people should pay attention to, especially in the USA. In Chinese, people have some taboos on discrimination on minor peoples, but not as evident as that in English nowadays.

How to Avoid Taboo——Using Euphemisms

The euphemism is a widely and frequently used figure of speech. It literally means "to speak with good words." The general characteristics of euphemisms—the use of pleasant, polite, or harmless- sounding terms in the place of those considered unpleasant, rude, or offensive. Since the euphemism is culturally relevant, namely, different cultures show different attitudes towards the same taboos, which is deep-rooted in a country's cultural environment, having an inherent association with the country's history, customs, values, national character, etc., and suggesting the basic characteristics of a culture in a comprehensive manner. Euphemisms are products of social language and embodiments of culture as well.

The purpose of using euphemisms is to avoid directly speaking out the unpleasant or taboo reference like death, the dead, the supernatural, etc. Euphemism is a kind of polite and roundabout mode of expressions.

Positive euphemisms and negative euphemisms

The positive euphemisms can also be called stylistic euphemisms or exaggerating euphemisms. In order to avoid thrill, to be polite or to achieve cooperation, British and American people, especially contemporary Americans, prefer using the technique of exaggeration to euphemize something unpleasant and embarrassing.

The positive euphemisms include many fancy occupational titles, which save the egos of workers by elevating their job status. For example, "exterminating engineers" for "rat catchers", "beautician" for "hairdressers." In China, there do exist occupational titles, in showing respect for others. For example, " 清 洁 工 "(sanitary worker/street cleaner), " 护 士 "(hospital nurse), and " 邮 递 员 "(postman/mailman) are often called euphemistically "环境美容师"(environmental beautician), "白衣天使"(angle in white), and "绿衣使者"(messenger in green). Hence, it might be said that quite a few positive euphemisms are doublespeak and cosmetic words. They usually appear in the political, military, and commercial vocabularies.

The negative euphemisms can be called traditional euphemisms or narrowing euphemisms. They are extremely ancient, and closely connected with the taboos. A euphemism and its corresponding taboo are in fact two faces of the same coin. They refer to the same thing though they have different looks, the euphemism having a much more pleasant face than the taboo. In many cultures, it is forbidden to pronounce the name of God. So there are euphemisms such as Jeeze, Jeepers Creepers or Gee for Jesus, Jesus Christ or Christ, goodness for God, or My Goodness for My God. The names of the tabooed subjects as the dead, and the animals that are hunted or feared, may also be euphemized this way. In Northeast China, the bear is called "老爷子"(grandfather) by people and the tiger is alluded to as the "猫"(cat) or "山神爷"(god of the mountain). Some Chinese call "黄鼠狼"(weasel) and "狐狸"(fox) as "黄仙"(weasel fairy) and "狐仙"(fox fairy) respectively.

Conscious euphemisms and unconscious euphemisms

Unconscious euphemisms, as its name implies, were developed long ago, and are used unconsciously, without any intent to deceive or evade. For example, now standard term as "cemetery" has been a replacement for the more deathly "graveyard" since the fourteenth century. "Indisposition" has been a substitute for "disease" for a long period; people seldom realize that its original meaning is incapacity for dealing with something. Take "dieter" for another example. The original meaning taking food by a rule or regulation has been substituted by the euphemistic meaning "the one moderate in eating and dining for losing weight." From the above examples we can conclude that unconscious euphemisms were developed so long ago that few can remember their original motivations.

Conscious euphemisms are widely employed, which involve more complex categories. When people communicate with each other, speakers are conscious to say tactfully, and the listeners understand their implied meanings. For example, when a lady stands up and says that she wants to powder her nose or make a phone call at a dinner party, the people present realize the euphemism means something else, that is, "going to the ladies' room."

A comparison of Chinese and English euphemisms

Substitution is to replace the impolite or unspeakable words with certain literally mild and pleasant words or expressions. So in English "be sent to the big houses" just means "be sent to prison"—perhaps most of the prisons are big houses. Another euphemism for "be sent to prison" is "be sent up the river," because Sing Sing state prison—the best known prison in the USA, is located at the upper reach of the Hudson River, which flows through the New York City. Other examples such as "live at the government's expense" is really "be in prison," and "wash one's hands," "powder one's nose," and "spend a penny" all mean "go to the WC."

The simplest is to make a straight substitution, using a word that has happier connotations than the term one wishes to avoid. Thus, "agent," "speculator," and "thrifty" have better connotations than "spy," "gambler," and "tight" despite the similar denotations between each pair of words. This is the most commonly employed strategy in encoding euphemism as well as the most frequently tool resorted to in decoding euphemism.

In China, instead of directly mentioning "上厕所," ancient Chinese people turned it into "更衣"(literally meaning "changing clothes"). And modern Chinese people occasionally refer to this as "办公"(literally meaning "doing office work").

We can pick up such examples as "吃双份饭"(to eat for two) and "孩子他爹"(literally meaning "the father of our children") euphemistically refer to "怀孕"(pregnant) and "丈夫"(husband) respectively.

In both English and Chinese, people also use abstract, general, and vague words and expressions to euphemize the oral taboos. To avoid using the word "fat," such words as "round" "plump" "well-fed" "full" "full-bodied" are employed in English. Similarly, we Chinese use "发福"(put on weight) or "富态"(portly) to replace "胖"(fat).

Though English and Chinese euphemisms are similar in quite a few ways in lexicon, the Chinese language has its unique way of euphemizing—using antonyms (反义词). Sometimes antonyms can increase the distance between euphemism and taboo so that euphemisms not only sound well, but also are easy to understand. Amusingly many things related to death are called "寿," like "寿材"(a coffin prepared before one's death) and "寿衣"(grave clothes). "监狱"(prison), a tabooed word in Chinese is called "福舍"(blessed house). In English, however, this device is not common; we can find only a few, for example, a fat chance means a slim chance, and a fat lot replaces very little.

The euphemism often consists in substituting a denial of the opposite idea for a positive word as well as a sentence. Thus, to replace "I think it would be better for us to start off a little earlier tomorrow morning," we may say "Wouldn't it be better for us to start off a little earlier tomorrow morning?" Another example is "He and truth are not on very intimate term." After careful consideration, you may find that the real meaning behind it is "He is a liar," or "He often tells lies." Still another example is the euphemism "plain" for "ugly," "senior citizens" for "elderly people," and "advanced in age" for "old."

4.4.3 Case for Practice

Case

A sales executive has taken her ex-boss to an industrial court claiming that his swearing forced her to quit her job. For over six months, Martha Johnson, 43, put up with the foul language of Jack Slater, managing director of a transport company, and his deputy, Darren Wiggins. Both men swear continually, the court was told. Yesterday

Ms. Johnson of Worthing, Sussex, who has recently taken up a new job, said, "I had a really wonderful job with the company but I just had to do something about the awful language. At least now I am in a place where people show respect for each other."

Mr. Slater told the court that bad language was part of his personality and also common in the transport business. "I can't stop swearing," he said. "I'm the fucking boss. My workers would all think I was fucking soft if I don't swearing." During the hearing the judge had to warn Mr. Slater several times about his language. The case continues tomorrow.

(1) Do you think Martha Johnson was over-reacting? If so, what do you think she should have done?

(2) Do you think Mr. Slater should be in court? If not, what do you think should have happened?

4.4.4   Further Reading

The term taboo can be traced back to the Tongan "tapu" or the "Fijian tapu" meaning "under prohibition," "not allowed," or "forbidden." It originally refers to those holy facts or objects which can not be spoken of or touched. In its modern use in Tonga, the meaning of "tapu" is sacred or holy, although often in the sense of being restricted or protected by custom or by law. For example, the main island in the Kingdom of Tonga, where the capital Nuku'alofa is situated, is called Tongatapu. In this context, it means Sacred South. The use of this word was first noted by Captain James Cook, a British sailor, during his visit to a place he named "the Friendly Islands" (now Tonga) in 1771. When he came to the islands in the South Pacific, he observed many strange social phenomena. For example, some objects can only be used by their leader or only by God, but some can only be used by common people; and some objects can only be used for special purpose, but some only for general purpose. In describing the Tongans, he wrote:

"Not one of them would sit down, or eat a bit of any thing... On expressing my surprise at this, they were all taboos, as they said; which word has a very comprehensive meaning; but, in general, signifies that a thing is forbidden... When any thing is forbidden to be eaten, or made use of, they say, that it is taboo."

He found out that the local people call the above-mentioned phenomena as tabu, which means to be holy or untouchable. Cook introduced the term into the English language, from which it achieved widespread popularity and was spelled as taboo. It is the way in which a society expressed its disapproval of certain kinds of behavior which are considered to be harmful to its members either for supernatural or for having such behavior will violate a moral code. For example, the Zuni, an Indian people in New Mexico, USA, regard frog as their god, therefore, the word "takka" (frogs) is forbidden during the religious feasts.

Notes

taboo	禁忌	abhorrent	令人讨厌的
sacred	神圣的	doctrine	信条
vulgarity	粗话	excretion	排泄
menstruation	月经	indecent	下流的
euphemism	委婉语	discrimination	歧视

Encounter Tips

◎ 除英国人以外，多数西方人忌讳星期六结婚，认为此日绝非黄道吉日。

◎ 欧美的老人，大多忌讳由别人来搀扶。他们认为这有损于体面，是受轻视的表现。

◎ 在欧美，"老"常使人联想起晚年生活的孤独与凄凉，所以常常避免用"old""aged"等字眼，而用一些悦耳的词语代替。如："seasoned man"（历练的人），"elder statesman"（政界元老），"senior citizens"（资深公民），"the mature, the longer living"（生活经历较长的人），"golden years"（金色年华），养老院也成了"a home for adults"或"an adult community"（成人社区）。

◎ 在欧美国家，男性称赞女性容貌、身材、穿戴、打扮是很平常的事，但在中国传统文化里这可以说是禁忌。

4.5　Exercises

4.5.1　Exercise A

Decide whether the following statements are true or false.

(1) Christianity has a strong influence in the cultural connotation of numbers in Western countries.

(2) People around the world have the same responses to the same colors.

(3) Chinese people use red to express happiness, luck, and prosperousness.

(4) To the ancient people, the cosmos is made up of four elements: earth, air, water, and fire.

(5) Number thirteen is regarded as an evil number, standing for misfortune in eastern culture.

(6) English cultures have been more strongly affected by the Greek and Roman mythology.

(7) Oak means the same to the Westerners as "橡树" to the Chinese.

(8) The taboo words on death in the west are influenced by Christian Doctrine.

(9) Belly and leg were taboo words in English history.

(10) The phoenix has negative connotations in the west.

4.5.2 Exercise B

Each statement below contains a color word. Find out which choice of four can explain the meaning of this color word.

(1) I don't think you can depend on Jack to do that job by himself. He's too green.

A. shy   B. inexperienced   C. timid   D. native

(2) A rainy day always makes me blue.

A. happy   B. sad   C. painful   D. frightened

(3) David is the black sheep of his family.

A. wastrel   B. hero   C. villain   D. monster

(4) They had to sell the firm because they had not been in the black for years.

A. lack of money   B. in the dark night

C. needing money   D. gaining money

(5) He is proud of his blue flood.

A. poor   B. noble   C. humble   D. rich

(6) I tried to attract his attention, but he was in a brown study.

A. in meditation   B. asleep   C. studying   D. dark room

(7) He was discovered in the act of breaking open a lock.

A. caught white-handed   B. caught black-handed

C. caught red-handed   D. caught green-handed

(8) The president was treated to the red carpet in America.

A. warm welcome   B. red cloth

C. protest   D. demonstration

(9) That was only a harmless lie. I didn't want to hurt her.

A. a red lie   B. a white lie

C. a purple lie   D. a black lie

(10) I hope she will soon be in the pink again.

A. look down   B. be good

C. cheer up   D. lose heart

4.5.3 Exercise C

Translate the following statements. Pay attention to the number words.

(1) at sixes and sevens

(2) on second thoughts

(3) by ones and twos

(4) Two heads are better than one.

(5) —Can you come down a little?

　　—Sorry, it's one price for all.

(6) He had one over the eight after he drank only half bottle of the wine.

(7) Ten to one he has forgotten it.

(8) Seventy times seven did I take counsel with my soul.

(9) I used to study in France in the year one.

(10) —Are you taking Pam out tonight?

　　—Ah, that's the sixty-four-thousand dollar question!

4.5.4　Exercise D

Work in small groups and find out the connotations of the following animals and plants in both English and Chinese.

(1) dragon, phoenix, owl, dog, peacock, chicken, bat

(2) oak, willow, pine, bamboo, plum

4.5.5　Exercise E

Read the following case, and discuss the questions.

　　Years ago, a kind of pen called "Bai Ling"(白翎) was made in Shanghai. It sold well in China. But when it was exported to some English-speaking countries, it didn't sell well. That is because of the brand "Bai Ling," which means white feather in Chinese. The white feather looks beautiful and lovely for Chinese, but it refers to a timid guy in English. No wonder nobody would buy "Bai Ling" pens.

　　A type of car called "NAVO" manufactured by General Motors Corporation (GM) came into Mexico. But "NAVO" means "it doesn't go" in Spanish. Who would like to buy a car which doesn't go? You can guess the results of the story.

(1) Why didn't the "Bai Ling" pens sell well in English-speaking countries?

(2) Why didn't Mexico like to buy "NAVO" car?

(3) Can you tell the reasons why "Bai Ling" pen and NAVO cars failed outside their native countries?

Chapter 4 Keys

CHAPTER 5

Cultural Differences in Nonverbal Communication

There's language in her eyes, her cheek, her lip, nay, her foot speaks.

—Shakespeare

In human intercourse the tragedy begins not when there is misunderstanding about words, but when silence is not understood.

—Henry David Thoreau

5.1 Nonverbal Communication

5.1.1 Pre-reading

Two business people are sitting at a negotiation table. One is from Africa and the other is from Europe. The African businessman is putting his index finger to his temple which means he is thinking how to start negotiating with his counterpart. The gesture seems to have annoyed the European businessman, who has got impatient and stands up and shouts, "Why do you say at the beginning of our negotiation that I'm crazy?" The African, himself, is confused and at a loss as to what has gone wrong.

Do you know why? What leads to their misunderstanding? Well, the true reason for this miscommunication is that the gesture, with the index finger, sent different messages to the two parties. When Europeans put their index fingers to their temples, they are suggesting a person is crazy. In most of Africa, Argentina, and Peur, it is a slight delaying tactic and means "I'm thinking about it." The same gesture in the United States can mean that someone is intelligent.

这个案例中交际双方的冲突在于对 "put one's index finger to his/her temple" 这个动作所表达的含意的不同解释，很多时候相同的体态动作、手势等非语言符号在不同的文化环境中表达不同的语义。在传递信息、表达语意时，除了使用言语交际，还会使用内容极为丰富的非言语交际，非语言行为是指言语行为之外的所有人际沟通方式，是人们利用面部表情、触摸、姿势、眼神、气味等非语言符号传递信息、增进了解的方式，它包括除使用言语行为以外的一切传递信息的方式。各国之间由于文化背景各不相同，交流中非语言交流的方式和含义也就有所差异，在跨文化交际中，非语言交际是一种不可或缺的手段，是跨文化交际的重要部分，很多人在跨文化交际中，比较注意语言交际行为的正确性、合适性和可接受性，却容易忽略非语言交际行为和手段的文化差异及其影响，然而值得注意的是非语言行为的差异比语言行为的差异所引起的文化冲突更为严重，并且英语语言表达越熟练的人，所发出的非语言交流失误，越容易引起误读。我们在与来自不同文化背景的人进行交流时，应重视这一必要的交际方式。

5.1.2 We Communicate with More than the Words We Speak

Nonverbal communication refers to all aspects of a message which are not conveyed by the literal meaning of words, including hand gestures, eye contact, posture and stance, facial expressions, odors, clothing, hair style, walking behavior, interpersonal distance, touching, architecture, artifacts, graphic symbols, preference for specific tastes, arts and rhetorical forms, vocal signs, color symbolism, synchronization of speech and movement, thermal influences, cosmetics, drum signals, vocal inflections, smoke signals, factory whistles, police sirens, time symbolism, timing and pose, and silence. Definitions of nonverbal communication differ from one expert to another. Simply, nonverbal communication refers to communication without the use of words.

Whether you realize it or not, your emotions are reflected in your posture, face, and eyes—be it fear, joy, anger, or sadness—so you can express them without ever uttering a word. We communicate with more than the words we speak. Words are only one part of communication. How we use these words is another part. It's often not what you say that counts but what you don't say. For example, if you hear someone's voice quaver and see his or her hands tremble, you may infer that the person is fearful or anxious, despite what he or she might say. Your general appearance is one form of non-verbal communication. So are your facial expressions, your gesture, your silence, and your touch. A wink, a subtle hand gesture, a scratch of the chin can all be signals that punctuate the spoken word. In fact, in most instances nonverbal messages arrive before the verbal and influence the flow of the interaction. Your personal experiences will show you how often your first judgments are based on the color of a person's skin, facial expression, manner of dress, or if he or she is in a wheelchair. Even how you select friends and lovers is grounded in first impressions. You often approach certain people because how attractive you find them, and of course, avoid others because of some rapid decision you make concerning their appearance. So, proper nonverbal signals can help reinforce the meaning of what one says, and improper nonverbal signals may contradict what one says and cause confusion.

Researchers have shown that the words a person speaks may be far less important than the body language used when delivering the verbal message. They estimate that less than 30% of communication between two individuals within the same culture is verbal in nature. Over 70% of communication takes place nonverbally. Some scholars even maintain that in face-to-face communication up to 93% of an oral message is communicated nonverbally and that the nonverbal elements are a much better indicator of the true meaning than the actual words are. We are not sure of that. But one thing we are sure about is that in face-to-face communication nonverbal signals are just as important as verbal messages.

Research indicates that sometimes nonverbal signals play a more decisive role than verbal messages in determining communicative effects. For instance, whether what you say is a joke or an insult depends on the facial expression and tone that accompany what you say.

Many people believe that nonverbal behavios are universal. It exists in every country of the world and among various groups within each country. It is true that people everywhere make use of nonverbal behaviors to express how they feel and that they all use it in an elusive, spontaneous, and unconscious manner. This sharing of nonverbal language often makes it possible for people from different parts of the world to understand each other better. But although most nonverbal communication is universal, many of your nonverbal actions are altered by cultures. Misunderstandings can occur when the speakers and listeners are from different cultures that generally do not share the same nonverbal codes. What is a gesture of joy in one culture may be considered a rude insult in another. Never underestimate the cultural differences in the interpretation of nonverbal forms of communication.

Nonverbal communication varies so significantly from culture to culture. Even if some expressions of nonverbal behaviors are universal and governed by biological necessity, the meanings attached to these expressions show great variety across different cultures. That is to say, the same nonverbal code may be interpreted differently by people from different cultures. Also people from different cultures use different nonverbal behaviors to express the same idea.

For example, we all laugh, but our culture teaches us when, how much, and under what circumstances we may laugh. The OK sign by the Americans may indicate money or zero, but to the Japanese and in South America this gesture has a sexual meaning. While physical contact between a male and a female is a common practice of social greeting in Western society, it is a taboo in some Asian cultures. In Western cultures eye contact can signify honesty, whereas in Asian cultures it may indicate rudeness.

In the United States people greet by shaking hands. Arab men often greet by kissing on both checks. In Japan, men greet by bowing, and in Mexico they often embrace. In most Middle Eastern and Asian countries, pointing with the index finger is considered impolite. In Thailand, to signal another person to come near, one moves the fingers back and forth with the palm down. In the United States, you beckon someone to come by holding the palm up and moving the fingers toward your body. In Vietnam the same motion is used for someone attempting to summon his or her dog. The Tongans sit down in the presence of superior; in the West, you stand up. Crossing one's legs in the United States is often a sign of being relaxed; in ROK, it is a social taboo. In Japan, gifts are usually exchanged with both hands, and in China, people also exchange cards with both hands. Muslims consider the left hand unclean and do not eat or pass objects with it. Buddhas maintain that great insights arrive during movements of silence. In the United States, people talk to arrive at the truth.

Cultural shocks are often the result of a lack of knowledge of another culture's oral and nonverbal communication patterns. And misunderstandings can be harder to clear up because people may not be aware of the nonverbal cues that lead them to assume that they aren't liked, respected, or approved. Successful interaction in intercultural settings requires not only the understanding of verbal messages but of nonverbal messages as well. Learning about the alliance between cultures and nonverbal behaviors is useful to students of intercultural communication. In this section we only list some of the most commonly used non-verbal means in human interaction.

5.1.3   Case for Practice

Case

One British businessman is in Iran. After months of doing the right thing—building relationships with Iranian colleagues, respecting the influence of Islam on negotiations, and avoiding any potentially explosive political small talk—the executive was elated once formal contract was signed. He signed the papers and turned to give his Persian colleagues a big thumbs-up. Almost immediately there was a gasp and one Iranian executive left the room. The British executive didn't have a clue as to what was going on—and his Iranian hosts were too embarrassed to tell him.

The explanation was really quite simple. While the thumbs-up gesture means "good, great, well-played" in Britain, in the Persian culture it is a sign of discontent and borders on the obscene. "I don't think I was ever more embarrassed in my life. I felt like a child who yells out a vulgar curse word without having any clue as to what it means," the executive says. "My colleagues accepted my plea of ignorance but the relationship was damaged. It wasn't that they thought I had truly meant the gesture as interpreted in their culture but rather that I was totally ignorant of it. I just never suspected there was anything wrong with it."

(1) What does "the thumbs-up gesture" mean in China?

(2) What does this story suggest to you?

5.1.4   Further Reading

Functions of Nonverbal Behaviors in Communication

Nonverbal communication has its own unique functions in interpersonal communication. We will sum up some important ways that nonverbal communication regulates human interaction.

Repeating

People often use nonverbal messages to repeat a point they are trying to make. If you were telling someone that what they were proposing was a bad idea, you might move your head from side to side while you were uttering the word "no." You might hold up a hand in the gesture signifying that a person should stop at the same time when you actually use the word "stop." If someone asks you where the city library is located, you can say something like that, it is at the corner of the second block on the left, and you can use your finger to point in the direction of the library to repeat what you said.

Complementing

Closely related to repeating is complementing. For example, you can tell someone that you are pleased with his or her performance, but this message takes in extra meaning if you pat the person on the shoulder at the same time. Physical contact places another layer of meaning on what is being said.

Emphasizing

Nonverbal messages can emphasize or accent the feelings or emotions conveyed by verbal messages by adding more information to the expressions. Loudness and tone of voice can be an example here. You can accent your anger by speaking in a voice that is much louder than the one you use in normal conversation. You can see how an apology becomes more forceful if your face, as well as your words, is saying, "I'm sorry."

Conveying

Nonverbal behaviors convey our emotions and our attitudes towards ourselves and towards the people we communicate with. For example, the phrase, "I would love to meet you and discuss this issue in more detail," can convey different meanings and attitudes depending on the nonverbal signals accompanying the words. Nonverbal messages can be as effective as verbal messages in conveying orders.

Regulating

We often regulate and manage communication by using some forms of nonverbal behaviors. For example, a parent might engage in "stern" and direct eye contact with a child as a way of "telling" him or her to terminate the naughty behavior while guests are in the house. Hand clapping by the instructor in a classroom demands the attention of the students. Turn taking is largely governed by nonverbal signals. In short, your nonverbal behaviors help you control the situation.

Replacing

We use nonverbal messages to substitute for verbal messages. If it is noisy at a big meeting, the speaker may stop for a few seconds as an alternative to say, "Please calm down so that I can speak." Instead of raising your voice by shouting "bravo" after a great performance of the orchestra, you may silently sit there with an awed expression. Your expression automatically indicates that the performance is excellent and that you are moved by the experience.

Contradicting

On some occasions, nonverbal actions send signals opposite from the literal meanings contained in our verbal messages. For example, you tell someone you are relaxed and at ease, yet your voice quavers and your hands shake. When you are sick and a friend asks you how you feel, you may say, "I'm fine" in weak voice and with a slouchy posture. Nonverbally, you are telling your friend that you are not fine, but, verbally, you give your friend an opposite answer. People rely mostly on nonverbal messages when they receive conflicting data like these, so we need to be aware of the dangers.

Notes

artifact	人工制品	graphic	图解的
synchronization	同步	elusive	难懂的
spontaneous	未经琢磨的	blunder	犯错
turning taking	话语轮换	quaver	颤抖
slouchy	没精打采的		

Encounter Tips

◎　填写表格和选票时，中国人以打勾或画圈表示同意或赞同，打叉则表示否定或不同意；而有些欧美国家则以打叉表示肯定或赞同。

◎　欧美国家的人若不断转动手上的戒指，则表示情绪紧张或不安。

◎　欧美国家课堂座位往往采用马蹄形或半圆形的空间安排，有利于教师生和学生之间的交流与讨论。

◎　中国学生往往比欧美国家的学生更容易沉默不语。例如，在教师提问题时以沉默相对，在报告做完后并不提问。对欧美国家的人来说，这是对讲话人不礼貌或不尊重的表现，甚至是一种侮辱。

5.2　Body Language

5.2.1　Pre-reading

At Heathrow, one of the world's top international airport, a Japanese asks an American passenger whether Heathrow has a luggage trolley service. It has. And as it happens, this service is not only first class, but free! So the American replies with the famous "OK" gesture. But to the Japanese, this signifies "money" and he concludes that there is a charge for this service.

Meanwhile, a Tunisian on-looker thinks that the American is telling the Japanese that he is a worthless rogue and he is going to kill him.

The ring-gesture can have further meanings. A Frenchman has just read an advertisement about the airport. He asks his wife "You know how much this airport cost the British taxpayer? Not a sou." And he makes the finger and thumb ring which to him means "zero."

本案例发生在英国的希思罗机场，案例中矛盾的起因是交流双方对 OK 手势的理解发生了偏差。由于各国人对这一手势的理解不同，在美国及欧洲，OK 手势被广泛地用于各种场合表示"好""是""同意""顺利"的意思；在法国表示"零"或"毫无价值"；在日本、缅甸、韩国，OK 手势就像硬币形状一样，表示"钱"的意思；在印度表示"正确""不错"；在突尼斯表示"傻瓜"；在泰国表示"没问题，请便"；在巴西表示"粗俗下流"；而在中国和世界其他很多地方则表示"零或三"，因此本来免费的推车服务，日本人以为要钱，而突尼斯人以为美国人认为日本人是毫无价值的废物要杀了他，而法国人则和妻子说修这个机场没花英国纳税人一分钱。可见，分歧有多大，误会就有多深。

体态语同语言一样，是文化的一部分，它是指由人体发出的具有表情达意功能的一套图像符号。包括人的面部表情、身体姿势、肢体动作和身体位置的变化。体态语是人类重要的交际手段之一，它可以加强、补充有声语言表达，并使语言信息具体化。但在不同文化中，体态语的意义并不完全相同，打手势时动作稍有不同，就会与原来的意图有所区别，对某种手势理解错了，也会引起意外的反应。

5.2.2 Body Language—Transmits Information Through Gestures, Actions, Facial Expressions...

When a Chinese converses with an American friend of the opposite sex, would it be indecent to be looking at the other person? Does nodding the head means "yes," and shaking the head means "no" in all cultures? These questions are not about verbal language, but about body language.

Body language is known as nonverbal behavior which transmits information through gestures, actions, and facial expressions. People communicate with each other by their body language in the ways of nodding, waving, eye contacting, shrugging and so on. These ways can sometimes express what the verbal language cannot directly.

Henry David Thoreau has once said, "In human intercourse the tragedy begins, not when there is misunderstanding about words, but when silence is not understood." We can learn to use our body language for a purpose. It is important to note that body language has different meanings in different cultures. How we can interpret body language depends on the situation, the culture, and the relationship we have with the person as well as the gender of the other.

Body language contains posture, gesture, eye contact, facial expressions, touch, and so on.

Posture

Posture communicates just as language does. Posture is a matter of how people sit, walk, stand, and move. The way people hold themselves gives important information. Body posture can be closed or open. Interested people always pay attention and lean forward. Leaning backwards demonstrates aloofness or rejection. A firm handshake will give the impression of assertiveness or honesty, but too firm can seem arrogant or challenging. Folding arms across your

chest or body is protective and will give the impression of a character who's closed, guarded, and defensive. People with arms folded, legs crossed, and bodies turned away are signaling that they are rejecting messages.

Posture offers insight into a culture's deep structure and reflects a person's attitude toward the people he or she is with. The manner of sitting, standing, and moving can also communicate a message and reflect a certain culture's lifestyle. In many Asian cultures, a bow is much more than a greeting, and it signifies that culture's concern with status and rank. For example, in Japan the bow posture is an indicator of respect. The person who occupies the lower status begins the bow, and his or her bow must be deeper than the other person's. The superior, on the other hand, determines when the bowing is to end. When the participants are of equal rank, they begin the bow in the same manner and end at the same time.

In the United States, where being casual and friendly is valued, people often fall into chairs or slouch when they stand. In many countries, such as Germany and Sweden, where lifestyles tend to be more formal, slouching is considered a sign of rudeness and poor manners.

According to Chinese tradition, people who are sitting have right to take charge of others: Monarch sits and officer stands, father sits and son stands, leader sits and employee stands, and so on. So the younger give the old a seat to show respect. But in America and Britain, people who are in charge of others have tendency to stand. They will make use of the height of space to indicate the high status. People who have high status choose to sit when they are conversing with you, which mean they want to create harmonious and equal atmosphere and lessen space. So adults will bend down when they are talking to children.

Gesture

Gestures refer to specific body that carries meaning. Gestures are the movements of hands, arms, and fingers that people use to describe or to emphasize. Gestures comprise a major form of nonverbal communication.

In a very general sense, we all use gestures to reinforce an idea or to help describe something. When we say, "That's an English book," at the same time we are pointing to the book. If someone asks us the way to the library, we point to the right, adding a little information about it, which will be clearer and more concrete. Some of us have such feeling, that is, in a class or speech, we become more interested in the speaker's motion than we do in his/her message when we see he/she pace back and forth in front of us. At last we may just remember the movement of the speaker, but get nothing about the information. The same is true in any context.

In our daily life, every one makes gestures, but many gestures have distinct regional and cultural features. What is acceptable in one culture may be completely unacceptable in another. One culture may determine that snapping fingers to call waiter is appropriate; another may consider this gesture rude. The gesture for applauding over the head in

America usually means arrogance to defeat the counterpart, while in Russia it is a symbol of friendship.

In China, holding up one's thumb means good, and raising one's little finger means bad. But Japanese will hold up their little fingers to express one is their lover. In America, waving one's hand means goodbye. But South Americans will not leave when they see this gesture, on the contrary, they will run towards you.

Americans often touch their temples to express somebody's cleverness. But this action means there is something wrong with one's mind or one is stupid to Chinese. Chinese are often surprised to see Americans lay their hands on their necks when they are full. Because it is a suicide action to Chinese, who used to express fullness by patting their stomachs. And another example, people from English-speaking countries turn around their rings constantly to show nervousness or uneasiness. Now people from Taiwan and Hong Kong also have this gesture. But if people in the mainland of China act like this, they will be regarded as showing off richness.

In Chinese culture, touching or pointing to one's own nose with raised forefinger signifies "It's me," or "I'm the one." In the Indian sub-continent, a woman sometimes uses the gesture of pointing her forefinger to her nose to express astonishment. In the Middle East, the same gesture stands for at your service, and can be employed by either sex, but is used predominantly by men. In Iran the gesture that stands for at your service is to put the palm of one's right hand over one's right eye. Nodding by moving one's head up and down, means a concurrence, a yes, in India, whereas the same gesture in, say, Kuwait would mean the exact opposite, a dissent, a no.

It is clear to see that the same gesture can have different meanings in different cultures, and people from different cultures will express the same meaning by different gestures. So it is necessary for us to know the cultural differences to avoid misunderstanding.

Eye Contact

The eye, the window revealing what is deep in one's mind, is full of rich expressions. Eye contact is direct and powerful. The eyes are always talking. Eye contact can express complicated feelings and is an important aspect of body language. There are many rules about eye contact: Whether to look or not to look; when to look and how long to look; who to and who not to look at.

Eye contact, like other elements in body language, as a result, is becoming complicated within that culture. People in Western countries expect the person they are interacting with to look at them in the eye during a conversation; however, staring at people or holding a glance too long is considered to be improper in most English-speaking countries, even when the look may be one of appreciation, because it may make people uneasy and embarrassed. But Arabs, on the other hand, look directly into the eyes of their communication partner, and do so for a long period of time, as they believe such eye contact shows interest in the other person and helps them assess the truthfulness of the other person's words.

The Japanese feel uncomfortable with direct eye contact, and they want to avoid it. Japanese often look at the other communicator's neck when they are in conversation. They believe eye contact is impolite. And Chinese consider gazing at people is an unfriendly behavior and is a challenge. Some South American Indians are used to look at different directions when they are talking.

Facial Expressions

Words are often accompanied by distinct facial expressions. The face provides vital clues to our own feelings and those of the people around us. In many cultures, when people are surprised, they may open their eyes wide and open their mouths. When they like something, their eyes may beam, and they may smile. When they are angry, they may frown  and narrow their eyes. While many facial expressions carry similar meanings in a variety of cultures, the frequency and intensity of their use may vary.

Smiles and laughter usually convey friendliness, approval, satisfaction, pleasure, joy, and merriment. This is generally true in China as well as in the English-speaking countries. However, in some situations the laughing of some Chinese will cause negative reactions by Westerners. For instance, a foreigner drops a plate in a restaurant quite by accident and feels embarrassed, but some Chinese onlookers laugh, which makes him discomfort and causes anger and bad feeling.

In fact, this laughter conveys a number of feelings: don't take it so seriously; laugh it off, it's nothing; such things can happen to any of us, etc. However, for people unaware of this attitude, the reaction to such laughter is usually quite unpleasant and often generates ill feeling towards those laughing.

The expression of anger also varies from culture to culture both in terms of intensity and type of expression. One of the milder forms of showing anger in Western cultures, such as frowning. Depending on the context, frowning can indicate anger, doubt, questioning of authority, suspicion, or disagreement. In cultures where open expressions of one's feeling are not appreciated, frowning may be much more subdued. The Japanese, for example, avert their gaze so as to hide anger.

Another way of showing anger is shouting and gesturing. Germans, Canadians, Arabs, and Latins often raise their voice when angry. The Japanese seldom do so. Instead, they may show their anger by sucking in their breath rather than letting it out with a scream. Some cultures use intense and expressive gesturing to show anger. Research in Korean companies has revealed the surprising fact that Korean managers sometimes show anger toward subordinates not only with verbal criticism but also with nonverbal acts of violence—even throwing coffee on a subordinate or causing physical injury!

Another facial expression is stretching out one's tongue. When Chinese realize that their behavior is unsuitable and feel embarrassed, they often stretch out their tongues and shrink their necks at the same time, especially girls and children. But Americans never do it. They think it is rude.

Touch

Touch refers to the way people exchange information by touching one's body. The manner of touch may serve as a reflection of one's attitudes and values.

In English-speaking countries, people are used to hugging or kissing each other in public between males and females, which is usually unacceptable and only exists between lovers and couples in private in China. In China, people greet each other with head nodding, smiling, hand shaking, and so on. Even good friends just hold hands for a short time or hammer softly on the other friend's shoulder.

In English-speaking countries, physical contact is generally avoided in conversation among ordinary friends or acquaintances. Merely touching someone may cause unpleasant reactions. If one touches another person accidentally, he/she usually utters an apology such as "Sorry, Oh, I'm sorry. Excuse me." Or they will be abused. In Western countries, people particularly mind their private space, which often represents people's privacy and intimacy. But some Chinese pay less attention to their private space. It is crowded in China because of its large population. So some Chinese have got used to crowded places and often show their understanding and tolerance.

5.2.3 Case for Practice

Case

The story is told of a teenage Puerto Rican girl in a New York high school who was taken with a number of other girls to the principal for suspected smoking. Although there was no proof of any wrongdoing and although she had a good record, the principal decided she was guilty and suspended her. "There was something sly and suspicious about her," he said in his report. "She just wouldn't meet my eye. She wouldn't look at me."

When she was questioned by the principal it was true that she kept staring at the floor and refused to meet his eye. And in English there is a saying "Don't trust anyone who won't look at you in the eye."

It so happened that one of the teachers had a Latin American background and knew about Puerto Rican culture. After talking with the girl's parents, he went to the principal and explained that according to Puerto Rican culture, a good girl "does not meet the eyes of an adult." Such behavior, he explained, "is a sign of respect and obedience."

Fortunately, the principal accepted the explanation, admitted his mistake and the matter was settled properly. This difference in interpreting a simple eye gesture was a lesson in cultural diversity that he would not easily forget.

Rules about eye-language are numerous and complex. What has been mentioned gives a good idea of this; we shall not go further into detail.

(1) Why did the principal decide the girl was guilty?

(2) What should the girl do when she talked with the adult according to Puerto Rican culture?

5.2.4　Further Reading

Finger Gestures Used by the Americans

The "Come Here" Gesture

With the palm up, the forefinger wiggled at the person summoned.

This gesture is rarely made to a superior, but is commonly used among peers, or in summoning service personnel (such as a waiter or porter). It is also sometimes used in sexual situations, when it is archaically referred to as a "come hither" gesture. It is confusing to some non-Americans, since most people of other countries use a full-hand scoping motion to summon a person.

The Peace Sign (Also Known as "V" for Victory)

With the palm out, foreign and middle fingers are pointed upwards and split into the shape of a V.

This sign achieved its greatest popularity in North America during the 1960s, when it came to signify peace. Winston Churchill popularized it in the U.K. earlier, as the "V for victory" sign during the Second World War.

The meaning of this sign does not change in the USA but it is accidentally done backwards (with the palm in rather than out). However, it becomes an obscene gesture in the UK when reversed in this manner. English-speaking Canadians may also recognize this meaning.

In a contemporary business setting, it is more likely to be used for its "V for victory" meaning.

Thumbs Up

With an outstretched fist, the thumb is extended straight up.

"Thumbs up" as a positive gesture quickly gained popularity in the USA, especially as a visual signal in noisy environments. Pilots unable to shout "all's well" or "ready" over the noise of their engines used it frequently. With a slight backwards tilt, this gesture is also used for hitchhiking. However, in most of the Middle East and parts of Africa (Notably Nigeria), this symbol can be obscene. In Japan, the thumb is considered the fifth digit; a raised thumb will order five of something!

The "OK" Sign

With the palm out, the thumb and the forefinger are curled into a circle, while the other fingers are extended upwards.

While this means "all's well" in North America, in France it signifies zero or nothing, and in Denmark or Italy it can be taken as an insult. In Brazil, Guatemala, and Paraguay, it is considered very obscene.

Pointing

A single outstretched finger (usually the index finger, sometimes the thumb) to designate an object or a person.

Although it's not polite to point, children—and many adults—frequently do so. Pointing at objects is not considered rude, but useful for foreigners who don't know the name of something. Pointing at people is not polite, perhaps because of its use in court, to point out wrongdoers. In many cultures, pointing is done with a toss of the head, a thrust of the chin, or even a pursing of the lips. In Asia, the entire open hand is used, except in Malaysia, where the thumb is preferred.

Notes

nonverbal communication	非言语交流	shrug	耸肩
interpret	解释	Monarch	君主
slouch	懒散	reinforce	加强
distinct	明显的	abuse	辱骂

Encounter Tips

◎　翘大拇指：在英国、澳大利亚和新西兰等国家，这一手势可以表示数字。另一种是旅游者要求搭车的手势，是一种表示请求的体态语。再一种就是侮辱人的信号：在希腊，如果将大拇指急剧翘起，就表示让对方"滚蛋"，是对人极大的不敬。

◎　目光接触：在美国，与他人交谈或向他人打招呼时，应目视对方。如果不看着对方，会被认为是羞怯、缺乏信心或不尊重别人。在韩国、日本、泰国及一些亚洲国家，正视对方却被视为不礼貌。因此人们从小就受到教育，不要正视对方，尤其应避免正视长辈、领导、老师等，以表示礼貌或尊重对方。

◎ 掩口: 用手捂着嘴打呵欠或嘴张开用手指拍拍嘴唇，在中国和英国都表示"枯燥无味""发困""该走了"。这个动作也正是英语国家在咳嗽、打呵欠、打喷嚏、打嗝和咀嚼时掩饰的规矩，其根本目的是不要让别人知道。

◎ 身体接触: 阿拉伯人喜欢相互触摸，甚至用鼻子嗅同伴身上的气味。在英国、美国、中国、日本、韩国等国家，一般朋友之间在公开场合很少进行身体接触，身体接触仅限于家庭内。除了迎接、到医院看病、到裁缝店做衣服等情况外，一般禁忌接触他人身体，否则会引起被接触者的不快或不安。不过中国由于现有的交通工具紧张，人们习惯于挤公共汽车和地铁。日本也是如此。中国人和日本人可以在公共汽车、地铁车厢里与不相识的人鼻眼相对，紧紧坐在一起，并不在意。而英美人对此却无法忍受。

5.3 Paralanguage

5.3.1 Pre-reading

In London's Heathrow Airport, airport staff who ate in the employees' cafeteria complained about rudeness by cafeteria employees from India and Pakistan who had been hired for jobs traditionally held by British women. And the Asian women complained of discrimination. A communication expert was asked to tape talk on the job to see what was going on, and then he had Asian and British employees listen to the tape together.

When a customer coming through the cafeteria line requested meat, the server had to find out if he wanted gravy on it. The British women asked, "Gravy?" The Asian women also said "Gravy." But instead of rising, their intonation fell at the end. During the workshop session, the Asian women said they couldn't see why they were getting negative reactions, since they were saying the same thing as the British women. But the British women pointed out that although they were saying the same work, they weren't saying the same thing. "Gravy?"—with question intonation—means "Would you like gravy?" The same word spoken with falling intonation seems to mean, "This is gravy. Take it or leave it."

这个案例中矛盾的起因是交流双方对语调的使用和理解发生了偏差。选择的文字得到了交际双方的认可，而在语调所表达的交际意义上双方产生了异议，也就是说在这里语调决定了交际的成败。英语是一种语调语言，英语语调是英语表达的灵魂，对交际意义的表达起到重要作用，而英汉语调系统的差异对我国英语学习者造成了一定的影响。像语调一样，音高、音质、语气，甚至叹气、咳嗽、沉默、哭、笑等都会对跨文化交际产生影响，他们同属于非语言交流中的副语言。副语言作为一种重要的非语言交流方式，在人类语言交际中起着极其重要的作用。它贯穿于语言交际过程的始末，伴随语言表达出信息的真正含义。

5.3.2 Paralanguage—"How" Something Is Said

All of us are aware that the meaning of what we say is contained, in part, in the words, or what we say, but that how we say things also contains powerful messages. The word "yes," for instance, may express defiance, resignation, acknowledgement, interest, enthusiasm or agreement according to the speaker's intonation, pitch, and rhythm, depending on how it is said. The "how" something is said is referred to as paralanguage, which includes intonation, emphasis, word and syllable stress, and so on.

Paralanguage is related to oral communication; it refers to the rate, pitch, and volume qualities of the voice, which interrupt or temporarily take the place of speech and affect the meaning of a message. It involves vocal elements (sound) but not verbal elements (words), that is, how something is said but not the actual meaning of the spoken words. Vocal elements of language differ from verbal elements in that: vocal elements involve sound and its manipulation for certain desired or undesired effects. Verbal elements are the particular words we choose when speaking. Thus, in saying "hello," the verbal aspect is the actual word "hello." The vocal aspect, or paralinguistic element, is the sound of the word when uttered: the inflection of the voice, the pitch, loudness, pace, stress, and the like. When we are speaking, both language (verbal aspects or words) and paralanguage (vocal aspects or sounds) will play significant roles in conveying our meaning.

Paralanguage also conveys emotions. It is easier for us to distinguish negative emotions such as impatience, fear, and anger than to distinguish positive emotions like satisfaction and admiration. An increased rate of speech could indicate anger or impatience; a decrease in rate could suggest lack of interest or a reflective attitude. Learning the nuances in speech will help to identity the real meaning of people from other cultures.

In intercultural communication, misunderstanding things like intonation, silence, volume, non-word noises may have as tragic consequences as misunderstanding the meanings of the words actually used. As E.M. Forster put it in his well-known novel A passage to India, "A pause in the wrong place, an intonation misunderstood, and a whole conversation went awry."

When we communicate with Westerners, what we Chinese speakers should care about is the cultural differences of vocal qualifiers, vocal segregates, vocal characterizers, and silence.

Vocal Qualifiers

The term "vocal qualifiers" refers to volume, pitch, tone of voice, and the overall intonation of the spoken word. For example, does the speaker raise or lower his/her voice at the end of a sentence? Does the speaker vary the speed of what he/she says, or does he/she speak very evenly? Does the speaker vary the volume between loud and soft: in other words, does he/she speak softly or does he/she shout? Does he/she have a mind to control his/her volume and pitch? Vocal qualifiers differ from culture to culture. The story told at the beginning is exactly an example of intonation.

Differences in volume of speech, are culture specific. Arabs, for example, speak loudly to show strength and sincerity. People from the Philippines, however, speak softly as they believe this to be an indication of good breeding and education. Thais also speak softly; they speak loudly only when they are angry, and loudness indicates impoliteness to  the Thais. Generally, people from English-speaking countries use a voice of softer volume than a Chinese people when telephoning or talking in public places, such as at the airport, bus stop, or on a plane, steamer, and bus. At the public places or even at the private places, some Chinese people like to turn on the TVs, radios, acoustic equipments to the greatest volume. But this will make people from English-speaking countries feel uncomfortable.

Differences also exist in the rate at which people speak. Americans living in the northern states usually speak faster than those in the south; Italians and Arabs speak faster than people of the United States do. People who speak slowly sometimes have difficulty in understanding the speech of those who speak rapidly.

Vocal qualifiers provide important signals in turn taking in a conversation. The changing of intonation, of pitch, and of volume, or using the asking intonation can indicate the turn-yielding cure. If everyone in the group is used to the same signals, the conversation can flow and speakers seem to take their turns almost automatically. The rhythm of the conversation feels natural. In contrast, if people use different intonation patterns, interlocutors may feel that the conversation is strained, that one side is trying to dominate or is not contributing to the discussion.

Vocal Segregates

All cultures use non-word noises such as "uhs" "ahas" "uhms" "eh" "lah," sucking in one's breath, and clicking one's tongue. These noises may be used as connectors between ideas; they also may be used to indicate that someone is ready to say something or that more time is needed to think things over. People often use " 这个 ", or " 那个 " in Chinese instead. The vocal segregates indicate formality, acceptance, assent, uncertainty, etc. Generally, the interpretation of these noises does not present a major hurdle in intercultural communication. The frequency of their use, however, varies from culture to culture.

Vocal Characterizers

Vocal characterizers include laughing, crying, yelling, moaning, whining, belching, and yawning. These send different messages in different cultures (Japan—giggling indicates embarrassment; India—belch indicates satisfaction; America—smile indicates happiness and agreement). Innate behaviors can change as we grow and learn our culture. For example, smile is universally recognized as a sign of friendliness, but it has other meaning to other cultures. Germans smile less than people from the US do, but it doesn't mean Germans are less friendly.

In Indonesians, laughing has a special function on some tense social occasions. People laugh to release the tension, embarrassment or difficult situations. They laugh to express their concern about others, their intention to put others at ease or to help others come out of the embarrassment. In Indonesia, people laugh even when they talk about the death or disasters of their friends or relatives. They laugh just to help their friends get rid of sorrow or bad emotions. But to Americans, laughing in such an occasion is surely an insulting, humiliating, and negative response.

Silence

Communication through silence plays an important role in all cultures. Silence can indicate agreement, disagreement, confusion, respect, sadness, thoughtfulness, and so on. The importance of silence as a communication tool and the interpretation of silence vary from culture to culture, but all cultures use silence at times to get a point across. "Silence in Asia has commonly been acceptable whereas in the West silence has generally been considered socially disagreeable."

Chinese believe that silence is preferable to conversation. It is through silence that one can discover the truth inside oneself. Contemplation and meditation take place in silence. There is even a Chinese proverb "Silence is gold." Chinese speakers are more likely to remain silent when asked questions they consider rude or inappropriate.

To most Westerners silence is the absence of communication. To them silence indicates that a rupture has occurred in the communication process. It makes them uncomfortable. When given a choice, Westerners tend to choose speaking over being silent. Silence is ambiguous; it must be interpreted, and the interpretation of silence is more difficult than the interpretation of words. They even think remaining silent when asked a question is rude.

If a conversational partner does not respond quickly to what a Westerner is saying, he/she is likely to continue talking. They often feel responsible for starting a conversation or keeping it going, even with strangers. Passengers on a train that makes an unscheduled stop in the countryside may start a conversation because they feel uncomfortable just sitting there. This is a problem for Chinese speaking in English for two reasons. First, Chinese communicators consider silence a message. They may remain silent or allow a significant pause before responding to what a speaker has said to indicate that the question is sensitive or unwelcome. A Westerner may not receive the message the silence is meant to convey. The other problem is that because English is a second language, it often takes Chinese speakers longer than native English speakers to form a reply. Native English speakers without taking this into consideration may rush to fill up the silence with more words.

Silence to Chinese is not empty. They may use silence as a very powerful communication tool. Whereas Westerners typically view silence as gaps in a conversation. This different attitudes toward silence can become a serious stumbling block in the progress of negotiations between businesspeople from China and the English-speaking countries.

All of these non-verbal (but tied to the voice) characteristics strongly affect how something is extracted by the other person, and how we interpret the words. They provide an additional context, and a very important one. The key here is that we need to understand that how we say things can be more important than what we say. When looking to diagnose conflict, always look at these to determine if the "how" is the cause, rather than the "what." Paralanguage reminds us that people convey their feelings not only in "what" they say, but also in "how" they say it.

5.3.3   Case for Practice

Case 1

Linda Carmichael lives in a Canadian city with her two-year-old adopted Chinese daughter Ming. Linda is a busy professional woman and a single parent who wants her daughter to speak Chinese and know the culture she was born into. For this reason Linda invites new Chinese immigrants to live in a spare bedroom in her house. She always interviews prospective housemates before they move in. She wants to avoid any misunderstandings by making her expectations clear, and she wants everyone who lives in the house to benefit. Among other things, she wants to see how Ming likes any new person who might live with them. She expects a new resident in her home to agree to share housework and to speak Chinese to Ming. In exchange Linda agrees to help with English and any other problems the newly arrived immigrant might face in adapting to life in Canada.

Linda liked 32-year-old Jiang Yumei, an engineer from northeast China, immediately when she came for her interview, and so did Ming. Jiang Yumei thought this would be an ideal place to spend the six months she had to wait until her husband and 4-year-old son could join her. They lived with Jiang Yumei's parents, where she and her husband had lived since they married. She had never lived apart from her parents except when she lived in a university dormitory, so she was pleased to be able to live with a family. She readily agreed to everything Linda said during the interview.

After a few weeks Linda noticed that Jiang Yumei seldom did any housework. She did not even clean up after herself, so Linda had more housework than before Jiang Yumei moved in. Linda helped Jiang Yumei with English and job applications, and practiced job interviews with her. At the same time Jiang Yumei did not seem to spend much time with Ming.

Linda gave Jiang Yumei some lighthearted reminders such as joking about how she hates housework or saying, "Ming, tell me what you and Aiyee did this afternoon."

This did not produce any positive results, so Linda decided to discuss the problem directly. One evening at the kitchen table Linda said, "I think we have some crossed lines of communication I understood that we had a certain agreement between us, but you obviously understood something different. Can we talk about it?"

Jiang Yumei was silent and stared at the table.

Linda tried again, "I hoped you would spend more time with Ming. You two got along so well at first. She likes you and is disappointed that you don't play with her."

Jiang Yumei did not say anything. She did not look at Linda. Her body stiffened, her face turned red, and she stared at the floor.

Linda tried again, "I'm not angry, just confused, tell me what you're thinking, I want to understand your point of view."

More silence.

Finally Linda could not tolerate Jiang Yumei's silence any longer. She was angry when she said, "You know, in this culture it's very rude to stay silent when someone is trying very hard to resolve a misunderstanding."

The next day Linda went to see her friend Liu Qian, who had lived in Canada for over a year. Liu listened to Linda's story and said, "She's angry!" This was a surprise to Linda.

"What is she angry about? Why won't she talk to me?"

Linda never found out. Jiang Yumei moved out soon after.

(1) Why did Jiang Yumei keep silent?

(2) What false assumptions did Linda make?

(3) Can you give any advice to each of these women to help them avoid similar misunderstandings in the future?

Case 2

Vu Nguyen was a Vietnamese studying English in the United States. He often visited the local public library to read the magazines and newspapers. One day he found a book he wanted to read at home. So he asked the librarian, "Excuse me, may I borrow this book?"

The librarian answered, "Why, of course. Just give me your card."

Vu smiled at her and nodded his head politely. He wanted to show he was listening.

The librarian kept talking. "That book is wonderful. Isn't that author great?"

Vu had never read anything by the author. But he smiled and nodded again to show his interest. Finally, he said, "I would like to borrow this book toady. Could you please tell me how to apply for a library card?"

The librarian looked confused. "Oh, I thought you said you already had one. I'll give you a temporary card for today. We'll send you your regular card in the mail. It will be about two weeks. Come right this way to fill out the application." The librarian held out her hand, palm, moving only her index finger to get Vu to follow her.

Now Vu was confused. He did not understand why the librarian had suddenly become so rude.

Vu smiled to cover up his confusion. As the librarian gave Vu the application, she said to him, "You look happy. You must be glad about your new library card."

(1) In the case, did Vu's smiling and nodding just show his politeness and listening carefully, or mean he had a library card?

(2) How did the librarian understand Vu's smiling and nodding?

(3) How did Vu think about the librarian's gesture (holding out her hand, palm, moving only her index finger to get Vu to follow her)? What does this gesture mean in most Asian countries?

5.3.4   Further Reading

Paralanguage refers to the non-verbal elements of communication used to modify meaning and convey emotion. Paralanguage may be expressed consciously or unconsciously, and it includes the pitch, volume, and, in some cases, intonation of speech. Sometimes the definition is restricted to vocally-produced sounds. The study of paralanguage is known as paralinguistics.

The term "paralanguage" is sometimes used as a cover term for body language, which is not necessarily tied to speech, and paralinguistic phenomena in speech. The latter are phenomena that can be observed in speech but that do not belong to the arbitrary conventional code of language.

The paralinguistic properties of speech play an important role in human speech communication. There are no utterances or speech signals that lack paralinguistic properties, since speech requires the presence of a voice that can be modulated. This voice must have some properties, and all the properties of a voice as such are paralinguistic. However, the linguistic vs. paralinguistic distinction applies not only to speech but to writing and sign language as well, and it is not bound to any sensory modality. Even vocal language has some paralinguistic as well as linguistic properties that can be seen, and even felt.

One can distinguish the following aspects of speech signals and perceived utterances.

Perspective Aspects

Speech signals that arrive at a listener's ears have acoustic properties that may allow listeners to localize the speaker (distance, direction). Sound localization also functions in a similar way for non-speech sounds. The perspective aspects of lip reading are more obvious and have more drastic effects when head turning is involved.

Organic Aspects

The speech organs of different speakers differ in size. As children grow up, their organs of speech become larger and there are differences between male and female adults. The differences concern not only size, but also proportions. They affect the pitch of the voice and to a substantial extent also the formant frequencies, which characterize the different speech sounds. The organic quality of speech has a communicative function in a restricted sense, and it will be expressed independently of the speaker's intention.

Expressive Aspects

The properties of the voice and the way of speaking are affected by emotions and attitudes. Typically, attitudes are expressed intentionally and emotions without intention, but attempts to fake or to hide emotions are not unusual. Expressive variation is central to paralanguage. It affects loudness, speaking rate, pitch, pitch range, and to some extent, also the formant frequencies.

Linguistic Aspects

These aspects are the main concern of linguists. Ordinary phonetic transcriptions of utterances reflect only the linguistically informative quality. The problem of how listeners factor out the linguistically informative quality from speech signals is a topic of current research.

Notes			
paralanguage	副语言	gravy	肉汁；肉卤
manipulation	（熟练的）操作；操作法；手法	go awry	失败；弄错
turn taking	话轮转换	turn-yielding cure	话轮放弃提示
contemplation	沉思；默想；冥想	meditation	熟虑

Encounter Tips

◎　　英语国家的人对体内发出的各种声音非常忌讳，如清嗓子、咳嗽、吐痰、打嗝、肚子咕噜叫、放屁。如果是控制不住发出声音，则应该表示歉意。

◎ 英语国家的人吃东西时，忌讳发出声音，如喝汤、吃面条等。面条要用叉子卷起来放到嘴里；喝汤时，要用勺子舀起来，然后倒进嘴里，而不是用嘴吮。

◎ 西方人认为沉默是人际交往中缺乏自信，甚至是患有"交际恐惧症"的表现，所以他们最忌讳交际中的沉默不语，强调在任何情况下，都应做出有声的反应，即使用话语的转换给说话者以信息反馈。

5.4 Object Language

5.4.1 Pre-reading

A group of professors from the United States went to Japan to attend a two-week seminar, and after their arrival moaned about the heat and the lack of air conditioning. The Japanese organizer didn't say anything at first, until some of the American professors began to show up in shorts and T-shirts. He politely asked them to dress formally, meaning suit, shirt, and tie. The Americans were already accustomed to wearing the casual clothing in their own country, so they tried to negotiate down the expected level of formality. However, the Japanese thought it was unacceptable, and insisted on the appropriateness of the dresses for the seminar lectures. The Americans finally had to give in and changed their clothing.

以上案例看似只是衣着观念上的不统一，实质反映出两个国家不同的文化个性。相对来说，美国人因为崇尚个性自由，日常着装喜好随意简便。炎热的夏天常常穿着短袖衬衣出入公共场合。而日本人在各种场合都非常注重着装礼仪，政府机关和大小公司一般都要求职员穿西装打领带，无论严寒酷暑。外国人到此，也得入乡随俗，否则会被认为无礼。此外，身体气味的掩饰、皮肤的修饰、家具、车辆及其他耐用非耐用物品所提供的交际信息，与衣着服饰的选择一样都属于非言语交际中的客体语。它不仅可以展示出使用者的文化特性，而且往往能揭示出其个性特征和心理状态。在某些特定的氛围下，甚至能传递出比有声语言更多的信息。

5.4.2 Object Language—Express Yourself by Objects, Especially Artifacts

In our daily life, many objects can communicate to others some nonverbal meanings either intentionally or unintentionally. These objects can be one's physical appearance, clothes, skin color, smell, accessories, cars, and even the arrangement of furniture. They are not just lifeless objects; contrarily, the users in different cultures invest different meanings in them. Thus, we can say the object language is an important medium in nonverbal communication.

Physical Appearance

When people meet for the first time, they immediately make judgments about each other based on appearance and dress. In his book, *You Are What You Wear*, William Thourlby states, "When you step into a room, decisions will be made solely upon your appearance; so to be successful, and to be sure decisions are favorable, keep in mind that you are what you wear and dress accordingly." Different cultures apply different standards. What is beautiful or appropriate by the standards of one cultural group may appear less beautiful or even unpleasant to members of another culture. Sometimes, our appearance and dress can influence how the others react to us.

Figure

In Western cultures, people tend to regard tall and slim women as beautiful. Being overweight in the United States lowers the chances of getting married and receiving higher education. However, in Tonga, being fat is a symbol of beauty and status, and this is also the case for some Africans, especially those of an older generation who prefer a more robust figure. While in the Tang Dynasty in ancient China, short or plump women are regarded as more attractive. However, it changed a lot with the passage of time, and the standards of thinness among Asian women are far more strict nowadays than those among white women. That is why so many young girls try various devices to reduce their weight.

Skin Color

Skin color is usually the source of racial discrimination. The typical example is the white and black segregation policy once held by America and South Africa. However, white skin is no longer the only preference in the Western world nowadays. Many people there regard a golden brown tan to be the most attractive and healthy hue for their skin. A sharp contrast is that East Asian cultures, particularly China, ROK and Japan, still prefer light skin.

Why? Perhaps part of the reason is that tanned skin in the West is often considered as healthy and rich, because it shows that the person has the money to go and enjoy holiday by the beach. But in China, light skin is generally accepted as the traditionally defined concepts of purity and elegance.

Hair

Many girls in China now dye their hair into varied colors, usually blond, in the belief that it makes them sexier. The sharp contrast is that in many Westerners' eyes, a girl with black hair is more charming and mysterious. Chinese women used to keep their hairstyle simple, often one or two braids. But nowadays, they become interested in choosing various hairstyles to demonstrate their personalities. A lovely young girl may prefer to wear her hair straight and leave some bang, but if she wants others to consider her as more mature, she will probably choose a big curly hairstyle.

Westerners are fairly concerned abut their own physical appearance. Many Western women wear different kinds of false hair in different occasions, in the belief that it will make them more beautiful and self-confident. While in China, wearing false hair is not a common practice. In most cases, a Chinese woman wears false hair only when she is bald.

Clothing

The basic function of clothing is to protect our body, keeping us warm and comfortable. Besides, it can reflect a culture's value orientation and plays an important role in people's daily communication.

As the English saying goes, "The tailor makes the man." There is also a Chinese proverb that says, "Clothes make the man as the saddle makes the horse." It is obvious to see the importance of clothes. Although the key to dressing today is convenience and simplicity, many cultures still evaluate a person on the basis of his or her clothes. In fact, what we choose to wear more or less conveys nonverbal clues about ourselves. A person with a sloppy appearance and dirty clothes, whatever the reason, conveys negative messages to people around him. By contrast, a person who is properly dressed demonstrates the ability and self-esteem, and can be more easily accepted by others. The clothing as well reveals a person's emotional feelings. The white wedding gown can create a joyful atmosphere. On the contrary, the dark suits at the funeral express people's sorrow and sadness.

Textures and lines of clothing as well convey silent messages. Soft textures suggest closeness, and crisp textures indicate efficiency. While lines of clothing, strict or flowing, can provide some indication of how rigid one's personality is.

Americans are known for their casual dressing in daily life. A shirt, a sweater, even a T-shirt and any kind of trousers are acceptable in the office, if neat and clean. Suit, shirt, and tie are not necessary except for some formal occasions. While in countries like England and Japan, people attach greater attention to the formality of dress. In most Arab countries, women should wear robes and veils to cover their bodies and faces. Otherwise, they are not allowed to appear in public.

People in English-speaking countries generally care more about what they dress than Chinese people do. When going to the church, attending the daytime ceremony or wedding, men are supposed to wear morning coat; when going to the concert, theatre or evening party, they are most likely to wear tuxedo. Western women also carefully choose dresses, hats, and gloves according to specific occasions. At an interview, one should not wear black leather skirt or miniskirt. Generally speaking, the Chinese pay little attention to the formality of dress, and sometimes dress casually when receiving the guests or going out shopping. However, wearing pajamas or slippers on such occasions is considered very impolite in the West and may cause misunderstanding in communication.

Different occupations also require different clothing. Professionals prefer tailored outfits and dress shoes, whereas blue-collar workers often dress in jeans or uniforms and boots. The military requires uniforms that define individuals as members of the group. In North and Western Africa, public speakers often wear long robes with big sleeves so that when they raise their hands, they will look bigger and more elegant.

Sometimes, clothes are the only visible clue to one's personality or cultural background, and small changes in dressing style may signal other changes that may be important in communication. Even when other indicators are more apparent, clothes continue to make a statement.

Smell

Nonverbal messages are conveyed not only through sight and hearing, but also through smell. The food we eat does affect the way we smell to others. For instance, tourists visiting India are often struck by the smell of Mutton curry throughout the country. Besides, hygiene and environmental factors also contribute to odors.

Body odor is a very sensitive issue for most Americans. They bath daily to reduce sweat and body odors, and clean their mouths after eating onion or garlic to make sure that their breath is free of food odors. It is very common for American women to use perfume each day. They tend to keep a distance from a person who has body odor or bad breath. Nevertheless, if someone uses too much perfume or cologne, it sends to others a "notice me" message.

Westerners may find the odor of Arabians offensive. While in Arab countries, human body's natural odors are quite acceptable. Efforts to overcome those odors, at least on the part of men, are sometimes considered unnatural. Actually, many Chinese people also pay little attention to their body smell, and just consider it as natural.

Accessories

Women's accessories like rings, glasses, handbags, and hats can help reveal one's interests, hobbies, status or lifestyle.

Ring

Rings are circles, which convey the meaning of unity in almost all cultures. In ancient times, they also signified magic power. Generally speaking, wearing a ring on the index finger expresses the person's desire for marriage, on the middle finger, indicates that he is already engaged, and on

the ring finger, shows to others that he is already married. If someone decides to remain single, he will wear a ring on the little finger. However, there are still some differences among cultures. Take the wedding ring for example. In most Western countries it is worn on the left ring finger, since people believe that the vein in the left ring finger is directly connected to the heart, which is a symbol of love. In Russia, Poland, Austria, Denmark, and some countries of former Yugoslavia, the wedding ring is usually worn on the right ring finger. In the Jewish wedding ceremony, the groom places the ring on the bride's index finger, and the ring is usually moved to the ring finger after the ceremony.

Choice of rings may affect the way your hand looks, and at the same time reveal your personalities. For example, the man who wears a big flashy ring is likely to be extroverted and outgoing, whereas the owner of a pink diamond ring may be a sensitive and romantic lady.

Handbag

A handbag, the most popular accessory in the West, is not only a means to transport personal items, but also an extension of a woman's essential self. Carrying a photo bag around probably shows that you are family-oriented; you value security as well as close relationships. The main features of someone who carries a tote are generous and sociable. A briefcase is a sign of efficiency and ability to multi-task. While a large canvas backpack expresses your casual and practical attitude, showing that you put comfort over style and are health-conscious.

In addition to the type and material, you can also tell a lot about a woman by the contents of her handbag, ranging from keys, credit cards, mobile phone, to sweets, medications, and magazines. It is clear that most women have their own preferences; nevertheless, they usually have multiple bags and outfits for different occasions.

Handbags are acknowledged as one of the necessities of life for Western women. We may notice that Hollywood film stars appearing on the red carpet always carry fashionable handbags, and these bags would soon become the focus of discussion by the audience. Nowadays, women in the East also pay more and more attention to the important roles of handbags in their daily communication.

Car

Personal cars, which can enhance accessibility and mobility, are the most important transportation tool in the Western world. At the same time, they are often used by Westerners as a means to show to others their cultural values, social status, lifestyle, and personality.

A luxury car may reveal the high standing its owner has achieved in the community. A notchback tells us that its owner may live in the suburb. An expensive and old-fashioned sports car suggests that its user is rich but conservative. People who drive big flash cars are considered extroverted and enthusiastic in general. While the person who owns a four doors car is probably a family man.

5.4.3 Case for Practice

Case

Risley was an Indian student who studied in an American university. He was easygoing and hardworking, and always achieved good grades in the courses. However, he found that his classmates did not seem very happy when he got close to them, especially after he did some exercises or ate something. When talking face to face, they tried to keep a large distance from him. He was quite upset. Later, one of his American classmates who knew him very well told him the reason: because he "smelled bad" and he breathed on others.

(1) Why did the Americans behave like this?

(2) What do you think Rialey should do when communicating with his American classmates?

5.4.4 Further Reading

Western vs. Eastern Clothing

Alteration of power and domination between the East and the West has occurred throughout the last two thousand years. The supremacy in art, culture, science, philosophy, and poetry flourished in the East in the ancient times while the Western world was sunk in the Dark Age. However, the pioneers of the Western imperialism pulled the Western world out of that abyss and it became dominant over the rest of the world.

Every walk of life developed gradually. Mechanization, new techniques, new methods, new trends, and modernization developed in both the East and the West. Both have traveled a long way, gone through many phases to finally stand at a position they are at present.

Trade and commerce has worked as an intermediary to bring these civilizations together and exchanges of ideas take place at a very large scale.

Clothing, way of living, and food differ from civilization to civilization. Various factors determine the trends prevailing in societies. No great civilization has ever been cosmopolitan but there is prominent distinction between their cultures, norms, religions, and beliefs.

Western clothing displays more of a casual style because basically the West is a secular society, therefore its clothing is a blend of wanton type. The West is the trendsetter of the present fashion world. Its clothing includes jeans wear, T shirts, skirts, pants, shorts, etc. Formal wear is only confined to three-piece suits. Religion does not define the dress code. What defines the Western clothing is anything that is comfortable and trendy. Whatever attracts, fits perfectly, drapes the body is worn. The Europeans more or less follow the same trend. Mix-matched dresses adorned with requisites are preferable anywhere in the West. Western clothing is ministered by the liberal thought of a free mind.

On the contrary, Eastern clothing depicts tradition and culture though it is fast changing. Religious beliefs, cultural obligations, and traditions determine the code of dressing in the East. Traditional and customary dressing is considered a vital thing in order to preserve what the Eastern mind believes in and wishes to pass on from generation to generation. But the fact that cannot be denied is that now the West and the East have started to adopt a new, modernized pattern of clothing which is a blend of all cultures brought together.

Notes

object language	客体语	racial discrimination	种族歧视
segregation	隔离	bang	刘海
robe	长袍	veil	面纱
tuxedo	小礼服	tailored	剪裁讲究的
outfits	套装	texture	质地
sloppy	衣着不整的	curry	咖喱
hygiene	卫生	body odor	体味
accessory	配件；配饰	extroverted	外向的
tote	手提包		

Encounter Tips

◎ 欧美国家的人非常忌讳闻到对方的身体气味，特别是由于流汗、口臭或因不良卫生习惯而出现的怪味。在吃过葱、蒜、韭菜等后要注意及时清除口中遗留的气味，同时，也要养成良好的卫生习惯，平时勤洗澡，并认真对待自己因某种原因而产生的特有的气味，以免给别人带来困扰。

◎ 欧美国家的人对某些场合的着装要求非常讲究，比如男士在室内戴帽子就很不得体。接待客人时，男主人穿着背心、短裤，女主人穿着类似睡衣的宽松式连衣裙都是不礼貌的。正式接待客人时，应该穿上礼服。此外，在西方社交活动中，请柬上往往对于着装有单独的说明，要特别注意。

5.5　Environmental Language

5.5.1　Pre-reading

A Malaysian lady flied to Germany for an important business meeting which was scheduled on Friday morning. It was late Thursday night when she arrived. Feeling rather exhausted after a long journey, she went to sleep at once. Unfortunately, she woke up late the next morning and to make the matter worse, she lost her way in the city. It was not until 1 p.m. that she found the right place. However, the German businessman told her that the scheduled meeting was already over, and he had other arrangements this week. The lady was very upset and had to wait until next week.

这个案例反映出东西方在时间观念上的差异。欧美人非常注重"准时"与"效率"，强调日程阶段性和计划性。为了利用好时间，他们精心地安排一天、一周，甚至一月的工作日程。准时开始、按时结束，严格遵守约定时间。而安排的时间结束后，不论完成与否必须停止，不能影响下一次的安排或让一个人等候。相比较而言，很多亚洲和拉丁美洲国家的时间观念较淡薄，强调的是人们的参与和所进行的交际活动的完成，而不是固守某个约定。他们认为只强调时间表而不问客观情况，只要时间一到便立即结束这项活动转向下一项活动的行为不太合情理。

5.5.2　Environmental Language—People and Their Environment Interact with Each Other

Environmental language consists of time, space, color, light, sound, signal and architecture, etc. Compared to artifacts, it is more endurable and cannot be moved easily. They are points that people and their environment interact with each other and are mutually influenced. Generally speaking, time and space are two fundamental research areas in environmental language.

Time

Edward T. Hall points out, "Time talks. It speaks more plainly than words. The message it conveys comes through loud and clear. It can shout the truth where words lie." Each of us has the same amount of time every day, but time can be viewed and used in different ways.

Time can be classified into several concepts, and what we discuss most are psychological time, cultural time, as well as Monochronic and Polychronic time.

Psychological time

Psychological time is how people feel, think, structure time and how it affects their daily life. It is natural that different cultures have different time orientations.

Past-oriented cultures, like China, Japan, and most Asian countries, are more concerned with traditional values and collective historical experiences. They tend to be slow in changing those things that are tied to the past. While people in present-oriented cultures usually consider the current experiences as most important. They prefer short-term benefits, and experience each moment as fully as possible. The examples are the Filipinos and many Central and South American people. The third category can be called as future-oriented cultures, which is best characterized by the United States and most post-industrial countries. They are generally optimistic about the future, and believe that they can control the consequences of their actions through planning.

Cultural time

Cultural time involves how we look at time due to the way we were brought up and the ways in which we currently live. It can be divided into technical, formal, and informal uses.

Technical time refers to the precise and scientific measurements of time, which is often calculated in units such as light years or atomic pulses. It is not closely related with interpersonal communication.

Formal time is the traditional way of viewing time like minutes, hours, days, weeks, months, years, and centuries. For instance, a year, a formal time, means three hundred and sixty-five days plus one-fourth day, which is accounted for by inserting leap year, or twelve months, as well as fifty-two weeks.

Compared with the former two, informal time is rather loose and flexible, varying from culture to culture. It is actually the individual interpretations of formal time, and is often associated with words or phrases like "soon," "right away" and "forever." Informal time is the most difficult cultural time orientation to understand, since different people may have different understandings of these abstract references. For example, as far as the phrase "long-term relationship" is concerned, Americans usually mean no more than two or three years; for Europeans, it would be more likely to be at least 10 years; while Chinese tend to consider it as a lifelong relationship.

Cultural time can also be divided into Monochronic (M-time) and Polychronic (P-time). The typical examples of M-time pattern are the Americans, most northern and Western European people. In these cultures, time is perceived as a linear structure. People there usually do things one by one, organize their activities by means of schedules and place considerable value on punctuality. A person's being late sends them the nonverbal message that he/she is impolite and lacks of consideration for others. They make good use of their time, and often carry a small calendar to help them remember their daily schedule.

By contrast, P-time cultures schedule several activities at one time, which is more flexible but less efficient. People change plans easily, and time is subordinate to interpersonal relations. Southern Europeans like French, Greek, and Italians often turn up to a meeting late and think nothing of it. People in Arabic cultures also have a more casual attitude toward time, and this attitude is related to their religious belief that God decides when things get accomplished. In the language of Sioux Indians, there is even no word for "time" or "late," reflecting a very relaxed attitude towards time.

Chinese people in general belong to P-time culture. Instead of tasks and schedules, human relationship is highly valued in China. There is an example showing how conflicts may arise if we are unconscious of these cultural differences. An American couple who have a lovely daughter teaches in a Chinese University, and many of their students like to go to their house to play with the little girl. The couple, although very friendly and hospitable, sometimes feel unhappy, because the students often visit them during lunchtime without making appointments. This causes a lot of inconvenience to them. Therefore, in order to better communicate with people from other cultures, it is important for us to consider the different attitudes toward time.

Space

Personal space

The way people structure their personal space is called proxemics. The study of proxemics is important in various fields, especially in business communication. Factors that affect personal space include sex, age, relationship, and more importantly, culture.

We may notice that when Americans and Chinese are waiting in a shop or at a ticket window, they behave differently. Americans usually keep a long distance from each other; even slight body touch will make them feel uncomfortable. By contrast, in the Chinese line, some body touch is acceptable and pushing and shoving is not rare.

Different cultures have different customs concerning how far apart people should stand when communicating with each other. Generally speaking, Americans tend to need more space than Latin Americans or Arabs. According to the theories proposed by Hall, there are four main categories of distance in America: intimate, personal, social, and public.

The following table provides some information concerning the four categories of distance.

Distance	Description of Distance	Vocal Characteristics	Message Content
0—6 inches	Intimate (close phase)	Soft whisper	Top secret
6—18 inches	Intimate (far phase)	Audible whisper	Very confidential
1.5—2.5feet	Personal (close phase)	Soft voice	Personal
2.5—4 feet	Personal (far phase)	Slightly lowered voice	Personal subject matter
4—7 feet	Social (close phase)	Full voice	Nonpersonal information
7—12 feet	Social (far phase)	Full voice with slight over loudness	Public information for others to hear
12—25 feet	Public (close phase)	Loud voice talking to a group	Public information for others to hear
25 feet or more	Public (far phase)	Loudest voice	Hailing, departures

Intimate distance is the closest distance often used in private situations. People who have a very close relationship, such as husbands and wives, lovers, and close family members, usually keep this distance. If someone is forced to be at this distance with a stranger in a crowded public situation, he would probably feel uncomfortable.

At personal distance, Americans usually hold conversations with friends, colleagues, and some members of their family. Actually, most of their everyday communication situations take place within this range.

Social distance is generally used for social gatherings and impersonal business. When an American student is in a class in which the teacher is leading a discussion, he will most likely feel more comfortable within this range of distance from the teacher. Closer than four feet, he may feel somewhat threatened. Farther away than twelve feet, he may feel separated and lose interest in the discussion.

Public distance is the longest distance in interpersonal communication, including the space in which a person feels comfortable in a public area or gathering. The amount of this space will vary accordingly. It is appropriate for highly impersonal situations such as the movies, theater, lectures, or sports events, indicating that there is little or almost no personal relationship between them.

Sometimes in communication, we consciously shift the distance between ourselves and others, and this actually serves as a sign to convey nonverbal meanings. The amount of the space also varies according to the situation. For example, when many people are crammed into an elevator, they will invade what would normally be considered each other's intimate space.

In a general way, people live in colder climates keep large physical distances when talking with others, whereas those from warm climates prefer close distances. Cultural values and thinking patterns also exert great influence on personal distance: Cultures which stress individualism usually demand more space than collective cultures like China and "tend to take an active, aggressive stance when their space is violated." Furthermore, due to the large population and limited public space, the idea of "personal space" is relatively weaker in China, and people sometimes seem insensitive to the accidental physical touch with strangers. An example is that when waiting for buses, Chinese people often follow another closely and push and shove to get on if it is crowed. This may startle the English-speaking people, and they consider it as invading their space. Besides, walking arm in arm or hand in hand is a way of showing friendship in China and other eastern countries, but often a sign of homosexual affection in the West. Therefore, it is important for us to bear in mind that most English-speaking people do not like strangers to get too close; otherwise they will feel very uncomfortable. Violation of their personal space may cause misunderstanding in interpersonal communication.

Territoriality

Territoriality is the study of how people define and maintain their possession of objects or areas. According to Altman, there are three territories in space.

(1) Primary territories: areas or possessions exclusively owned, used or controlled by a person or group of people, like a family's house, a bedroom, and a study. Violation of such territories is serious.

(2) Secondary territories: areas or possessions over which people have only partial control, such as a table in a bar and a seat in a classroom.

(3) Public territories: areas that are open to anyone, and the ownership is temporary, such as elevator, park, beach, library, and public telephone.

Territory can be defined by walls, hedges, filing cabinets, furniture, etc. Different concepts of territory sometimes cause conflicts in cross-cultural communication. In English-speaking countries, people attach great importance to territory, especially at home: The wife is generally in charge of the kitchen; the husband usually spends much time in the study; children also have their private bedrooms, and sometimes lock the doors to protect their privacy. They prefer to do lots of things in their own territory— watching the game, listening to the music or reading a book.

Western people also prefer to have their own office rooms if necessary, at least they would use active plates to divide the office into several parts. They are careful in protecting their territory, and will be unhappy if others intrude without permission. To them, it is somewhat confusing why Chinese people like to move two desks close together and sit near each other.

Seating arrangements

Differences exist in seating arrangements among cultures. Americans, when in groups, tend to talk with those sitting opposite them rather than those beside them. This pattern also influences how they select group leaders: in most cases, the person sitting at the head of the table is chosen. While the Chinese prefer to sit side by side on couches and talk with each other.

Seating arrangements on a dinner party also have cultural and historical roots. In ancient China, the king always sat facing south during the ceremony or the discussion of governmental affairs, while the ministers were all facing north when meeting the king. Thus, the word "south" gradually has the meaning of power and position, and in Chinese people's mind, the seat facing south in a formal banquet is  usually reserved for those who are respectable or powerful, while the seat facing north is considered less important. However, owing to the evolution of dining furniture, the seat of honor in China is now the one facing the entrance door, or in the center facing east. The seats on the left-hand side are in turn the second, fourth, and sixth, etc., while those on the right are numbered third, fifth, and seventh, etc.

What merits special attention here is that because of the deep-rooted confusion thought, Chinese people usually pay more attention to the seniority and social rank, but somewhat lack the respect for women. In an ordinary family dinner, the guest of honor is always the eldest member of the family, and on formal occasions, the one with the highest social status; while women are not even allowed to sit with men at the table in some remote areas for a long time, especially in feudal societies.

By contrast, in Western countries, seating arrangements take on different meanings from the past to the present. The most honorable guest once sat on the left side of the host, since in ancient times there were lots of assassinations for political and social reasons, and assassins usually held daggers in their right hands. Therefore, it was comparatively easy for the host to protect the guest on his left hand in case of the attack. However, with the development of civilization, this old style of assassination has been extinct for a long time. People's perspective towards left and right changed, and so did the seating arrangement in meetings or banquets. In general, the seat on the right side of the host is regarded more honorable than the one on the left side.

Nowadays, at a Western dinner party, seat arrangements are usually based on gender. The distinguished female guest generally sits to the right of the host, while the distinguished male guest sits to the right of the hostess. In most English-speaking countries, if a woman and a man come to a restaurant, the man should invite the woman to sit on his right. Therefore, when inviting a Westerner to a banquet, we should take notice of these differences and arrange seats accordingly.

Exterior Architecture and Interior Design

Architecture and interior designs throughout the world reflect the concepts of their builders both geographically and culturally.

There are obvious differences between Chinese and Western architecture. From ancient period to modern time, "toward south" is one of the most important principles in Chinese architecture. Since China is located in the northern hemisphere of the earth, in order to get the maximum sunlight, the

house should be built with its façade facing south. But most people in English-speaking countries don't take that into consideration. They may choose the house orientation according to their own wishes.

Cultural values also have influence on architecture. Take "Siheyuan" (四合院) for example. It shows some fundamental characteristics of Chinese culture. Chinese people believe that the universe is composed of five elements, that is, metal, wood, water, fire, and earth, therefore this traditional type of Chinese architecture is structured according to this concept that embodies unity and balance. It is actually an open-air living room, where family members can take a rest or talk with each other, creating a sense of warmth and intimacy. Chinese people's choices of internal layout, the ornaments, and the color of furniture, are also for the sake of harmony and good fortune.

In contrast, Westerners place more emphasis on coziness than harmony. They make full use of their space, sparing no pains to add dressers, filing cabinets and closet organizers to maximize the storage space. On average, they have more bathrooms than people in any other country. Many homes have big, open kitchens and vaulted ceilings. They also prefer natural and environment-friendly materials for interior decoration.

Sound

Sound is one of the main elements in environmental language. It provides nonverbal cues that enable people to recognize important aspects of our surroundings and react accordingly.

Various sounds in public occasions can help attract our attention: Sirens in the street make people alert; soft music in restaurants conveys the message of "welcome"; while the loud sounds made by percussion instruments in discos can arouse the excitement.

Businessmen in Western countries pay more attention to the use of different sounds to create great expressive force and achieve commercial purposes, for example, playing some suitable tape and TV programmes may attract people to come closer to the counter and enhance their surrounding atmosphere. A research shows that sounds emitted from the environment are really important to the customer experience. They help to create bonds between consumers and products, influencing the speed at which people shop and their willingness to buy. On the other hand, sounds may as well influence the working attitudes of the shop assistants.

Among so many kinds of sounds, music perhaps has the most powerful effects on our daily life, for better or for worse. Country music can lead to depression. Classical has the power to encourage; yet punk rock may increase tension. People in the West like to play various kinds of music in parties or other social gatherings, which may create a warm atmosphere and smooth the interpersonal communication; In addition to that, the use of music in hospital is now becoming more and more popular in the United States and some European countries. It helps to reduce the anxiety of the patients and silently pass on to them the comforting words—Relax, take it easy, and you will be fine soon.

So to speak, using suitable sounds in specific occasions are especially important. Otherwise, misunderstanding and uneasiness may arise in daily life. Let's say, the hubbub of voices and mechanical noises in front of the counter will probably make customers annoyed, and at the same time slow down the working pace of the shop assistants. The sounds of loudspeaker, if improperly used, are very disturbing to people nearby, and may distract them from their conversations or tasks. In cross-cultural communication, we should also notice that people in Japan and English-speaking countries prefer quiet environment, especially in public. When travelling in a Japanese bullet train, you can hardly feel people around you. People there seldom talk with each other or on mobile phones in the carriage, and what you can hear is only the light sound of page flipping.

Lighting

Application of lighting not only affects the personal experience of the viewer, but also the social communication in public spaces.

Proper lighting level facilitates communication. Bright light in open space generally produces cheerful effects and encourages people to carry out activities, whereas dim light may create an atmosphere of relaxation and restfulness. In English-speaking countries, for a dinner party, a bridal event, or a romantic dinner for two, people tend to use soft lighting to fill the room with comforting atmosphere, and create a feeling of intimacy. According to Western researchers, soft light also gives good facial modeling to people wearing make-up.

Colored lighting can better enhance an atmosphere, affecting people's mood and attitude. Red, orange, and yellow convey a sense of warmth, while violet, blue, and green usually suggest coolness and may provide a refreshing feeling. What's more, people under red lighting tend to have a sense of urgency, and thus react more quickly than usual.

On the other hand, a poor lighting environment can reduce the accuracy of messages and affect people's judgment in communication; harsh light and shadows on the face may distract the viewer's attention; while flickering light somewhat creates a horrible effect.

Typically, lighting in a department store should be two to five times stronger than that in a private room, since people's eyes are drawn automatically to the bright thing in their field of vision. Besides, shopkeepers generally choose the high, florescent lights to make the display "stand out" and look inviting. Therefore, in some occasions when communicating with customers, lighting actually speaks more than words and contributes to greater marketing results. What merits special attention here is that nowadays the display light is seldom thrown on a certain goods in a direct way, but focuses more on enhancing the overall shopping atmosphere.

Lighting is also used as an important environmental language on the stage both in the East and West. Every scene requires different lighting techniques to convey the right message. It gives an idea of the mood especially when there are no words spoken. For example, the choice of front lighting, side lighting, and background lighting may stress the different characteristics of the performers, while the use of floodlight and the change of dark and bright light, will probably reveal to the audience their fierce mental struggle. The important thing to keep in mind is that the light should be relaxing to the audience. If the light is positioned into people's eyes, it will be an unpleasing experience.

5.5.3 Case for Practice

Case

Magid was an Arabian working in a company in the USA. One Sunday morning he was at home and didn't have much to do. He thought of his good friend, Jock, an American who he used to study with. They had not seen each other for a long time though they lived in the same city. And he had told Jock that he would come and visit him a long time ago. Now this Sunday morning seemed like a wonderful time for him to fulfill his visit. Without informing Jock of his visit, Magid went to Jock's house and rang the doorbell.

At the same time, Jock, after a whole busy week, was just looking forward to spending his Sunday reading and relaxing himself. Just as he started to read in his most comfortable chair, the doorbell rang. He opened the door and to his surprise, it was Magid who was standing at the door. He didn't look completely happy to see Magid. Then, after a few seconds, he smiled and said, "Hi, Magid. Come on in." They drank coffee and chatted about their life after their separation. Magid stayed about four hours and decided to leave. Jock walked Magid to the door. They said good-bye to each other and Jock thanked Magid for coming. After they left each other, both of them felt a little uncomfortable.

(1) Why didn't Jock look very happy to see Magid although they hadn't met for a long time?

(2) Why did both of them feel a little uncomfortable after they left each other?

(3) Can you give any advice to Magid before he visited Jock?

5.5.4 Further Reading

The Message in Distance and Location

Professor Hall's particular concern is the misunderstanding that can develop because people from different cultures handle space in very different ways. For two unacquainted adult male North Americans, for example, the comfortable distance to stand for conversation is about two feet apart. South Americans like to stand much closer, which creates problems when a South American and a North American meet face to face. The South American who moves in to what is to him a proper talking distance may be considered "pushy" by the North American; and the North American may seem standoffish to the South American when he backs off to create a gap of the size that seems right to him. Hall once watched a conversation between a Latino and a North American that began at one end of a forty-foot hall and eventually wound up at the other end, the pair progressing by "an almost continual series of small backward steps on the part of the North American… and an equal closing of the gap by the Latin American."

The problem is that, relatively speaking, Americans live in a non-contact culture. Partly, this is a product of our puritan heritage. Dr. Hall points out that we spend years teaching our children not to crowd in and lean on us. We equate physical closeness with sex so that when we see two people standing close together, we assume that they must be either courting or conspiring. And in situations where we ourselves are forced to stand very close to another person—on a crowded subway, for example, we're careful to compensate. We avert our eyes, turn away, and if actual body contact is involved, tense the muscles on the contact side. Most of us feel very strongly that this is the only proper way to behave.

Hall has suggested that the degree of closeness neatly expresses the nature of any encounter. In fact, he has hypothesized a whole scale of distances, each felt to be appropriate in the United States for a particular kind of relationship. Contact to eighteen inches apart is the distance for wrestling or intimate talk—here, even a discussion of the weather becomes highly charged. At this range, people communicate not only by words but by touch,

smell, body heat; each is aware of how fast the other is breathing, of changes in pallor or texture of the skin. One and a half to two and a half feet is the close phase of what Hall calls personal distance. It approximates the size of the personal-space bubble in a noncontact culture. Four to seven feet is close social distance. In an office, people who work together normally stand this far apart to talk. However, when a man stands four to seven feet from where his secretary is sitting and looks down at her, it has a dominating effect. Far-phase social distance, seven to twelve feet, goes with formal conversation, and desks of important people are usually big enough to hold visitors to this distance. Above twelve feet, one gets into public distance, appropriate for speechmaking and for very formal, stiff styles of speaking.

When a number of people cluster together in a conversational knot—at a party, for example, or outdoors on a college campus—each individual expresses his position in the group by where he stands. By choosing a distance, he signals how intimate he wants to be; by choosing a location, such as the head spot, he can signal what kind of role he hopes to play. When the group settles into a particular configuration, when all the shifting around stops, it's a sign that nonverbal negotiations are over. All concerned have arrived at a general, if not temporary, agreement on the pecking order and the level of intimacy that's to be maintained, and perhaps on other relationships as well.

Notes

environmental language	环境语	linear	线的；线形的
proxemics	空间关系学	territoriality	领地观念
assassination	暗杀	northern hemisphere	北半球
siren	汽笛声	percussion instruments	打击乐器
emit	发出	distract from	使分心; 分散 (注意力)
facilitate	使便利	dim	暗淡的
restfulness	宁静	harsh	刺眼的
flickering	闪烁的；摇曳的		

Encounter Tips

◎ 欧美国家的人对体触非常敏感。在说话、排队时要注意与其保持合适的距离，即使在特定情况下触碰在所难免，也应该表示歉意。

◎ 欧美国家的人非常重视个人物品的所有权，不要随意触摸他们的衣物、手表、汽车等私人物品，或者问东问西。

◎ 邀请欧美国家的客人吃饭时，要注意座位的安排，并尊重他们的习惯，尽量不要让两个同性坐在一起，一般是男女交叉安排。

5.6 Exercises

5.6.1 Exercise A

Decide whether the following statements are true or false.

(1) Nodding the head means yes, and shaking the head means no in all cultures.

(2) In most Western countries, people pay less attention to their private space.

(3) Staring at people or holding a glance too long is considered to be improper in most English-speaking countries.

(4) Most South American countries belong to past-oriented cultures which emphasize current and short-term benefits.

(5) Social distance is the longest distance among the four categories of personal space, and can often be seen in some social gatherings and impersonal business.

(6) Silence is ambiguous, for it can be interpreted as agreement, disagreement, confusion, respect, sadness, and so on.

(7) Some small accessories like handbags and glasses can also reflect their owners' Characteristics and cultural backgrounds.

(8) People in English-speaking countries prefer to move two desks close together and sit near each other in their office.

(9) In a Western banquet, seats are usually arranged according to gender.

(10) It is universally accepted by Japanese people to wear a miniskirt in an interview.

5.6.2 Exercise B

Find out as many expressions and proverbs as possible relating to time in English and Chinese respectively. Then sum them up and do an analysis of them.

5.6.3 Exercise C

Decide which of the following clothes may be suitable to wear for attending formal Western banquets.

(1) evening gown   (2) leather skirt (3) tuxedo   (4) dark suit   (5) blouse
(6) cocktail dress   (7) sweater   (8) jacket   (9) tailcoat   (10) blazer

A: men (   )

B: women (   )

5.6.4 Exercise D

Read the following case and point out the mistakes Zhang Lin actually made here.

When on a business trip in London, Zhang Lin was invited by her English colleague Sara to go to a banquet at 6:00 p.m. on Friday. The invitation card mentioned the dress code as formal, so Zhang Lin decided to wear her favorite business suit. However, the taxi driver made a mistake in finding the right way. When Zhang Lin arrived at the banquet, it was already 6:20 p.m. As soon as seeing Sara, Zhang Lin moved a chair to sit down next to her, and began to chat happily with her. Sara was a pretty girl, but had some grey hair much earlier than people of the same age, and she kept dyeing her hair for years. Suddenly, Zhang Lin noticed that Sara had some visible grey hair again, and quickly told her so. Sara seemed unhappy, and changed the topic away.

5.6.5 Exercise E

Read the following case, and discuss the questions.

Peter is the General Manager of an American company in China. Recently, Chen Kaijun, one of the Chinese managers made a mistake at work that caused some difficulties requiring a lot of effort to fix. Chen Kaijun was very upset about what had happened, and came to Peter's office to make a formal apology.

Chen Kaijun went into Peter's office after being told, smiling before he spoke. "Peter, I've been feeling very upset about the trouble I've caused for the company. I'm here to apologize for my mistake. I'm terribly sorry about it and I want you to know that it will never happen again." Chen Kaijun said, looking at Peter with the smile since he walked into the office.

Peter found it hard to accept the apology. He looked at Chen Kaijun and asked, "Are you sure?"

"Yes, I am very sorry and I promise this won't happen again," Chen Kaijun said, with a smile even broader than before.

"I'm sorry I just can't take your apology. You don't look sorry at all!" Peter said angrily.

Chen Kaijun's face turned very red. He did not in the least expect Peter to take it negatively. It was desperate to make himself understood. "Peter," he managed to smile again, "please, trust me. No one can feel sorrier than I do about it."

Peter was almost furious by now, "if you're that sorry, how can you still smile?"

(1) Why was Peter so angry about Chen Kaijun's sincere apology?
(2) What do you think of Chen Kaijun's smile when he said sorry for Peter?

Chapter 5 Keys

CHAPTER 6

Intercultural Communication in Business Situation

The single greatest barrier to business success is the one erected by culture.

—Edward T. Hall and Mildred Reed Hall

Live together like brothers and do business like strangers.

—Arab proverb

6.1　Intercultural Business Writing

6.1.1　Pre-reading

Case 1

Two paragraphs are extracted from two business reports about the same issue, one by a Chinese, and the other by an American.

Paragraph 1

We have conducted a survey about the opening of a chain department store. The survey shows over 75% of plaza shoppers indicated they would shop at the store. Moreover, all the adjacent and surrounding small businesses supported the location of such a store in the plaza. So, I dare say that a chain department store located in Crown Plaza would be successful.

Paragraph 2

Our survey indicates that a chain department store located in Crown Plaza would be successful. Firstly, over 75% of plaza shoppers indicated they would shop at the store. Secondly, all the adjacent and surrounding small businesses supported the location of such a store in the plaza.

人们在构思段落、篇章时，往往会受到其思维模式的影响，表达同一意思，其遣词、造句却不尽相同。在本案例中，段 1 先把几句支撑句层层写出，接着最后才引出主题句，这是典型的按中文逻辑写成的段落。而段 2 则把主题句放在开头，支撑句紧接其后，这是典型的按西方逻辑写成的段落。这主要是因为西方人习惯演绎 (deductive) 的思维模式，而中国人则偏爱归纳性 (inductive) 的思维模式。

Case 2

Compare the following two letters, the first one by a Chinese student, and the second by an American.

Letter

INTERNATIONAL FACTORS

Circus House

124 Wanchai Road

Wanchai, HONG KONG SAR

13 December, 2020

Sales Manager

Empore Typewriters

190C Wai Yip Street

Kwun Tong
Kowloon

Esteemed Sir,

Reference is made to our purchase of recent date 25 LuxTak laser printer (model no. T54). Herein enclosed is a copy of our order number H817112. To date, said machines have performed in line with our expectations. However, we beg to inform you that it has come to our attention that these machines are becoming increasingly susceptible to malfunction. We request and require, therefore, that your kind selves undertake to replace, at your earliest convenience, all of these machines with your newer model, viz. T55. In the event that you prove unwilling to comply with our request, we shall be obliged to reconsider any future transactions with your kind selves.

Awaiting the favor of your early response, and assuring you of our best attention at all times, I remain.

Yours faithfully,

Simon Tse
Simon Tse
Office Manager
ST: dg

Letter 2

INTERNATIONAL FACTORS
Circus House
124 Wanchai Road
Wanchai, HONG KONG SAR

13 December, 2020

Mr. Albert Chan, Sales Manager
Empore Typewriters
190C Wai Yip Street
Kwun Tong
Kowloon

Dear Mr. Chan,

Subject: Faulty laser printers (model No. T54)

In September, this company bought 25 LuxTak laser printer (model no. T54) from your branch Wanchai—see our order number H817112. Until recently, these machines acted perfectly, only requiring occasional clean.

However, we have started to notice that breakdowns are becoming increasingly common with this model. Twice in the last week, we have had to return faulty machines to you. Clearly, there is a problem with this model that only becomes known after a few months' service. This is not satisfactory.

We would, therefore, like you to replace all of the machines which we bought, with your new model T55 laser printer, which, we understand, does not have the same design fault.

As you know, we do a large amount of business with your company, and we have always been happy with your service. It would be a pity to spoil this good relationship.

I look forward to receiving your reply soon.

Yours sincerely,

Simon Tse
Simon Tse
Office Manager
ST: dg

　　中国人在写商业信函时，往往受一些传统观念的误导，诸如，商务信函是正式文体，应该用深奥的词汇、复杂的句式，以使书信显得礼貌、高雅与专业。初用英语进行商务写作时，很多中国人都会走入一些误区，没有把握好礼貌、高雅与专业的度，导致写出来的信晦涩难懂。西方人收到这类书信时，会感觉不知所云。第一封信便是个典型的案例，这封信函中所使用的许多词语非但不能帮助理解，反而使其更加难懂，满篇都是过时的商业行话，用语高度冗余，言不及义。

　　而第二封信虽然同样正式恭敬，但文体却简单得多，简洁明朗，读起来较容易理解。

　　这两封信说明了用正确文体写作的重要性。用英语进行商务写作时，要有意识地避免写作中母语文化的干扰，从篇章大局把握，在整个语体风格上与国际商务写作保持一致。

6.1.2　Intercultural Business English Writing

The ability of writing effective business English documents is gaining greater importance in this global economy. As an essential communication way in various activities in the international arena, business English writing is done more frequently and in a more complex manner. At work in administration, business or management, writing is one thing that you must do every day. Success in your career depends largely on your ability to express your thoughts clearly, simply, and persuasively. Therefore, you should try to improve your use of words, so that your writing works for you and helps you to achieve your goals.

Business English writing mainly includes business letters, memos, reports, and product proposals. The purposes of writing are to distribute information, to give instructions or orders, to respond to memos and letters, to complete forms or to keep records, etc.

When writing intercultural business documents, there are many routine ways you must observe in order to maintain smooth cross-cultural interaction. With some knowledge of the basic cultural difference, you are likely to succeed in a cross-cultural business communication. In the following pages, our discussion will be centered on different connotations of words, discourse patterns, and writing styles between Chinese and English business writings.

Choose the Right Word

Be aware of different cultural connotations of words

Whatever you write, first you should have a vocabulary that provides for clear communication of your ideas and thoughts. You need to know the type and level of your audience and adjust your vocabulary accordingly. It is worthwhile to constantly work at improving your knowledge of words.

However, it is quite difficult for you to choose suitable words to convey your intended meanings, especially when your audiences are foreigners. That is because when selecting a word, only taking into account its denotation (the primary, surface meaning, or explicit meaning) is not enough, you should also consider its cultural connotation (the implicit meaning or the implication of a word).

Stemming from a certain cultural background, language itself is a product of culture and it is influenced and shaped by culture. Language and culture are interwoven with each other. Owing to the differences in the social and natural environment, custom, religion, and history, cultural differences will be inevitably embodied in language. Different nationalities have their own peculiar culture. Vocabulary, a major part of language, is the distinct tool of carrying cultural information and reflecting the cultural life of human society. Many words have specific cultural meanings.

People have long noticed that, when the denotative meaning of a word is the same in both cultures, problems may be still incurred if its connotative meanings differ. Take the word propaganda as an example. When addressing a group of people with different cultural backgrounds, we Chinese are inclined to express "今天我想向大家宣传一下我们公司的经营理念" like this, "Today, I would like to propaganda our managing conception." Hearing this, many Westerners would be shocked; some even leave their seat right away. What is the problem? Actually, Chinese "xuan chuan" (宣传) is not equivalent to the English word propaganda. In the Chinese culture, xuan chuan is quite neutral in meaning, meaning to explain to the people in order to convince them, and then ask them to take actions accordingly. However, the English word propaganda has a negative value, always sounds pejorative, meaning to cheat, to deceive by exaggerating or covering the fact.

Then how can we choose the appropriate word, especially when our readers are with different cultural backgrounds? Here are some tips.

Use simple words

Try to employ the simple words which usually don't have cultural connotations. If the reader cannot understand or misunderstand your words, you may seem "intelligent" by using long and difficult words, but the message you are trying to deliver is lost. For example, we should write "extra" or "more" rather than "additional," "help" rather than "assistance," "show" rather than "demonstrate," "use" rather than "utilize." Although sometimes you may need technical words, you should choose the simpler word instead of the complex word whenever you can. For instance, many people tend to write "All of these splendid commodities utilize a bare minimum of electrical energy," instead of writing the simpler one "All our products include a 25% energy saving device." However, the former will not make you sound smart but confuse the reader and make you look dumb.

Breaking the habit of using complex words and replacing them with shorter, everyday words can help make the essay easier to read and encourage you to explain your ideas in more specific terms.

Improve your vocabulary

A good dictionary and a complete thesaurus (a reference book of words and their synonyms) are your best sources for finding the right word. Use these reference works often. They can enhance your business vocabulary and help you express yourself clearly and accurately in your writing. What is more, it may help you avoid causing embarrassment and conflict in intercultural communication.

Structure Your Paragraphs

Be conscious of the different discourse patterns

A good business document must be well organized. You must plan in advance everything you want to say. When organizing paragraphs, it is believed that the Westerners prefer the deductive pattern of discourse, while the Chinese favor the inductive one. When writing paragraphs, the Westerners tend to stick to one idea in each paragraph and place that idea in the opening sentence, and then develop that idea with a series of specific illustrations, whereas the Chinese like to provide lots of relevant material first, even with some digression sometimes, and then use a concluding sentence to summarize the preceding information at the end.

Example

The One Westerners Favor	The One the Chinese Favor
The T-shirt promises a good market. It can be seen everywhere and on everyone. Women and little children wear T-shirts, as do teenagers, university students, and men from all walks of life. T-shirts are worn on the playground, at the beach or in the town. They can also be worn for work. Yet T-shirts remain relatively inexpensive and long wearing as well as easy to care for. Smart but comfortable and convenient to wear, they have become one of American's newest ideas on fashion.	Today, T-shirt can be seen everywhere and on everyone. Women and little children wear T-shirts, as do teenagers, university students, and men from all walks of life. T-shirts are worn on the playground, at the beach or in the town. They can also be worn for work. Yet T-shirts remain relatively inexpensive and long wearing as well as easy to care for. Smart but comfortable and convenient to wear, they have become one of American's newest ideas on fashion. So I believe T-shirt promises a good market.

But can we simply conclude that Westerners are direct and the Chinese are indirect in communication? Are there any exceptions? Read the following letter, and then you can find the answers.

Dear Mr. Wilson,

Every customer has a right to expect the best product and service from Caring Plastic Material. Every Caring material is the result of years of experimentation.

I have routed your letter of August 10th attached with photos to our production department. After careful inspection in our laboratory, we find that the materials Series 0150 you intended for refund were apparently exposed to a long-time sunlight. As we have noted from the beginning as well as mentioned in our advertising, Series 0150 cannot be shined for a long time.

However, Series 215 can withstand exposure to all sunlight. They share all the merits of Series 0150 and are sunlight-proof and waterproof. They are also economical. If you need further details and any help we can offer on your selection, please call us at 01-45-4318188 or send us an e-mail at caringmaterial@yahoo.com.

Frankly yours,

Apparently, this letter is written in an indirect order (inductive sequence). The writer didn't tell the reader that he/she could not refund directly at the first paragraph of the letter, but inferred it implicitly by explaining the reasons first. That is because negative messages are received more positively when an explanation precedes them.

Actually, you can organize your business messages either deductively or inductively, depending on your prediction of the receiver's reaction to your main idea. Here are some guidelines to help you choose the appropriate discourse pattern.

Deduction in good news and routine messages

Good news or routine messages follow a deductive sequence (direct order). To present good news or routine information deductively, you should make a point up front; tell the reader what your message is about in the opening line, followed by supporting details, and end with goodwill.

Induction in bad news messages

It is preferable to write bad news messages in inductive sequence (indirect order). The indirect order is especially effective when you have to say "no" to a request or when you must convey any disappointing news. That is because an explanation may convince the reader that the writer's actions are reasonable and understandable. In fact, an explanation cushions the shock of bad news.

Induction in persuasion

Persuasion is the art of influencing others to accept your views. Persuasive messages aim to influence readers who are inclined to resist. In persuasion, you should follow the inductive order: begin with words that set up the strategy—needs, appeals, emotion, and credibility, then present the strategy (persuasion), using persuasive language and you-approach, and end the writing by describing precisely what you would like to do, restating how the audience will benefit by acting as you say.

Watch Your Style

Notice the different writing styles

The style of business documents has to do with the language and the tone you use. As business documents receive a functional reading, the expectation we bring to a business document differ from those we bring to any other kind of writing. We read not to entertain but to discover what the writer wants us to do or to know. Therefore, we expect to encounter ideas, not to have to decipher awkward, or needlessly complex expressions. In addition, we expect economy of expression: Business writing isn't poetry, and we do not treasure the writer's choice of words. Finally, we  expect the document to make a point: Business writing isn't detective fiction, and if the point isn't in the first paragraph, we stop reading the sentences in order. We begin to scan. In other words, the most effective business writing is concise, vivid, and clear. It does not waste the reader's time. It uses active verbs and nouns and is free of clichés, jargon, and awkward phrases that confuse the readers and complicate the message.

As a result, for the Chinese writers, a radical adjustment in thinking is quite necessary. We Chinese are often plagued by a host of complicating assumptions when writing to the Westerners. For example, many people feel compelled to begin with background, forgetting that their foreign readers of business documents scan until they find the main point; many are used to using big and vague words, forgetting that Westerners prefer to read little but concrete ones; many endeavor to write flowery formal words, forgetting that their Western readers like the conversational style.

You can learn to be more aware of your language and avoid outworn expressions, wordy phrases, vague terms, and other lapses in style. Here are some suggestions for your consideration.

Keep your words concrete

Chinese are used to vague or abstract words, while the Westerners prefer the concrete ones. The Westerners feel uncomfortable with the vagueness and ambiguity, which is often associated with limited data in their eyes. In their view, vague words are not persuasive; using vague words is a sign of lack of survey or research. So, when writing to Westerners, you should keep your words concrete.

Concrete words refer to something specific, often something we can see, hear, touch, taste, or smell. Vague or abstract words refer to concepts or generalities, philosophies, or ideologies. The more abstract the word or phrase is, the more removed from our ordinary experience and the more likely we will misunderstand the term. The more concrete the word is, the less room there is for misinterpreting the message.

The following are some examples.

Vague	Concrete
Management has admitted the need for greater levels of productivity in the assembly area.	Management agrees that assembly workers need to increase their productivity by 20%.
In view of the company's current economic situation: The company anticipates that net sales for fiscal 2021 will be higher than net sales in 2020.	With company sales up 10% and inventory reduced by 12%: The company anticipates that net sales for fiscal 2021 will be about 13% higher than net sales in 2020.

Vague or abstract words leave the questions "How much? What kind? Which one?" unanswered. For example, "greater levels of productivity" means little. How much greater? Read through your letters for abstract words and phrases that appear to say something but actually say little. By using concrete words, you answer readers' questions with specific information.

Keep your words brief

As business writing is a kind of formal writing, Chinese were taught to be polite and indirect, and even to use flowery but unnecessary words in writing, whereas, in Western culture, time is money, especially in the business circle, so it is highly valued that you keep your message brief and concise.

Brevity may be the soul of wit, but some people have acquired and used wordy expressions without thinking. These wordy expressions pad our messages and add nothing to the meaning or impact what we have to say. Concise writing, on the other hand, saves the reader time and effort in understanding your letter.

We Chinese often use unnecessary words and phrases to give our writing a more "dignified, polite, or professional" tone. When such expressions are eliminated, the message comes through more concisely. Here are some tips that can help keep your messages brief.

Firstly, avoid empty phrases such as:

Empty	Brief
In about a week's time...	In a week...
It is a matter of prime importance...	It is important...
The reason I take the train is that...	I take the train because...

Secondly, use adverbs and adjectives sparingly. When you need to use modifiers, make sure they work for you and do not simply add words to your sentences. A well-placed adverb or adjective can heighten the impact of your letter. Overused modifiers weaken your meaning and give the message a flat, timeworn tone. For example,

Poor	Better
She gave a quick and highly emphatic reply.	She gave a quick, emphatic reply.

6.1.3 Case for Practice

Case 1

Dear Mr. Smith,

We are in receipt of and would like to thank you for your letter and catalogue of June 21, 2020. After close examination we have come to the conclusion that your products are of no interest to us but we wish you every success in your future endeavors.

Sincerely,

Case 2

Dear Mr. Green,

We are sorry to have your complaint about the poor performance of our Xingxing disks.

You claim that ten of the disks are unable to store data. Under separate cover we are sending you ten new disks which we hope is not inferior to the one you submitted to us under our guarantee. They were tested beforehand for any obvious defects.

Less than 2.5% of our total production is unsatisfactory, and we are usually inclined to feel that the user of the disks is at fault, not the disks. Since it is possible for some defective disks to slip by our rigid inspection process, we follow the practice of replacing any damaged disks that are called to our attention.

It is unfortunate that you have had this inconvenience. We trust you will experience no further difficulties with our products.

Very truly yours,

Try to improve the above two letters according to the knowledge you have learned in this chapter.

6.1.4　Further Reading

Passage 1

Make Your Business Writing Conversational

As a kind of formal language style, business English writing is featured by stiffness and definiteness with strict wording and logical structure. Most of what we find dull in business correspondence isn't what we say, but how we say it. Just because we work for an institution is no reason why we have to sound like one. The most effective business correspondence, like the best writing anywhere, is short, clear, and personal. Phrases such as "prioritized evaluative procedures" and "modified departmental agenda" only make readers work harder to understand the message.

To help you write in the same voice you would use when you speak, consider the following suggestions:

(1) Don't write any word that you wouldn't say. "Perusal," "Pursuant to," and "As per your request" are examples of this kind of writing.

(2) Don't substitute the impersonal "one" for "you," "we" or "I." When we speak, we rarely say "one must" or "one should"; we say "I must" and "you should."

Business correspondence is a written form of conversation, which is in pursuit of clearness and concreteness. When we Chinese write English business documents, we should be cautious about the negative effect our native language has on our writing. We should make our writing style in consistent with international English business writing.

Passage 2

A Reader-oriented Writing Strategy

Getting a clear picture of your readers before you start to write is very important in intercultural business writing. The better you know about your readers, the better you can direct your writing. Once you have identified your readers, you will be able to aim your message at their specific needs. But, remember, not all audiences have the same needs, especially when your audiences are from different cultures. What has to be said to people from one culture may not necessarily have to be said to people from another. Writing in the cross-cultural context demands us to attain some intercultural awareness.

After you've finished your writing, ask yourself these questions:

Is it easy to understand? Does it say what I want it to say in a simple, clear, and straightforward way?

Is it organized in a logical way? Does my opening sentence focus the reader's attention in the directions I want him or her to go? Does each sentence build in some way on the one that came before it? Are there any illogical surprises? Does any material need to be added, moved or omitted? To begin answering these questions, proofread your writings from the reader's point of view. Ask yourself, "What's in this writing for the reader? Why should the reader agree with me?"

Does it contain any unnecessary words? The more words we can eliminate from our writing, the more power we preserve.

Is it complete? Does it contain all the information the reader needs to know? Not every reader needs to know all the information that exists on any one subject.

Is it accurate? Have you exaggerated anything, been unfair in any way or failed to distinguish between fact and interpretation? If you do anything to break your reader's trust, they will never trust you again.

Notes

cushion	缓冲	decipher	译解
radical	重要的	plagued	折磨；麻烦；困扰
outworn	过时的；陈腐的		

Encounter Tips

◎ 西方人习惯演绎的思维模式，而中国人偏爱归纳性的思维模式。因此，在写文章段落时，西方人喜欢把主题句放在开头，支持句紧接其后；而中国人倾向于先写支撑句，后归纳出主题句。

◎ 当用英语进行商务写作时，就要有意识地避免写作中母语文化的干扰，从篇章大局把握，在整个语体风格上与国际商务写作保持一致，避免使用深奥的词汇、复杂的句式以及过时的商业行话，尽量使用简单易懂的语言与文体。

6.2 Intercultural Business Negotiation

6.2.1 Pre-reading

Walther Habers worked for many years as commodities trader in Rotterdam. On a business trip to Milan, he waited almost two hours for his 10:00 am appointment. When the Italian commodities buyer finally came out to meet him, it was time for lunch. Two hours later, after lunch, Habers walked back to the office for the meeting. By this time Habers was inwardly furious. He would miss his afternoon appointments. Being well traveled, he understood that time was treated differently in Mediterranean cultures, but this was his first experience in the thick of it. Although he eventually made the sale, Habers swore he would never again allow such a waste of time. The buyer from Milan, however, was never aware of any problem and thought the transaction had been a great success.

全世界对时间的观念是不一样的，有的甚至是截然不同。如德国人、荷兰人对待时间的态度就与同属欧盟的意大利人不同，前者属于对时间抱有直线式观念，即一次只从事一项主要的活动，他们认为时间是宝贵的，应该好好利用，不能浪费，他们总是高效、精确地组织商务活动；而后者则认为时间是可以变通的，不太愿意对时间进行严格计量和控制，他们对时间的流逝往往熟视无睹，他们更关注现在，因为他们喜欢现在就能生活得很充实。因此在上面这个案例中，来自鹿特丹的商人 Walther Habers 在意大利米兰的遭遇就清楚地表明了不同文化间商务活动中可能会遇到的理念、习惯等的差异。一般来说，在单一的文化背景下，谈判过程是可以预见并准确把握的。然而跨文化谈判比单一文化背景下的谈判更具有挑战性，因为跨文化谈判是一种属于不同文化的不同思维形式、不同沟通方式、不同行为方式的谈判行为。所以从事跨文化商务活动就要重视和了解谈判双方的文化差异，尊重和理解对方以期商务活动顺利进行，并提高谈判效率。

6.2.2 Cultural Conflicts May Affect Intercultural Negotiations

In modern society, intercultural negotiation involves discussions of common and conflicting interests between persons of different cultural backgrounds who work to reach an agreement of mutual benefit. As intercultural negotiations take place in different cultural environments, an effective negotiator has to learn about the specific  cultural, political, economic, religious, historical background knowledge for a successful negotiation. That is to say, during intercultural negotiations, negotiators from different cultures have to concern about many intercultural factors, such as different senses of value, ways of thinking, communicating, and awareness of law, which can be understood as cultural conflicts in intercultural communication. These intercultural conflicts may directly affect the results of an intercultural negotiation. In a word, it is really not an easy job to get a mutual satisfactory result in an intercultural negotiation. One should always make full preparations for an effective negotiation. The intercultural conflicts in business situations are usually shown in the following aspects.

Different Senses of Value

Different cultures may hold different attitudes toward the power of individuals. And in cultures that value individualism, the individual is always competitive rather than cooperative and personal goals are higher than group goals. Each individual has his or her own ideas, thoughts, etc. They usually prefer making individual decisions promptly and decisively. While collectivism always emphasizes on views, goals, etc. of the in-group and gets ready to cooperate with in-group members. They trust making group decisions.

In intercultural communication, British, French, German, Scandinavian, Swiss, Australian, Canadian, and the US cultures tend to value highly in individual power. While in other cultures, like Japan, ROK, China, Singapore, they tend to sum up all the ideas, opinions within the groups, and then make a decision.

Different cultures have different power distance values as well. In the high-power-distance culture, the authority is regarded as a high power in life. The people are not equal in such culture. Lower-ranking people have to show their respect to people in high-status positions. While in the low-power-distance culture, people expect to be respected and valued based more on personal attributes than on their position or titles. That is to say, people in power often try to look less powerful than they really are in such culture. Some countries whose ranking systems are very strict, like the Philippines, together with Malaysia, ROK, Japan, Panama, Mexico, and many Arab countries have been identified as the high-power-distance culture. In these countries, you should show respect to the most senior person in the group, who will also be their spokesperson. The personal wills of high ranking people will affect the result of negotiations greatly. So it would be more beneficial to avoid misunderstanding or failure to mutual communication.

In the low-power-distance culture, like the UK, Australia, France, the USA, negotiators may be more objective rather than powerful during business negotiations. They often pay more attention to data, facts, and figures rather than relationships or emotions in the course of the negotiations.

The values of time differ from one group to another. Some cultures like Americans, view time as an extremely precious resource so as not to be wasted. So do Germans, Swiss, and Canadians, etc. Time is money for them. People in such cultures always value time greatly. All the activities including appointments and business negotiations begin at the settled time. Being late is regarded as laziness and irresponsibility. While other cultures like Middle East or Latin America have totally different attitudes toward time, they think time is causal. And they often mix up private time and working time.

Different values of time may lead to different styles of negotiation. However, punctuality is essential and important in business situations, whichever culture you are from.

Different Ways of Thinking

Westerners including Americans tend to think from the particular and small to the general and large. However, in other countries, it is sometimes common for people to begin with a general idea and then move to more particular facts. In business situations, Westerners think deals are deals. They seldom associated them with friendship or relationships. They put more emphasis on outcomes rather than process. While in some Asian cultures, they think differently. They may consider relationships more than negotiations. That is to say, processes are more important than outcomes. Thus, different ways of thinking may cause intercultural conflicts as well as different attitudes and strategies in the course of the negotiations.

Different attitudes toward "face" also result from different ways of thinking in different cultures. In many Asian cultures "face" is deeply valued. To save or give face is regarded as a great honor as well as deep respect. To cause someone to lose "face" is even a threat to the group order. The importance of "mutual or group face" interests is particularly emphasized. In Western culture, the loss of "face" only means "personal" failure. Thus, saving or giving "face" is a good way to avoid conflicts in "face-valued" culture and help make a negotiation further.

Different Ways of Communicating

In general, some cultures focus on expressing ideas and opinions through verbal message clearly and directly, which is defined as low-context communication. While other cultures with the concept of high-context communication emphasize on conveying through the context (e.g. social roles, positions) and nonverbal channels (e.g. pauses, silence, tone of voice) of the verbal message. Thus the businessmen from totally different cultures may misunderstand each other.

For example, Chinese (characteristically defined as high-context) may keep silent to mean "I don't agree with you." It is not polite for a Chinese to refuse something or someone directly. Chinese would consider their own and opponents' faces, while keeping silent for Americans (characteristically defined as low-context) means refusal of communication. It seems impolite, or even rude. If Americans will make a rejection of something or somebody, they would say "no" directly. What different attitudes towards the "silence" between Chinese and Americans!

Different cultures also have different attitudes toward communicating distances— space. Space is the distance from one person to another. The language of space is powerful. How close can we get to others? What is a proper distance? The acceptable size of space varies greatly from culture to culture. This can cause intercultural conflicts when people communicate with each other. Relatively speaking, private space is the closest while public space the widest. Different cultures have different standards to measure the proper space with different people. A proper distance in one culture may be regarded as an uncomfortable one in another.

Generally speaking, the Middle East and Latin American cultures prefer closer space when they are in business situations as well as in daily communication. Americans and British share larger space. Usually, the smaller the space is, the closer the relationship is. In intercultural business, a safe, proper, and comfortable space should be measured and adjusted according to the mutual relationship.

These different ways of communication may affect the process of negotiations, and sometimes may cause misunderstanding between negotiators from different cultural contexts.

Different Awareness of Law

Different cultures have different awareness of law. Some cultures prefer performing strictly according to laws, while other cultures may take more flexible measures to settle problems or disputes. The purposes of negotiations are reaching an agreement. In business situation, different cultures may have different ideas with the styles of agreements, which greatly depend on their attitudes toward the formal and legal documents. Once you've found a solution, finalize agreements, and make sure everyone understands what's expected. In some cultures such as America, Germany, and China, detailed and written agreements are expected at the end of negotiations; in others, for example, for Saudis verbal agreements or a handshake is accepted. While for some cultures, like Nigerians, agreements are written but regarded as flexible.

Different Cultures Show Varied Behaviors in Business Negotiations

During intercultural business negotiations, negotiators would face their counterparts from different cultures. It is crucial to familiarize with various styles of business negotiations long-established in different cultures and adopt flexible and appropriate negotiating strategies to win a successful negotiation.

Egypt

(1) Egyptians prefer to do business with those they know and respect, therefore they expect to spend time cultivating a personal relationship before business is conducted. Who you know is more important than what you know, so it is important to network and cultivate a number of contracts.

(2) Egyptians believe direct eye contact is a sign of honesty and sincerity.

(3) Egyptians are emotive and use hand gestures when they are excited. In general, they speak softly, although they may also shout or pound the table. This is not indicative of anger; it is merely an attempt to demonstrate a point. This doesn't mean rude; it means powerful.

(4) Egyptians are tough negotiators. Do not use high-pressure tactics.

Japan

(1) Japanese prefer to do business on the basis of personal relationships. Never refuse a request, no matter how difficult or non-profitable it may appear. The Japanese are looking for a long-term relationship.

(2) In general, under business situation being introduced or recommended by someone who already has a good relationship with the company is extremely helpful.

(3) One way to build and maintain business relationships is with greetings/seasonal cards.

(4) It may take several meetings for your Japanese counterparts to become comfortable with you and be able to conduct business with you.

(5) You may be awarded a small amount of business as a trial to see if you keep your promise. If you respond quickly and with excellent service, you prove your ability and trustworthiness.

ROK

(1) Koreans prefer to do business with people with whom they have a personal connection. In ROK the main purpose of the first meeting is to get to know each other. Sensitive matters may be avoided discussing directly usually through the intermediary that first made the introductions. Relationships are developed through informal social gatherings that often involve a considerable amount of drinking and eating.

(2) It is a good idea to send both an agenda and back-up material including information about your company and client introduction prior to the meeting.

(3) Koreans treat legal documents as memos of understanding.

(4) Since there is a tendency to say "yes" to questions so that you do not lose face, the way you phrase a question is crucial. It is better to ask "Can we expect shipment in 3 weeks?" than "When can we expect shipment?" since this question requires a direct response.

Russia

(1) Meetings and negotiations are slow. Russians do not like being rushed.

(2) Russians respect age, rank, and position. The most senior person reaches decisions. Russian executives prefer to meet with people of similar rank and position.

(3) Russians see negotiations as win-lose. They do not believe in win-win. Russians view compromise as weakness. They will continue negotiating until you offer concessions. They may lose their temper, walk out of the meeting, or threaten to terminate the relationship in an attempt to coerce you to change your position.

(4) Nothing is final until the contract is signed. Even then, Russians will modify a contract to suit their purposes.

Saudi Arabia

(1) Decisions are made slowly in Saudi Arabia. Do not try to rush the process of the business negotiations. Most decisions require approval of several layers. It takes several visits to accomplish simple tasks.

(2) Saudis are tough negotiators. Decisions are made by the highest-ranking person.

Decisions are easily overturned.

(3) You may need to compromise on a point during negotiations if someone's dignity is at stake.

(4) Your Saudi host may interrupt your meeting or conversation, leave the room and be gone for 15 to 20 minutes for the purpose of his daily prayers.

The United Kingdom

(1) Punctuality is important in business situations. In most cases, the people you are meeting will be on time. Scots are extremely punctual. Call if you will be even 5 minutes later than agreed.

(2) In general, meetings will be rather formal. Meetings always have a clearly defined purpose, which may include an agenda. But there will be a brief amount of small talk before getting down to the business at hand.

(3) If you plan to use an agenda, be sure to forward it to your British colleagues in advance for them to review it and recommend any changes.

(4) Be prepared to back up your claims with facts and figures. The British rely on facts, rather than emotions, to make decisions. Make certain your presentation and any materials provided appear professional and well thought out.

(5) Decision-making is slower in England than in the United States; therefore it is unwise to rush the English into making a decision.

(6) Maintain eye contact but not long and a few feet of personal space. It is considered inappropriate to touch others in public. Loud talking should be avoided.

(7) After a meeting, send a letter summarizing what was decided and the next steps to be taken.

The United States

(1) Americans are direct. They value logic and linear thinking and expect people to speak clearly and in a straightforward manner. Try to get to your point more quickly and don't be afraid to be more direct and honest than you are used to. Americans will use the telephone to conduct business that would require a face-to-face meeting in most other countries. They do not insist upon seeing or getting to know the people with whom they do business.

(2) Arrive on time for meetings since time and punctuality are so important to Americans. In the Northeast and Midwest, people are extremely punctual. In the Southern and Western states, people may be a little more relaxed, but to be safe, always arrive on time, although you may have to wait a little before your meeting begins.

(3) Meetings may appear relaxed, but they are taken quite seriously. If there is an agenda, it will be followed. At the conclusion of the meeting, there will be a summary of what was decided, a list of who will implement which facets, and a list of the next steps to be taken and by whom. If you make a presentation, it should be direct and to the point. Visual aids should further enhance your case. Use statistics to back up your claims, since Americans are impressed by hard data and evidence.

(4) With the emphasis on controlling time, business is conducted rapidly. Expect

very little small talk before getting down to business. It is common to attempt to reach an oral agreement at the first meeting. The emphasis is on getting a contract signed rather than building a relationship.

6.2.3 Case for Discussion

Case 1

As business director for a private university, Hsuan Park was in charge of negotiating the rent of a dormitory during the 1996 Atlanta Olympic Games. Although he had lived most of his life in the United States, Park used a negotiation style often employed by high context cultures such as his native ROK.

A national news organization wanted the 23-room house for three weeks and offered $30,000. Park didn't respond. The news organization then offered $45,000. Park didn't respond. Totally exasperated, the US news organization made their final and absolute offer of $60,000, which Park accepted.

He later told a colleague, "Initially, I didn't respond because I was considering their offer, and I wasn't sure what to do about it. After they upped the offer so quickly, I waited to see what their final price might be."

(1) Where was Hsuan Park from?

(2) Why didn't Hsuan Park respond when the US news organization offered the first price?

(3) What made the offer up so quickly?

Case 2

A group of the US businessmen are visiting China and are exploring the possibility of building a factory in China. While the Chinese are showing them sites, the US people ask the level of the available water pressure. The Chinese are perplexed and ask why. The US people say because they need to be sure the water pressure is sufficient to fight fires for insurance purposes. The Chinese answer that they have sufficient water pressure but want to know why the US people are speaking of bad luck before they begin the project because that will assure bad luck.

Differences in perception will lead to failures in negotiations. What one culture sees as planning and necessary, another culture may perceive differently.

What will you perceive in this situation?

6.2.4 Further Reading

Strategies for an Effective Negotiation

Step 1: Always be prepared. Remember the more you know, the more effectively you can negotiate. When you're negotiating, you should know: (1) What you must have; (2) What I would like to have; and (3) What it would be great to have.

Step 2: Set objective negotiating standards before you begin bartering. Make sure all parties agree on objective standards before you begin. That is, lay the ground standards.

Step 3: Work with, not against, the people you're negotiating with to develop mutually beneficial solutions. The only way to ensure a feel-good result is for everyone involved to look for mutually beneficial solutions. If they really believe you want to play fairly with them, they will usually try to play fairly with you.

Trust is a necessity if groups are going to establish trust together to their mutual benefits and all groups seek to establish trust with the other parties in the negotiation process. Each group may, however, establish trust on a different basis. The following table can show the bases of trust for the seven cultural groups.

Americans	Americans look to the past record of those with whom they are negotiating and trust in sanctions.
Chinese	As a critical element in negotiation with the Chinese, trustworthiness is assessed on the basis of past record.
French	Trust emerges slowly, usually as a result of one's deeds.
Japanese	Trust rests on past record and otherwise on intuition.
Mexicans	Evaluations of trustworthiness are based initially on intuition, then on past record.
Nigerians	Trust is an essential element of successful negotiation in Nigeria, and is based largely on friendship (past record).
Saudis	Trust is an extremely important factor, and depends on personal friendship.

Step 4: Finalize all Agreements. Once you've found a solution, finalize agreements, and make sure everyone understands what's expected.

Negotiations are entered into only for the purpose of reaching an agreement. In some cultures, written agreements are expected; in others verbal agreements or a handshake is accepted. We will be familiar with the forms of agreements for the seven cultural groups.

Americans	Detailed written agreements are expected and are to be legally binding.
Chinese	Together with a concern for the spirit of agreements, the Chinese prefer written agreements that appear very general to Americans.

French	Detailed, legally binding written agreements are preferred.
Japanese	Japanese tend to prefer brief, written agreements that set forth basic principles, but a gentlemen's agreement often has even more force than a legal contract.
Mexicans	Mexicans tend to prefer implicit agreement.
Nigerians	Generally, agreements are written but regarded as flexible.
Saudis	Bound by their words, Saudis prefer to comment their agreements orally.

Step 5: Follow through. Once the solutions have been developed and the agreements signed or otherwise finalize, follow through to the end of your bargain.

Notes

objective	客观的	mutually	双方地
beneficial	有益的	necessity	必要
trustworthiness	诚信	assess	评估
evaluation	评价	intuition	直觉
legally binding	具有法律约束力的	implicit	含蓄的
bound by	受……限制	comment	解释

Encounter Tips

◎ 国际商务谈判大多用英语进行，而谈判双方的母语往往又不都是英语，这就增加了交流的难度。在这种情况下，我们要尽量用简单、清楚、明确的词句，不要用易引起误会的多义词、双关语、俚语、成语，也不要用易引起对方反感的词句。为了避免误会，我们可用释义法确保沟通顺利进行。释义法就是用自己的话把对方的话解释一遍，并询问对方我们的理解是否正确。最后，为确保沟通顺利的另一个方法是在谈判结束前做一个小结，把到现在为止达成的协议重述一遍并要求对方予以认可。小结一定要实事求是，措辞一定要得当，否则对方会起疑心，对小结不予认可，已谈好的问题又得重谈一遍。

◎ 亚洲人的谈判焦点不在于眼前特定的交易，而在于建立长期合作的人际关系。因此，在谈判初期，双方谈判的内容涉及个人的和更宽泛的事情，直到彼此建立信任、增进了解之后才可以谈论谈判主题。对欧洲和北美国家人而言，谈判焦点在于谈判的实质性内容，在于交易，而非人际关系。一般而言，在双方相互寒暄之后，他们会直言不讳地直入主题，说："让我们开始讨论实质性的问题吧。"

6.3 Intercultural Business Protocol

6.3.1 Pre-reading

Texas agronomist, Tom Goodroy, was invited to Mexico to share technical information with a farmers' co-op. Used to wearing jeans and a Western shirt, he was unsure of how to dress for the trip. He asked the advice of an expert in cross-cultural communication and was told to wear a suit on the plane, so that he would be appropriately attired and thus respectful of the representatives who would meet him at the airport and escort him to the meetings. Tom was skeptical… After all, he would be meeting a bunch of farmers.

On his return, Tom called the consultant and said, "You were right about wearing the suit. Even the taxi drivers wore ties!" His trip was a success.

在不同的文化中，在不同的商务情况下，适宜的着装是不同的；如果着装不恰当，可能招致误解乃至生意失败。因此，出席需要与其他文化进行交流的商务会议，事先询问好适宜着装十分必要。在本案例中，如果这位美国官员因为去墨西哥只是与当地农场主交流而穿着牛仔裤和 T 恤，可能这次旅行会使他本人感到尴尬。应该重视了解当地文化习俗、礼仪礼节。重视一些看似小事的细节，会在商务活动中起到意想不到的效果。

6.3.2 Understanding Different Protocol

Webster's College Dictionary defines protocol as "the customs and regulations dealing with diplomatic formality, precedence and etiquette" and etiquette as "conventional requirements as to proper social behavior." According to Chaney and Martin, etiquette refers to "manners and behavior considered acceptable in social and business situations." Protocols refer to "customs and regulations dealing with diplomatic etiquette and courtesies expected in official dealings (such as negotiation) with person in various cultures." In a word protocol is what to do in a given situation.

In modern world, a well-honed sense and appreciation of appropriate protocol can make you stand out in a competitive global market. If you want to be a successful business person, you need to know enough about the correct behavior of a particular country so that you don't unintentionally offend its customs. Understanding the basics of protocol and etiquette is an important skill.

Though it is impossible to identify all protocols of a particular culture, one still has to understand proper protocols and behave appropriately and gracefully to try not to lose face or even lead to misunderstanding and failure to the negotiation as well.

Initial Contact

First impressions are made only once but are remembered for a long time. They are your manner of dress, your professional appearance, the color of your dress or tie, your body language, handshake, posture, amount of eye contact on introduction, where you put your hands, how you accept a card and how you present yours as well as the actual content of the card.

Naming systems

Names are our most precious asset. Names set us apart—they are what make us different from others. Of course, remembering names and using them to address others is one of the most important yet different elements of protocols. One of the best strategies is: Be aware that there are differences in global naming systems and differences can often be subtle. If you are not 100% certain, ask.

The procedure of making introductions varies from culture to culture. First names are used almost immediately by people from the US and the Great Britain, but introductions are more formal in some other cultures. Titles are used when introducing people in Germany, Italy, and China; they often indicate the person's profession or educational level. In Asia the surname precedes the personal name, and in many Hispanic cultures most people will have two surnames, one from their father and one from their name. There are also issues of formality and it is not always clear which is to be used and when.

Men and women from Latin America will often add their mother's maiden name to their surname so you could use the next to the last name when addressing them. When women marry, they drop their mother's surname and add their husband's father's surname. When in doubt ask what name is to be used.

Appointment-making

The ways in which you make initial contact and an appointment can range from a brief telephone call to writing a formal letter of request or the use of a "go-between". The manner in which the initial contact is made and the amount of the advance notice between the contact and appointment are key factors you must consider in another culture.  When dealing with another culture, the date you plan your business trip is also of major importance.

In El Salvador (萨尔瓦多) and much of Latin America, including Mexico, appointments must be made at least a month in advance by mail or telephone and then verified one week before the meeting. If you want an appointment in Egypt, you must send a letter of introduction to an Egyptian who can facilitate obtaining an appointment. In Africa, the use of an intermediary is also essential, especially when approaching someone of a higher status. To do business in Saudi Arabia, you must have a sponsor acting as an intermediary, making appointments, and arranging meetings.

Card-exchanging

An exchange of cards is an expected part of most introductions in Europe. Other parts of the world in which an exchange of cards is the norm include the Middle East, the Pacific, Asia, and the Caribbean. In Asia, especially in Japan, the exchange of cards is a meaningful ritual rather than a casual informality. Unlike the Japanese, Americans don't always exchange cards, unless there is a reason to contact the person later. They are more concerning your product than your card.

Today, bilingual cards are the norm, with one side printed in your home language and the other side in the foreign language in which you are dealing with. Please ensure that the side using the local language is face up. Use both hands when presenting your card; position the card so that the person can read. If presenting to a multitude of people at the same time, you should give your card to the highest-ranking leader of the delegation.

Social Entertainment

Much of the world's business is done while enjoying social events rather than in a bland office environment. How can we act properly and gracefully at the dining table? The following tips are hoped to be helpful.

Dining practices

The dining protocol includes what to eat, how to eat, when to eat, and where to eat, etc. The dining protocol in different cultures reflects different cultures' underlying values. The purpose of dining with business associates is not merely to eat or drink, but to extend the business meeting through the mealtime. It is an opportunity for an enjoyable interchange in association with the pleasure of eating or drinking.

Time and place of dining also vary in different cultures. In some parts of the world, the main meal is at noon while in others the main meal is in the evening. Lunchtime in many cultures is from noon to 2 p.m., but in Mexico, lunchtime is 2 p.m. to 4 p.m. and is the main meal of the day. In some cultures, business meals are eaten in private homes while in other cultures they are usually eaten at restaurants.

The manner of eating is widely diverse. You will have your own plate of food in Western dinner table, while in China the dishes are placed on the table and everyone shares. Tahitian food is eaten with the fingers. In the Middle East, be prepared to eat with your fingers if your host does, but use the right hand only.

In Bolivia, you are expected to clean your plate; Egyptians, however, consider it impolite to eat everything on your plate. Dining in Japan, especially in Japanese homes, requires sitting in a kneeling position on a tatami mat. Men keep their knees 3 or 4 inched apart; women keep their knees together. Being able to lower yourself to a position and rise from it gracefully requires practice.

Strict Muslims do not consume pork or alcohol. Orthodox Jews eat neither pork nor shellfish. Hindus do not eat any beef because the cow is considered sacred. People from countries such as India are often vegetarians because of personal or religious beliefs.

Drinking protocol

Drinking is always involved in many social entertainments. Different cultures have various attitudes towards alcohol drinking. For example, Muslims have a complete shunning of alcohol, while alcohol is a part of Chinese folklore and has a long history. In modern China, alcohol maintains its important role, despite many social changes. It still appears at almost all social activities, the most common occasions being business dinners, birthday parties, wedding feasts, and sacrifice ceremonies in  which liquor must be the main drink to show respect and express happiness. In Japan or ROK, it is traditional for the host and the guest to take turns filling each other's cups and encouraging each other to gulp it down. Do as Romans do when you are in Rome.

Perhaps the best-known drinking culture in the world is in Russia. No Russian meal is complete without vodka, which is a big business in the country. People in many countries drink beer quite often, but with different preference. In the US beer drinkers prefer their brew cold, while in the UK and much of Europe, beer is served at room temperature.

Seating arrangement

As for the seating arrangements, in business dining or negotiation, the primary principle is to achieve your goal: Honor your important business guest with a seat next to the host or as close as possible so that the host can communicate with him/ her.

Still different cultures have different seating forms. Sitting at a long table, the most important people sit at the center of each long side, facing each other. The most important guest sits to the right. Men and women alternate in this way, with the least important guests seated farthest from the hosts. Remember right-hand side is always preferred side.

In Asia, tables are usually either circular or square. The honored guest is seated facing the door. Someone's left-hand side is preferred side.

In Middle Eastern Cultures, seating is usually circular, but not necessarily around a table. Guests might sit on the floor. Someone's right-hand side is preferred side. Women usually sit separately.

Tipping

Tipping is acceptable in some countries and not necessary or even not allowed in others. Therefore there are tipping culture and non-tipping culture. In the tipping culture, a tip of 15% of the bill was considered to be a generous tip in numerous situations like fine restaurants. In many European restaurants, 10% to 15% has been already added to the bill. You can leave extra if the service was especially good, but it isn't usually necessary to tip the cab driver, the bellhop, and other service personnel who may carry your luggage, summon a cab, perform other service such as delivering food or small appliances to your hotel room. If the service is very bad, you are not expected to leave a tip but should report the situation to the manager. Leaving a few coins—insult tipping— shows a lack of respect and is inappropriate regardless of how poor the service is.

However, in the non-tipping culture, tipping can offend or insult the people of that culture. In Australia and New Zealand, tipping is frowned upon—virtually non-existent. People in China and Japan, too, consider helping you with your luggage as a gesture of hospitality and would "lose face" if you tipped them. Observing cultural differences in tipping can be helpful for you to communicate in a proper and graceful way.

Business Scheduling

When scheduling business activities, you have to take into consideration various rules of engagement with people from other culture. The first thing you should know is their typical hours of work, lunch and break times so as to make arrangements at a proper time.

Office hours vary in different countries. Customarily hours of work in most countries are 9 a.m. to 5 p.m. But in Iran, for example, business hours are from 9:30 a.m. to 1 p.m. and 2 p.m. to 5 p.m., Monday through Friday. In some South American countries such as Brazil and Colombia, the workweek is 8 a.m. to 6 p.m., Monday through Friday.

The Lunch period is also different. In the US firms it may vary from 30 minutes to an hour, and break times are usually one 15-minute period in the morning with a second 15-minute period in the afternoon. Europeans have a one to one and a half hours' lunch break, 20 minutes morning and afternoon breaks, and 15 minutes at the end of the workday for cleanup time. Thus, their nine-hour workday is, in reality, a seven-hour workday.

Next, an awareness of the holidays and holy days of other cultures is important in scheduling business activities. Respecting the customs associated with these special days can be a polite and appropriate behavior. On such occasions as Christmas and New Year, sending greetings appropriately would be a very polite behavior which can facilitate business relations. But when a firm starts doing business in a different culture, it must ask when and if it is appropriate to send greetings and who should receive a card. In most cultures it would be appropriate to send best wishes for the New Year or season's greeting for the holidays.

Others

In addition, superstitions—a belief that special charms, omens, or rituals have supernatural powers is another point you should not neglect. In many cultures, bad luck and even death are associated with certain numbers. People from the USA, for example, think that 13 is an unlucky number. Most American hotels do not have a 13th floor.

Friday the 13th is regarded as an unlucky day. Some Chinese believe that the number 6 represents happiness, 8 represents making a lot of money, and 9 represents a long life. Now that you know this, try to schedule important events on the days that represent good luck.

6.3.3 Case for Practice

Case

At an international airport in an Arab country, a Chinese engineer had his luggage checked and been impressed by the friendly attitude of the Arab customs officer. He wanted to express his appreciation and, as he knew no Arabic, he thought he'd shake hands with the officer. Unfortunately, both the engineer's hands were full. He was holding a small traveler's bag in his left hand and a larger piece of luggage in his right hand. So the engineer quickly put the traveler's bag into his right hand and extended his left hand for the handshake with the officer.

Then, something unexpected happened. The officer's face turned pale and the smile disappeared. Instead of giving the expected handshake, he slapped the engineer's extended hand and walked away angrily.

(1) Why was the Arab officer angry?
(2) If you were a businessperson, what could you learn from this case?

6.3.4 Further Reading

Passage 1

Cocktail Party

The cocktail party is perhaps a typical US symbol of entertainment, but an unfamiliar social phenomenon to many other cultures. Thus it may cause problems in intercultural business communication.

A US manager may invite employees, clients, and customers so that they get to know one another. The goal at a cocktail party is to meet as many people as possible. Nobody expects to get into deep discussions. In fact, it would be rude to monopolize any one person. One makes small talk and "walks the room," exchanging business cards and phone numbers so that one can get into contact later and establish future business relationships. At purely social cocktail parties, friends catch up or become reacquainted; new friends are introduced. At business-related cocktail parties, new contacts are made, business cards exchanged, and connections renewed.

To Europeans the cocktail party is a curious phenomenon. In Germany, for example, one invites only as many people as one has chairs for. To invite crowds and expect them to stand would not be hospitable and thus not acceptable. The art of small talk is not a forte of most Europeans either. They tend to view the US style of entertaining as superficial and lacking sincerity.

A US firm that hosts a cocktail party in Japan creates all sorts of problems because the cocktail party is based on the premise that one can walk up to anyone in the room and introduce oneself. In Japan, with its hierarchy and protocol for how to address others, it is almost impossible to introduce oneself without knowing the age and status of the other person. What it intended as a friendly gesture by the manager from the United States may cause discomfort and embarrassment for the Japanese guests.

People of different cultures may have different interpretation to the length of the cocktail party. For example, invitations in the United States may announce "Cocktail party 5:00—7:00 p.m." Americans find this arrangement very considerate and efficient. The guests know that they don't have to reserve the entire evening for the event; they can make other plans for the rest of the evening. But it's unthinkably in cultures where hospitality is supposed to be unlimited, because to invite someone for a set time period is rude.

Passage 2

Everyday Etiquette for Office Life

Most bosses expect their employees to get along with another and, more important, to get along with clients and customers. This means that however important your job skills are, they may not count for much if you don't also have some people skills. Fortunately, getting along with people usually boils down to simple, everyday courtesy.

Representing Your Employer

When you work for a company, you are its representative to the outside world. For this reason, everyone from a secretary to a CEO should know how to greet visitors and make them feel comfortable.

Both men and women should stand to greet visitors who come into their office. Coworkers also
should be given a warm greeting, but you need not rise each time when one comes into your office. For a visitor, though, your hand should be extended just as it would be if you were host in your own home. Ask the person to sit down; and if there is a choice of seats, you may want to wave him into one.

Many managers and executives sit behind their desks when talking to coworkers and customers, but it is more gracious to move a conversation out to a sofa or two occasional chairs. Visitors should be asked whether they would like a beverage. If the answer is yes, the manager should get the drink or ask a secretary or assistant to get it.

Office Greetings

Although corporate cultures vary from business to business and even from region to region, the exchange of daily greetings is a ritual everywhere. Coworkers usually say hello first in the morning and then simply smile when they pass each other for the rest of the day. No further verbal greeting is called for, and no one should take offense when a colleague doesn't stop to chat. It is considered rude, though, not to acknowledge fellow workers when you see them, even if it is for the fifteenth time in one day. You can nod or smile, but don't look the other way when you see someone.

Office Chitchat

Beyond routine greeting, how much people chitchat during the day generally depends on the atmosphere of the work environment. A formal, rigidly organized workshop may allow little room for casual conversation, while one that is informal and loosely organized leaves room for this kind of socializing. Sometimes talk is encouraged or discouraged by the nature of the work. An assembly line that involves heavy equipment or noise, for example, doesn't promote collegial chitchat, while an underworked sales staff may spend most of its workday talking.

In many workshops, the chitchat, especially that of extracurricular nature, is frowned on by management, and with good reason, since workers do have jobs to perform. Then the problem for an employee who wants to appear friendly is how to disengage from the friendly chatter without alienating coworkers.

When you must cut short a conversation to get to work, it helps to announce your reason in a friendly manner. For example, you might say, "I'd love to talk more, but I've got to finish the year-end budget report," or "Can't talk right now. I have to finish these estimates."

If you disengage graciously, there should be no problem expect for those relatively few workers who don't get the message. In these cases a little less friendliness is called for. Don't smile broadly; don't stop to initiate a conversation. When a talker walks by, quickly say, "Hi there," but don't look up from your work expectantly. With time, they should get the message.

Notes

represent	代表	executive	管理人
gracious	亲切的	beverage	饮料
corporate	公司	ritual	形式
acknowledge	答理	chitchat	闲聊
socializing	社交	collegial	合意的
extracurricular	业余的	alienating	疏远的
budget	预算	expectantly	期待地

Encounter Tips

◎ 国际商务谈判是正式场合，需要穿着正装。服饰要求高雅大方、端庄严肃。男士外装应为较深色的西服套装，全身上下的颜色应不多于三种。女士可着西装套装或礼服。发型应精心修饰，与实际身份相符。化妆浓淡适宜，与环境协调，力戒浓妆艳抹。

◎ 选择合适的打电话时间，一般在以下时间不宜打电话：(1) 三餐时间；(2) 清晨七点以前；(3) 晚上十时半以后。交谈以三分钟为宜。

◎ 在涉外商务交往中使用的名片通常不提供手机号码和私宅电话，只提供办公室电话。

6.4 Intercultural Design of Advertising and Trademark

6.4.1 Pre-reading

With the rapid development of China's economy, more and more foreign companies are coming into Chinese market and their popular brands have been well received by Chinese consumers, such as Sprite, Ford, Coca Cola, Nike. In the same way, Chinese manufacturers come to realize the importance of a good brand name, especially a good design of advertising and trademark for helping the products enter the overseas market. However, concerning the intercultural design of advertising and trademark, it is not just about promoting the product itself, but also considering the diversity of different nations' faith, cultural background, political system, ways of thinking, and consuming concepts.

Trademarks with "sun" are very popular in some English-speaking countries, such as Sunergy, Sunjoy, Sunrider, Sunett, Suniwell, Suntroy, Suntour, and Sunwoods. It may sound strange for our Chinese, but for those living in countries with large population believing in Christianity, these trademarks may arouse their buying desire. Culture penetrates every aspect of our daily life. Some people even argue that humankind can't live without culture. As part of our daily life, trademark is inevitably influenced by culture.

随着中国经济的快速发展，越来越多的外国品牌进入中国，如雪碧、福特、可口可乐、耐克。与此同时也有很多中国品牌进驻国际市场。在这个过程中，由于品牌的产地和推广地拥有截然不同的文化积淀，产品商标的设计和广告推广都不仅仅是单纯的产品推介。因此，跨文化广告与商标设计就有着非常重要的地位。例如，在英语国家中，带有"太阳"商标的产品都非常畅销，这与国外信仰基督教人数众多，崇拜太阳的文化有关，"太阳"的商标能够提高消费者的购买欲。

6.4.2 Design Affected by Cultural Differences

The design of advertising and trademark is the sign of products. Intercultural design of advertising and trademark consists of language effect and culture effect. Therefore, from the perspective of cross-cultural communication, intercultural design of trademark and advertisement should be consistent with the custom and culture of the two languages.

Generally speaking, if we pay enough attention to the difference between Chinese and English design of advertising

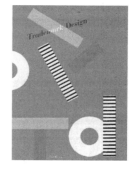

and trademark, we may find that Chinese people tend to be more indirect and prefer the use of modifiers, while English people prefer to use direct and concise expressions.

"You" Attitude

The design of Chinese advertising and trademark usually adopts the "I" centered attitude and emphasizes the publicity of their products and services. However, the design of English advertising and trademark focuses on "you" attitude. Usually they concern more about the cultures for which the product is intended, and their selling point is how the products are able to do for the customers and how the advertising would make people feel. Coca Cola, for instance, boasts "tastes good and makes you happy," while The Ford Motor Company has chosen a translation that means "happy and unique or special." These tactics in selling products attract Chinese customers, because they believe those things are good sign and could bring them good luck.

You may find out that the successful intercultural design of advertising should not only consider culture, history, values, but also norms and traditions when promoting the product into another foreign target market. McDonald varies its offerings by selling beer in Germany, wine in France, mango milk shakes in Hong Kong, China and mutton pie in Australia.

Individualism

Many societies, like the United States, consider individualism positively and regard it as the basis for creativity and achievement; some others consider it with disapproval. The design of Chinese advertising and trademark thinks highly of the public feelings, while the design of English advertising and trademark cares more about individuality.

Chinese culture focuses on the unity, while Western culture values the individualism and characteristic, which also reflects in the advertising, such as Nike's "just do it," and "I can." The success of Nike's advertising is partly because the brand boasts personal pursuance, effort, and individuality.

You may point out that Nike is also quite popular in China. Yes, we cannot deny the fact that China as a society is collectivist. However, to fulfill the social needs, culture must continuously evolve to reflect the best interests of a society. It is common that more and more youth groups feel at ease to accept foreign ideas. Thus, in the design of cross-cultural advertising and trademark, the advertisers should also be aware that culture is dynamic.

Blind Faith

The design of Chinese advertising and trademark values people's physiological need and tradition, at the same time, the design of English advertising and trademark pays attention to people's spiritual life and creativity. Language is the carrier of culture and people's spiritual life. Having been strongly influenced by the doctrines of Buddhism, most Chinese regard death and the loss of fortune as very unpleasant topics. When the famous foreign brand of men's accessories "Goldlion" first appeared in the

Chinese market with the name " 金狮 ," it was not sold well. Because the name sounds very close to " 今死 " " 金失 " " 尽输 " in some Chinese dialects. And then "Goldlion" was translated in another way. The source brand name was taken apart into gold and "lion." The first part was literally put into " 金 " to be faithful to the original, while the latter adopted the method of semantic transliteration and was put into " 利来 ," meaning bringing profit. From then on, "Goldlion" achieved great success in Chinese market.

It is well-known in China that " 黑猫 " is a famous brand name of mobile sprayer. However, when translating into English, "black cat" is not proper for the countries where people generally believe in Christianity. Since some Christians regard black cat a taboo image and the word "cat" already implies the meaning of "a mean unpleasant woman."

Colors, even the same one, symbolize variously from country to country; and symbols in different cultures also influence people's purchasing behavior. Companies should be particularly sensitive to the choices of color in the international advertising.

Just like pink is associated with femininity in the United States, yellow is considered the most feminine color in some other parts of the world. People in many Latin American countries disapprove of purple because people in these countries usually relate purple with death; by contrast, purple signifies elegance and quality in China.

Different Concerns

Most Chinese learners of English mistake the writing of English advertisments for the translation of Chinese ones. Being unfamiliar with the style of advertising English, they cannot but resort to translation of the original Chinese version into English. Such advertisments might impair the images of the advertisers and our country if they appear in the international market. For when shoddy English reaches customers, they may judge the products or services to be shoddy too. English advertisments of this kind should be eradicated, or improved, or rewritten. Look at the following corrected version of an erroneous advertisment.

> *Longyan Salted Crisp Peanuts are specially prepared with the imported advanced equipment and superior technology. It is extremely popular in the Chinese district of Hong Kong and Taiwan, and some Southeast Asian countries.*
>
> *(Peanuts)*

Although this improved advertisment is grammatically correct, it cannot possible hit its goal. It is not likely to secure the attention of any potential foreign buyers, because it is colourless. Note that advanced technology is given excessive emphasis in this advertisment. This may appeal to potential Chinese buyers but probably not to people of English-speaking countries. What is valued in their food advertisments is generally the products' natural flavor and freedom from pollution. Therefore, cultural differences should also be taken into consideration in our composing of English advertisments. For this purpose, therefore, a market research and a study of the target audience should be conducted before we write English advertisments. On this basis, we can recompose the

Longyan Peanuts advertisment as the following:

> *Give me Longyan Peanuts, or let me go nuts.*
>   *Why are Longyan Peanuts so popular at home and abroad? The crack lies in*
> *our state-of-the-art technology. The cutting edge innovations. Together with*
> *the traditional recipe. They are unrivalled. Next time, when your kids nag for*
> *some nuts, easy-to-crack, give them Longyan Peanuts.*
> *Longyan Salted Crisp Peanuts*
> *Savour the Epicurean-delicacy Flavour*
> *Oh-so-good-to-be-alive*

This version is undoubtedly far more effective than the previous one because it embodies some background information and linguistic devices. The parody in the headline will immediately conjure up in the reader's mind the familiar line by the famous American poet Patric Henry, "Give me liberty, or give me death." Meanwhile "peanuts" rhymes with "nuts" and therefore helps enhance the attention value and memorability of the ad. It is often the case that people may feel more comfortable to accept the familiar things. Western people with the cultural background of knowing Patric Henry's poem, or even the rhythm of the parody previously may be easier to understand the advertisment and memorize the products.

6.4.4　Case for Practice

Case 1

There is a well-known foreign brand of beverage in China, that is, Coca Cola. The Chinese meaning of "Coca Cola" is " 古柯 ," which is a kind of tropical shrub. At first, when we Chinese heard this name, nobody wanted to drink it. Cocaine, an illicit drug, is refined from Coca's leaves. But nowadays it has made a great profit in the Chinese market. Why? Mostly because they advertised the brand as " 可口可乐 ."

The newly designed trademark not only eliminate customers' fear, but also coincident with the pronunciation. What's more, it has a good and significant meaning—tasty. "Cola" is translated into " 可乐 ," which accords well the with Chinese nation's traditional deep love for a lucky name. We Chinese always attach importance to the name's meaning; we usually try our best to get a good name that contains many active meanings. " 可乐 " is undoubtedly the best choice. And as a whole, "Coca Cola" is an alliteration, " 可口可乐 " also sounded harmoniously. They are easy to read loud and remember. Whenever we hear the name " 可口可乐 ," we will get a cool feeling. So we can say this brand is a successful trademark.

(1) Why did they choose to design Coca Cola's Chinese trademark as " 可口可乐 " instead of " 古柯 "?

(2) What does "可口可乐" mean in Chinese?

(3) Can you explain the brand Sprite in a similar way?

Case 2

In September 2004, a highly creative but controversial advertisement aroused a national fury upon the Japanese well-know Nippon Paint (立邦漆). The picture named "Dragon" was initially published in the International Advertisement, which vividly presented the audience an inspiring advertisement but its glaring shortfalls unconsciously resulted in an earthquake among the public and fundamentally ruined its creativity as a whole.

In a typical Chinese gazebo, there were a couple of columns standing tall and upright. The color of the left one was bleak on which a symbolic dragon could clamber. Yet, the color of the right coated with the Nippon Paint was significantly shinning, where consequently the dragon fell down. The accompanying footnotes interpreted this image as the competitive edge of Nippon Paint products.

The originality of the mentioned picture was highly evaluated by advertisement specialists. However, the falling dragon strongly offended Chinese national dignity and surely annoyed the overwhelming majority. Fresh evidence provided us that according to an online survey conducted by China Advertisement, by 15:06, September 28, among 1,053 voters, 36.1% suggested advertisement originality should respect Chinese national culture; 38.27% thought this advertisement ignored the bond between advertisement and cultural elements; 2.66% criticized the advertisement staff for lacking the basic knowledge of Chinese history.

(1) If you are the audience, will you feel insulted by its design when you read the advertisement?

(2) As far as you are concerned, what image does dragon stand for in Chinese culture?

(3) In your view, what is the major reason in this case that annoys the majority?

(4) Can you give more such kind of examples?

(5) Do you think unawareness of cultural differences in advertising is a serious problem or not? Why?

6.4.5　Further Reading

Passage 1

When American Express writes to potential customers for its credit card in the

United States, the letter begins with mention of milestones on the road to individual success. Results-oriented cultures value measurements of success like the carved stones on English highways that told travelers how far they were from London, the presumed goal of every journey. American Express tells readers of the letters that only those who have already achieved a certain "measure of financial success" merit their credit card, along with the benefits American Express offers. One of the benefits it offers, to those who have already proven by their results that they merit it, is no set-spending limit in advance. Another benefit is the ease of application: Just complete the short form and sign. People who are busy obtaining results want simple steps to set the credit card. The letter uses a symbol, a centurion that is recognized as a logo of American Express. His helmeted profile signals responsibility, fearlessness, and strength.

When American Express writes to potential customers in Mexico, however, the emphasis is on membership in the society of cardholders. Not everyone can appreciate the card's true worth, the letter says. Members are only those who can—and by implication the receiver of the letter is one of that select group. "Now you, like (equal to) those" can count on the incomparable services and benefits of the card. The reader is invited to take a few minutes to look at how the credit card can help in various situations. The letter urges the reader to "ask anyone" about the wide acceptance of this card in fine establishments. The message is that anyone in the know recognizes the membership that this credit card confers.

The letter goes on to say, "you have seen" that cardholders don't need to worry at the moment of paying, when taking family or friends out, because there is no credit limit. In Mexico, the bill for dining or entertainment is never shared; one person hosts the rest. Avoiding embarrassment from not being able to pick up the tab because the credit card is maxed out is a selling point in Mexican culture. (Ads. in the US do mention "no spending limit," however.)

"Surely anyone knows that the medical and legal assistance you can obtain when traveling is worthwhile," says the letter. With a few phrases the letter sketches a host of knowing people who form an in-group of cardholders. A nonverbal symbol, the image of the card itself—badge of membership—appears, but no rugged, individualistic centurion. The appeal is to Mexican collectivism.

Furthermore, although both are direct mail sales letters, the United States letter underlines specific phrases for emphasis so as to make the main points stand out. The Mexican letter is gracious in tone and has no underlined points or bullets to grab the reader's attention. The reader instead is guided through various scenarios in which she or he will benefit from being a cardholder.

Passage 2

The Problems in Trademark Translation and Their Solutions

A trademark is a distinctive sign which identifies certain goods or services as those produced or provided by a certain entity or person. Trademarks can be distinctive words, phrases, logos, symbols, slogans or other things that identify the source of the product and make it distinctive. Trademarks can consist of letters, numbers, sounds, smells, colors, or even product shapes used to promote and distinguish the product in the marketplace. Trademarks allow companies and businesses to distinguish their products and to prevent consumers confusion among products, and protect the meanings they've chosen to identify their products or services.

As the world evolves into the global village, many countries are directly tied to an international system of economic interdependence, and most countries have at least one asset within their borders that is needed by another country. No country is completely self-sufficient. Foreign companies or multinational ones manufacture many of the products, from the cars we drive to the clothes we wear, even the soft drinks. Multinational corporations increasingly participate in various international business arrangements. In today's market economy, competition is universal. That the product has a proper and attracting trademark (or brand name) would be more competitive in the international market.

The translation of the trademark is a very practical translation action with high commercial value. It also transmits the culture from the SL (source language) to TL (target language).

The Problems of the Culture in Trademark Translation

As translation is between two or more languages and different languages contain and convey different cultures. The cultural dissimilarities are the most important barriers in cross-cultural communication such as the trademark translation. Chinese trademarks have cultural characteristics. Many translators are not aware of the cultural differences and don't pay attention to the possible barriers.

In Chinese, "喜鹊" has the meaning of "reporting the coming of spring and happiness." In English magpie (喜鹊) gives us the association of jaw and prolixity. Almost for the same reason, in Chinese, " 凤 凰 " represents luck and beauty, while in English, phoenix means rebirth. It gives them the feeling of waking up from death. White Elephant translated from " 白象 ," is regarded as rubbish in Western country. Another example, "dragon" is always the symbol of riches, honors, power, authority, and luck in the several thousands years' history in China. It is one of the most respectable animals to the Chinese. There are many Chinese idioms and stories about dragon. All the things linked with dragon are good and righteous. However, most Westerners consider dragon as the embodiment of evil and disaster. Suppose we Chinese people don't know the culture difference between us and Western countries, and we use "White Elephant" or "Dragon" as the trademark of some of our products which will be exported to foreign countries, what kind of effects will we get? It will surely cause great embarrassment or even losses.

Take More Negative Translated Trademarks for Example

" 蓝天 "—lamp, in Chinese it is a commendatory term or at least a neuter one, and is widely used as trademarks by various products. When exported to foreign countries, it was translated into "Bluesky." However, in the international market, its sales were very bad. Because the blue sky means being worthless in English.

" 金鸡 "—alarm clock. Its translated version is "Golden Cock." At the first sight of this version, many foreigners could not help laughing, because cock has a very vulgar meaning and is a very strong slangy word. So there are few people who bought this kind of clock. If the word "Rooster" replaces it, it would be much better, because "Rooster" can be accepted easily and in the meantime expresses the meaning that this alarm clock is as timely as a rooster to wake you up.

" 芳芳 "—the lipstick, was translated as "Fang Fang." In China " 芳芳 " is a beautiful name indeed, which are used to name girls. But in English "fang" means a dog's long sharp tooth or a snake's poison tooth. Who dares to buy this kind of lipstick? What about the free translation "Fragrance" or the transliterated version "Fun Fun"?

" 西子 "—the fancy soap, is translated as is "Shitze," which is pronounced like Shits. "Shits" in English is a very negative word. Who would like to use the soap whose name is sound like shits for washing?

" 卡卡 "—the trademark of a kind of China-made biscuits, was translated as "KAKA." When the products arrived Russia, the Russian loaders got shocked to find that all the boxes printed with "KAKA," because in Russian, "KAKA" refers to shit!

" 马戏 "—playing cards, transliterated as "MAXIPUKE," which turns out to be a funny English trademark, indicating " to puke maximally"!

" 大白兔 "(Rabbit)—is associated with "insecurity or a person who plays a game badly."

" 乌鸡白凤丸 "—"Black Cock White Phoenix Pills," together with an introduction of the product: "Black Cocks provide the vital tonic for women." The translator of this brand must have not realized that he/she is actually destroying the image of the famous brand!

" 宜而爽 "—a famous brand of textile products, is translated as "A Natural Fit and Comfort." A well-known brand of napkin " 心相印 " is translated as "Mind Acts upon Mind." Although both their meanings are closely equivalent to those of the original ones, the trademarks are too long to be good trademarks.

Transliteration, the usual method in English-Chinese trademark translation, often brings customers a kind of foreign style, indicating high quality of products. When those trademarks first occur in the market, they might inspire customers' curiosity. Since they are easy to read and remember, they became popular in China. However, having come across too many trademarks with a foreign style, customers will become less interested in them. Nowadays, we have too many trademarks transliterated with such Chinese characters as "特""斯""克," for instance, "赛特""飞亚特""阿尔法特""迪斯""真维斯""高斯""伊莱克斯""别克""星巴克."

Some Examples of Successful Translated Trademarks

The meaning of a trademark includes two parts: referential meaning and associative meaning. A well-translated trademark should not only sound pleasant, but also convey beautiful "referential and associative meaning" to customers.

The most successful example is "可口可乐" (Coca-Cola). The translated version not only imitates alliteration like the original one, but also helps to arouse favorable associations of customers. The translated version has become even more successful than the original trademark. Another example is "可伶可俐" (Clean & Clear), which also achieves satisfactory effects through the similar method.

The formal beauty of a translated trademark mainly refers to its pleasant pronunciation. Different pronunciation may arouse different psychological reactions. Many English-Chinese trademark translations sound beautiful and clear in terms of pronunciation. For instance, "派克" (Parker), "柯达" (Kodak), "夏普" (Sharp), and "捷安特" (Giant).

A cosmetic brand "Relvon" is rendered as "露华浓," which is cited from a famous classic Chinese Tang poem by Li Bai, "云想衣裳花想容, 春风拂槛露华浓." The translated trademark not only sounds similar to the original trademark in pronunciation, but also indicates that the cosmetic will bring beauty and elegance to women. Another brand of detergent product called "Safeguard", is translated into Chinese as "舒肤佳," ingeniously indicating the feature of the product. In fact, many foreign trademarks are good examples, such as "飘柔" (Rejoice), "高露洁" (Colgate), "奥妙" (OMO), "锐步" (Reebok), "雪碧" (Sprite), "潘婷" (Pantene), "雅芳" (Avon), "玉兰油" (Oil of Olay), "汰渍" (Tide), "席梦思" (Simmons), "奔腾" (Pentium), "固特异" (Goodyear), "佳洁士" (Crest), and "强生" (Johnson's). All those translations bravely break the bound of the original meaning. They cleverly combined phonetic transcription and semantic manipulation by exploiting the advantage of Chinese characters to fit the different features of different products.

Some Chinese trademarks are also well translated in the similar way. "瑞鹊," a brand of plastic utensil has its English name called Richway, which not only avoids possible unfavorable association aroused by literal translation, but also brings customers good blessings. Some other Chinese trademarks are also well rendered. For instance, "雅戈尔" is translated as Youngor, "方正" as Founder, "万家乐" turns to be Macro, "海信" as Hisense, "美的" as Midea (a clever combination of my idea), "华帝" as Vantage, "格力" is translated as Gree (looking similar to agree), "西泠" as Serene, and "回力" as Warrior.

Sometimes, according to different aesthetic values of different translators and various product features, the same trademark can be translated into different versions. For example, the trademark "Best" have several versions like "百思特" "百德" "倍舒特" which are the trademarks for pagers, hot water heater, and napkins respectively. "超级" (the brand of a kind of oatmeal) and "优博" (the brand of a kind of milk powder) are the different renderings of "Super." Another example is "Welcome," which is translated as "卫康" and "胃康" respectively for the different products of contact lens and toothpaste.

Sometimes, translators will change the original meaning of trademarks in translation according to Chinese psychology and logic. For instance, a famous French perfume called Poison, is rendered into Chinese as "百爱神". GoldLion is not literally translated as "金狮," because in Chinese, "金狮" sounds the same to "金失," which means to lose money. It is translated as "金利来," which turns to mean to earn more money.

The English trademark of "宏基" is Acer, which is a newly-coined word. It breaks the traditional rules in trademark translation and fully exploits the advantage of English language. Since "A" is the first letter in the alphabet, the trademark initiated by "A" often occurs in the beginning part of product list, thus can easily draw the attention of customers. Acer looks similar to Ace, so it would easily arouse the association of outstanding and excellent.

"Legend"(联想), "Serene"(西泠), "Frestech"(新飞), "MAXAM"(美加净), "Skyworth"(创维), "Shinco"(新科), and "Gree"(格力) are all examples of successful trademark internalization.

Notes

parody	模仿诗文	Nippon Paint	立邦漆
gazebo	凉亭	distinctive	区别的
prolixity	冗长的；啰唆的	neuter	中性的

Encounter Tips

◎ 进行跨文化广告传播时，应该努力挖掘文化间的共性：人类所推崇的精神和常见的情绪。例如，M&M 巧克力糖果广告就是一个成功利用文化共性进行推广的案例。"只溶在口，不溶在手"这句广告语几十年来在三十多个国家和地区获得极佳的广告效果，几乎没有文化背景的障碍。究其原因，是这则广告抓住人们都怕融化的糖果弄脏手的心理特点以及运用对比强调了巧克力的口感，这是大多数文化都能欣然接受的。

6.5 Intercultural Marketing Communication

6.5.1 Pre-reading

Gillette Company wanted to open up markets in Iran—a country in the Middle East with its electric razor. But the sales were not desirable when the products first entered into the market. Later the company changed its marketing strategy and made some innovations on its products. Then the company promoted the newly designed shaver which could trim the moustaches and encouraged the consumers in Middle-East countries to use Gillette products and become its loyal customers. Since then, the company has made up the deficits and got surpluses.

本案例阐述的主要内容就是营销中的跨文化因素。Gillette 公司的剃须刀进入中东国家伊朗时市场销售情况并不好，后来公司改变经营策略，把产品进行改进，推广可以修理胡须的剃须刀，并鼓励中东国家的消费者使用 Gillette 的产品，才慢慢扭亏为盈。Gillette 公司在伊朗反败为胜的遭遇涉及文化因素在营销中的重要性。因为伊朗像其他阿拉伯国家一样，男性蓄胡须是一种生活时尚，大多数男性喜欢蓄胡须，但蓄胡须不是让胡须无限长下去，越长越好，而是要经常修整，使胡须样子好看和整洁。因此在他们的日常生活中需要能修理胡须的工具，而不是能把胡须剃得干干净净的剃须刀。

6.5.2 "4Ps" of Marketing Mix

Cross-cultural marketing is defined as the strategic process of marketing among consumers whose culture differs from that of the marketer's own culture at least in one of the fundamental cultural aspects, such as language, religion, social norms and values, education, and the living style. Cross-cultural marketing demands marketers to be aware of and sensitive to the cultural differences; to seek out cultural similarities in order to identify opportunities to implement a modified standardized marketing mix; to spot "cultural shift" which might point to new products that might be wanted by customers or to increase demand. That is, if marketers want to be the winners in cross-cultural marketing they must create the marketing mix that meets the consumers' cultural values. Marketing mix is one of the major concepts in modern marketing. Marketing mix is a set of controllable, tactical marketing tools that the firm blends to produce the response it wants in the target market. The marketing mix consists of everything the firm can do to influence the demand or its product. The many possibilities can be collected into four groups of variables known as the "4Ps": product, price, place, and promotion.

Product

Product is anything that can be offered to a market for attention, acquisition, use or consumption and that might satisfy a want or need. There are three levels of products—

core products, actual products, and augmented products. The core product stands at the center of the total products. It consists of the core-problem solving benefits that consumers seek when they buy a product or service. The actual product may have as many as five characteristics: a quality level, features, design, a brand name, and packaging. The augmented product may be additional consumer services and benefits around the core and actual products.

Products are inevitably affected by culture. First, product acceptance is affected by culturally-based attitudes toward change. This is best summarized by Kotler: An American would like to get a hamburger for food, PierreCardan for clothes, and a Mercedes for cars. But in different societies, the demands can be satisfied in different ways. An inhabitant of Bali takes mango for food, rags around the waist for clothes, and seashell necklace for respect. Second, culture is felt in the process of selling. When products are sold to the area where people have no concept of the product, concept should be promoted first; when products are sold to the area with different cultures where people have consumed the product, special attention should be paid to people's taste. For example, before Chinese people had concept of shampoo, P&G made introduction by saying that different shampoos enjoy different features and functions aimed at different users: Some could make the hair smooth and sleek, others could reduce dandruff or provide nutrition. When the concept kept locked in the mind, P&G poured its products into the market and enjoyed a great success. Another company called General Food Company prepares different flavor of coffee according to consumers' different tastes: Coffee with milk for the British and black coffee for the French. When it comes to the cultural factors of product, it often refers to the translation of languages and the use of symbolic icon and color. Many multinational companies have successful translation of brand names: Coca Cola, Pepsi Cola, Lucky film, Youngor suits, and Warrior sports shoes, etc. However, there are many unsuccessful examples of brand name translation: "White Elephant" is a mistake in brand name translation and explains the unpopularity of "White Elephant" battery in the world market. "White Feather" is also an unsuitable word for a brand name, as "to show the white feather" means sneak away at a critical juncture and conjures up unfavorable imagination. General Motor once promoted its car in Latin America under the brand name of Nova, meaning a new star, but failed. Because the word "Nova" in Spanish means "Don't move." How can people buy a car that can't move? Discovering the problem, the company took immediate action by changing the brand to Savage, meaning fierce or violent, and quickly removed the crisis. What's more, it is required in some countries that the label should be printed in at least two languages while in other countries, foreign language is prohibited. Also, the symbolic icon in the logo is worth our attention. Here is another example, an American fashion company wanted to sell its perfume to Latin America by advertising that it was as fragrant as camellia. But it never expected poorer sales. Why? Locally, camellia is the flower used at funeral.

Price

Price can be defined narrowly as the amount of money charged for a product or service, or more broadly, as the values that consumers exchange for the benefits of having and using the product or service. Despite the increased role of non-price factors in the modern marketing process, price remains an important element in the marketing mix that produces revenues; all other elements represent costs. Price is also one of the most flexible elements of the marketing mix. There are three general approaches to set price. They are the cost-based approach, the value-based approach, and the competition-based approach, of which the value-based pricing, relying on consumer's perception of value to drive pricing decisions, is most related to culture. As difference in culture will lead to different perception of value, the product which is expensive and valuable in one country may be considered to be worthless and valueless in another country. Therefore, companies should apply a variety of price-adjustment strategies to account for differences in consumer segments and situations and expectations in different world markets. Besides, the influence of cultural difference on pricing is reflected on customers' number preference and taboo. Here are some examples. It is a universal American psychological set that odd number is smaller than even number, thus the price in odd number appears lower than that in even number. Japanese also like odd number but dislike the price ending with the number 9, as in Japanese, the pronunciation of 9 sounds like that of "bitterness." In China, especially in Hong Kong and Guangdong Province, consumers prefer the price ending with the number 8, but dislike the price ending with the number 4. So when Hong Kong Disneyland launched Chinese traditional wedding parties, it took full consideration of local people's psychology and priced the wedding dinner respectively at RMB 8,888, 10,888, and 12,888. Meanwhile, consumers in different cultures have different attitudes toward bargaining. For example, in ROK and Japan, where honesty is highly value, consumers will not raise any question about the price, so companies usually price the products transparently. But in other countries, consumers like bargaining and are used to asking for a lower price than the original one, and then in these countries, companies should raise the price accordingly and leave room for consumers to bargain.

Distribution—Place

Distribution channel is a set of interdependent organizations involved in the process of making a product or service available for use or consumption by the consumer or business user. First, disparity in culture can affect distribution. In 1998, the world biggest retailer Wal-mart entered ROK. For the purpose of large expansion and cheap land, the market was not set up near the neighborhood; instead, the newly built market was more faraway and inconvenient than other supermarkets. Wal-mart had hoped to attract consumers with its low price. However, Korean consumers are not sensitive to price but convenience. Wal-mart's low prices were not appealing at all. Thus, Wal-mart suffered great failure in ROK. Second, cultural factors can also be felt in the expansion of distribution channel. Let's take KFC and McDonald for example. Globally, KFC lags behind McDonald in expansion, but in China, KFC  enjoys the larger expansion and more rapid development. The outcome attributes to the franchise pattern "Not start from zero." That is, transfer a mature and operating restaurant to a new franchisee. Such franchise pattern can reduce the investment risk and save the new franchisee a lot of time-and-energy-consuming work such as site choosing, recruitment, training, and employee management. It is attractive to the Chinese investors who are not adventurous and would not like to take risk in investment.

Promotion

Modern marketing calls for more than just developing a good product, pricing it attractively, and making it available to target customers. Companies must also communicate with current and prospective customers. For most companies, the question is not whether to communicate, but how much to spend and in what ways. A company's promotion mix consists of the specific blend of advertising, personal selling, sales promotion, public relations, and direct marketing tools that the company uses to pursue its advertising and marketing objectives. Of the five major promotion tools, the cultural difference is most likely to affect advertising. On one hand, differences in culture can explain different attitudes toward advertising. For example, in Spain, people believe good wine needs no bush. That is, they don't think good products need advertisement. So the more advertisements the company makes, the more likely the products will be considered to be of low quality. However, in the USA and Japan, consumers think more advertisements mean more abundant capital and better financial condition and better-quality products. The above examples show that companies should consider the consumers' different attitudes toward advertisement to determine how much to spend on advertisements. On the other hand, cultural differences will also affect the components of advertisements, such as the theme, music, picture, language, appealing method, and media.

Additionally, cultural differences can affect the information communication. Because of cultural differences, information in the advertisement will be distorted in the process of coding and decoding and cause communication barrier. The "Kneel Down" advertisement of McDonald was questioned and revolted by Chinese consumers. As in the mind of Chinese people, kneeling stands for righteousness and moral integrity, as the Chinese saying goes: A man should have dignity and not grovel or bow down. So though Mac only had wanted to make the advertisement humorous and relaxing, it could not deny the fact that the advertisement insulted Chinese consumers. Finally, consumers from different cultural backgrounds will adopt different attitudes toward promotion methods and promotion tools. For example, Spanish will usually associate coupon with government relief, thinking it's a shame to use coupons. French consumers on the contrary prefer coupons and two-for-one offer promotion. British consumers welcome sales promotion; American adventurous and risky consumers are interested in lottery and cash award competition. In Western countries, consumption loan is widely-adopted promotion, as people in these countries often overconsume. However, in China, due to Chinese traditional consumption of "keep ends meet," many Chinese consumers hold the cautious attitude towards consumption loan.

6.5.3 Case for Practice

Case 1

George enjoys a reputation of a cultural translator. That is, he can explain what the message really means instead of what it sounds like in the context of other culture. One day, George was presented by a puzzled American the following message: After signing a contract with a US-based retail coffee outlet, a Saudi prince was handed a wet rag to clean the counters at the coffee shop. The US executives had insisted that he go through training just like everyone else. At that moment, the prince decided he did not need an American coffee chain in his portfolio. The American could not understand what went wrong. But he kept nodding his head as he listened to George's explanation.

It is not unusual and George can always give satisfactory explanations to the cases dealing with cultural differences. One such case was when " 蓝天 "(Lang Tian), a popular brand of tooth paste in China and the southeast of Asia, wanted to enter American market under the brand name of Blue Sky or Blue Heaven, George immediately pointed out that it would fail in America market. He proved right! And another case was about Lux. Lux is called " 力士 "(Strong Man) in China, a name contradicting the image of a young lady on its package. When the brand first entered the Chinese market in the early 1980s, a Hollywood actress was employed in one of earliest Western TV commercials. While bathing herself in a large bathtub (certainly an exotic scene to the Chinese viewers at the time), she said in a soft seductive voice "I only use Strong Man. How about you?" This proved to be a huge success and Lux became a household name within weeks. However, in Taiwan Lux is called " 丽士 "(Beauty), a name that matches with the image of young woman. Both names are pronounced with the exactly same sound and tone. This means that Lux has two different names with totally different images in the same language. So far, George's explanation has been convincing. It's no wonder he earns himself a reputation as cultural translator.

(1) Can you guess what George's explanation for the first case is?

(2) What's wrong with the brand name of Blue Sky or Blue Heave?

(3) Why was Lux called " 力士 "(Strong Man) instead of " 丽士 "(Beauty) in the early 1980s?

6.5.4　Furthering Reading

The Art of Renaming Brand

Renaming brands in a foreign market is no straightforward process. It can be a creative and value-added process when cultural issues and brand positioning are taken into consideration along with linguistic factors. It provides the international brand a rare opportunity to re-cast the brand in the new market; create a unique global-local image with built-in positioning attributes that enhance the brand equity of the original.

A study on brand renaming has found that there are three common renaming methods: Mixed translation is used most often (46%), followed by free translation (29%) and direct translation (25%). Direct translation maintains the phonetic link between the two names, i.e. the new name sounds like the original, but it has no specific meaning in Chinese. Free translation, on the other hand, gives a meaningful Chinese name but loses the phonetic link with the original. The mixed method seems to be the most popular one among the three as it creates a new name that both sounds like the original and has a meaning in Chinese.

Other things being equal, a brand name that has some meaning to the consumer will be more easily recalled.

Of 100 brands, three quarters are given a meaningful new name. Chinese names place more emphasis on meaning than sound. A meaningful name is crucial in developing both a mental image and favourable associations. Mercedes Benz is " 奔 驰 "(Speed On). The sound and visual image of two characters (particularly, " 驰 " with a horse as radical) generate associations of speed, dynamism, performance, and capability—the exact attributes that the German brand symbolizes. Brand positioning is another important consideration. In the case of Canon, consider its old name " 卡 侬 "(based on direct translation) with its new name " 佳能 "(based on mixed translation). Though sounding very close to Canon, " 卡侬 " has no meaning in Chinese. In contrast, " 佳能 "(means the best calibre in Chinese) is strategically desirable: It sounds appealing and generates an association of high quality.

The dilemma faced by the international brand is not about whether to choose a suitable Chinese name (it is a necessity in the majority of cases), but whether to maintain a Western image or to create a more localized image. For example, Nike and Reebok have adopted very different brand image strategies. Nike maintains a standardized "fitness and performance" image in all of the markets it serves. Nike is translated into Chinese directly as "耐克," a name that has no specific meaning (though the first character means something is durable) but has a distinctive foreign or Western image and sounds more appealing. Its rival Reebok, on the other hand, customizes its image on the basis of national differences. It is rendered as "锐步"(Dashing Step), a meaningful name that lacks a foreign image.

The challenge for international branding is to find a fine balance between the two strategies, as there are risks at both extremes. A pure global image that is alien to the national culture will not appeal to local consumers. On the contrary, a totally localized image will not benefit from brand assets of the original and find it hard to differentiate itself from the local competition. Unilever is a good case in point. A global brand, according to its chairman Michael Perry, is simply "a local brand reproduced many times." For many years, the company has been actively pursuing localized branding strategy in China, localizing all its international brands and acquiring successful local brands. Most Chinese consumers probably have no idea about Unilever's origin, which is perceived as a multinational company with a Chinese identity as its name suggests: "联合利华"(United Benefit China).

Notes

marketing mix	营销组合	core product	核心产品
actual product	可触知产品	augmented product	增值产品
dandruff	头皮屑	warrior	勇士
camellia	山茶	cost-based approach	成本导向定价
value-based approach	价值导向定价	competition-based approach	竞争导向定价
distribution	渠道	Good wine needs no bush.	酒香不怕巷子深

Encounter Tips

◎ 跨国商务活动的顺利开展和成功与否很大程度上依赖于语言的交流。一个拥有多种语言的国家,营销策略上可以使用不同的语言,如在瑞士推销产品,在商品包装上最好同时印有德、法、意三国文字。

◎ 把握某一文化的审美价值观念,在开展国际营销中对产品式样和规格、色彩的偏好和禁忌都有重要的意义。如在西方文化中,白色代表纯洁,但在远东某些地区,白色是丧事的象征。

6.6 Intercultural Corporate Culture

6.6.1 Pre-reading

Infosys (an Indian IT giant) needs to create a globally diverse top management to overcome Indian ethnocentric corporate culture. Diverse multinational, multiethnic top executive will be able to create a polycentric corporate culture and only then Infosys will be able to reap maximum benefit from its globalization strategy.

It's not just Infosys that faces this problem. The Siemens CEO Peter Loscher warns about the immediate need for "global diversity" of its managers or the company might risk losing its competitiveness.

"The management boards are all white males. Our top 600 managers are predominantly white German males. We are too one-dimensional," Peter Loscher said in an interview with *Financial Times*. His comments underline a crucial issue for many German companies, who have benefited enormously from globalization but still have nearly uniformly home-grown management and supervisory boards.

Since Siemens is a large German company with conglomerate diversification strategy, future growth is mainly dependent rising affluence in Asia and Latin America. As long as its management is one dimensional, it becomes very natural to view its global operations, sales and management with the German colored lens. This distorted view can lead to missed growth opportunity. It's good that the CEO of Siemens sees "ethnocentric corporate culture" as a main stumbling block in their globalization strategy.

本案例阐述的主要内容是经济全球化浪潮中的企业文化。企业文化是企业的经营管理哲学，体现企业的竞争实力、竞争精神和整体形象。企业文化是由其传统和风气所构成，同时，文化意味着一个企业的价值观，这些价值观构成公司员工活力、意见和行为的模范。它是全体员工所接受和认同信守的。伴随着经济全球化的浪潮，来自世界各地跨国公司员工为企业带来不同的文化。而包含文化多样性的跨国公司企业文化为公司的发展注入活力，并使之持续发展。

6.6.2 Cultural Variability at Work Place

The globalization economy urges the individuals and communities from different cultures to work and communicate with each other. Therefore, people not only have to study a particular culture, but also have to know how different cultures influence the attitude and behavior, as well as their association interaction.

Now let's take a look at various cultures from the dimensions of culture by Hofstede: power distance, uncertainty avoidance, individualism versus collectivism, masculinity versus femininity. The power distance refers to the extent to which employees accept that their boss has more power than they have and the extent to which they accept that their boss's opinions and decisions are right because he or she is the boss. It shows how much subordinates can consent or dissent with bosses or managers. Uncertainty avoidance is the lack of tolerance for ambiguity and the need for formal rules. That means people trying to set up rules to face to the uncertainty. Individualism is a concern for oneself as an individual as opposed to concern for the group. The priority of self-concern or group-concern varies from different cultures. Masculinity is about the sexual inequality. Masculine societies define gender roles more rigidly than feminine societies.

Occidental Culture

In most Western countries, power distance is rather low. It is felt in "Eiffel Tower culture" in the international management. In this hierarchical system, each higher level has a clear and demonstrable function of holding together the level beneath it. Higher-educated employees hold much less authoritarian values than lower-educated ones. The obedience showed from the subordinates to the superiors is not as much as the oriental way. The leadership can be called as hierarchy and consensus. Employees can have different opinions with his/her boss. And when he/she got different ideas, he/she can go all the way up to the boss and discuss the problem. This is a good thing and usually company may explore all the potentials of its employees, because sometimes the subordinates may have the better idea of the business.

There is low uncertainty avoidance in Western countries because of high job mobility. For example, people in Denmark and the US think that when they change their jobs, they can get more experience because they like challenge.

Most Western employees demonstrate a high individualism. They like to work with their own plans for defending their interest. Their spare time and work time are separated clearly. They do not like to be interfered by others. People do not cooperate at all. They just simply work in their own ways, follow their own rules, and achieve their own objectives. It is good for a company to gather as many ideas as they can when starting a new program. But how to manage these individuals to reach the group goal should be the awareness for managers.

Oriental Culture

Oriental corporate culture is a high power distance culture, sometimes called "power-oriented" culture. This hierarchism, greater centralization culture is also associated with the family culture, where managers act like the caring father. Managers, entitled with more privileges, make the decision, and are always esteemed by the subordinates. It is not regarded appropriate if subordinates have a disagreement with their managers, especially in Malaysia, Japan, China, and India. Employees get their promotion in terms of age and experience.

There is high uncertainty avoidance in most oriental countries such as Japan and

China. In these countries, people prefer a stable job. They feel safe and proud when they keep working hard at the one place. Under this circumstance, an excellent manager should keep his employees away from unpredictable risks. And the employee would like to work within groups rather than independently because of the less risk-taking.

Arabian Culture

The Arabs have a very strong sense of community. The society is characterized by a vertical integration, where human relationship is based on a person's hierarchical position, status, educational background, seniority, and gender. It is also relatively higher in collectivism and lower in individualism. Members place more emphasis on the welfare of the tribe, group or organization than realizing individual's potential. Each tribe, group or organization perceives itself as a well-knit community. When decisions are made under the influence of the Sharia Law, there is no potential for conflict, at least in theory, during the implementation stage and it increases employees' commitment to the decisions. It can also enhance employees' commitment to the organization. The consensus approach may also result in team-building.

Global Corporate Culture

Building a strong global corporation involves recognizing the differences among employees from a variety of nations. But the real key to developing a cohesive global corporation is to find a way to effectively communicate a common set of values and principals consistently across national, cultural, and linguistic boundaries. In other words, corporate culture must be established to find a single standard, a single way of doing business that must transcend national and cultural boundaries.

Corporate culture is a worldwide system of shared goals, values, and behaviors suitable for all company staff with different races, different value views in a complicated and power-decentralized environment, such as the tenet of "IBM means service," or Matsushita's "to recognize our responsibility as entrepreneur, to pursue the improvement, to enhance the public welfare, to devote to the sustaining development of our world."

A Global Corporate Culture usually has the following characteristics.

Being regardless of nationality, race, color, creed

In recruitment, selections and evaluation of staff members and providing remuneration and benefits to staffs, the global companies usually apply the same standard in the global field and ignore the cultural differences.

Being respectful for cultural difference

The global company admits the affiliates into the cultural system of the enterprise headquarters. Wherever the global company set up branches, it

must obey local cultures and regulations and respect the staffs' customs, religions, etc. Otherwise it is hard for it to get an adequate environment neither of personnel nor of business.

Constructions of Corporate Culture

Steps of construction

The corporate culture is not built in a day. It usually follows three steps: culture contact, culture selection, and culture identification. During the period of culture contact, the cross-cultural corporate will be aware of cultural differences. Only when people have such awareness can they come up with effective methods to deal with cultural differences. The second step is called culture selection, during which people will select those cultures that agree with their own and at the same time accept the best features of other cultures to have complementary advantages. Finally comes culture identification. It begins with management level and popularize among the staff. Culture identification is the result of culture selection. It is the bond and universal ethical principle orientation of the corporation. It's the motive power of the corporate culture formation.

Measures of construction—cross-cultural training

The ability to work and manage in a cross-cultural environment comes from cross cultural training, which aims to help avoid cultural conflicts, ensure smooth communication and right decision and increase efficiency. Cross-cultural training can help maintain good and stable interpersonal relations in the organization, enhance the cooperation and cohesion. The main contents of cultural training include: cultural sensitivity training, language learning, cross-cultural communication, conflict handling, and cultural environment simulation. Cultural sensitivity training (also called T-group training) was founded by American psychologist Leland Bradford. It is designed to improve the interpersonal relation and break down the cultural barrier. There are many ways to improve trainees' cognitive competence and adaptive capacity in different cultural environments. For example, trainees with different cultural backgrounds can be gathered together for special training such as case study, group discussion, and role play. Through T-group training, trainees learn not to be prejudiced against each other, but how to effectively communicate and impact each other, raise awareness of their own feelings and emotions, the roles they play and the interrelation, better understand cultural differences, and enhance the cross-cultural cooperation consciousness. In language learning, trainees should grasp the relation between language and culture; in cross-cultural communication and conflict handling, trainees should understand that the communication is a dynamic process and the cultural conflict has dual impact; in cultural environment simulation, trainees should put themselves in other people's shoes, compare and analyze different cultural patterns so as to better understand foreign cultures.

Principles of construction

To make sure the cross-cultural corporate culture develop along the right path, the cultural construction should follow the two basic principles:

Be realistic

The cross-cultural corporation should take actions that suit local circumstances while building the cross-cultural corporate culture. It should pay attention to the host nation's macro culture environment and the corporation's micro culture environment. The application of other enterprise's corporate culture doesn't work.

Be cautious

The importance of the corporate culture and its constancy is worth building with great care. The corporate culture should be built on the basis of mutual understanding, respect, and trust after the comprehensive understanding of cultural differences. The corporation should also be careful to adopt the strategy of long-term development to make sure such open corporate culture can have sustainable development.

6.6.3 Case for Practice

Case

A Canadian bank employee described his Filipino boss's approach to management.

While working at the Royal bank, I had a most unbearable and suspicious manager who had authority over all administrative employees, including me. The problem was that he seemed to totally distrust his subordinates, he constantly looked over our shoulders, checking our work, attitudes, and punctuality. Although most of his employees resented this treatment, they recognized that he was an extremely conscientious supervisor who honestly believed in what he called "old-style" management. He really thought that employees are lazy by nature. He therefore believed that he must pressure them into working. As the manager, he felt justified in treating his employees severely.

But as a group, the employees thought of themselves as basically trustworthy. However, we decided that since our boss showed no respect for us, we would give him the same treatment in return. This resulted in a working environment filled with mistrust and hostility. The atmosphere affected everyone's work: Employees became less and less willing to work, and the manager increasingly believed that his employees were lazy and that he needed to be severe with them. Luckily, this situation caught the eye of the boss, who resolved it after lengthy discussions. Only then did it become clear that we were not seeing the situation in the same way. From the manager's perspective, he was simply showing his caring and involvement with his subordinates. As he explained, Filipino employees who were not treated like this might have felt neglected and unimportant. Unfortunately, we were not Filipinos and, as Canadians, did not respond as many Filipinos might have responded.

(1) How do you comment on Canadian employees?

(2) How do you comment on Filipino manager?

(3) What are the conflicts between Canadian employees and Filipino manager?

6.6.4 Further Reading

Passage 1

Culture is the values and practices shared by the members of the group. Company culture, therefore, is the shared values and practices of the company's employees. Every organization— businesses, government agencies, nonprofit organizations, even colleges—has a culture. An organization's culture is constructed by the people who found and change the organization.

Company culture is important because it can make or break your company. Companies with an adaptive culture that is aligned to their business goals routinely outperform their competitors. Some studies report the difference at 200% or more. To achieve results like this for your organization, you have to figure out what your culture is, decide what it should be, and move everyone toward the desired culture.

Company culture evolves and changes over time. As employees leave the company and replacements are hired the company culture will change. If it is a strong culture, it may not change much. However, since each new employee brings his/her own values and practices to the group the culture will change, at least a little. As the company matures from a startup to a more established company, the company culture will change. As the environment in which the company operates (the laws, regulations, business climate, etc.) changes, the company culture will also change.

These changes may be positive, or they may not. The changes in company culture may be intended, but often they are unintended. They may be major changes or minor ones. The company culture will change and it is important to be aware of the changes.

You can begin to analyze an organization's culture by asking the following questions.

(1) Are there lots of levels between the CEO and the lowest worker or only a few? How do people get ahead? Are the organization's rewards based on seniority, education, being well liked, making technical discoveries, or serving customers?

(2) Are rewards available only to a few top people, or is everyone expected to succeed?

(3) Does the organization value diversity or homogeneity? Does it value independence and creativity or being a team player and following orders? What stories do people tell? Who are the organization's heroes and villains?

(4) How important are friendship and sociability? To what extent do workers agree on goals, and how intently do they pursue them?

(5) How formal are behavior, language, and dress?

(6) What are the organization's goals? Making money, serving customers and clients, advancing knowledge, or contributing to the community?

Passage 2

Learning the Corporate Culture

One of my colleagues had left his company. The quit reason that he wrote has become the uppermost excuse for those who want to quit their jobs at present. This is a good topic that attracts me to analyze the true meaning of corporate culture. Let's share.

To use a simple analogy, fitting into a company's corporate culture is like buying a new pair of shoes. You want shoes that provide comfort, match you personal style, and last long enough to get you where you want to go. If the shoes are not a good fit, you probably won't get very far, and you will feel miserable.

The same holds true when shopping for a career, and ultimately, a place of employment. You want to look for and select a corporate environment that makes you comfortable, reflects your taste and style, and allows you to function and move along with ease. Whether or not you'll be happy working at a particular company will largely depend on how comfortable you are with the company's corporate culture. Like a pair of new shoes, the company and you have to fit just right.

I'm from Wal-mart which is a company who has its own tastes, preferences, and style. People in there has their individual right to express what they want to say, which we called "Open Door Policy." And compare with those R&D companies, you'll find that it is easy to go through all the process and get the final approval quickly if you send your new idea, even the result has been rejected. You feel more passionate when you are working in this kind of environment.

Every place has its culture, and no two are ever alike. A company's culture reflects the operating tastes, preferences, and the style of the company's chief executive. He or she ultimately sets the tone and shapes the working environment. It may include the way people address, act, present themselves, conduct their work, and interact with the public. Individually and collectively, these factors will likely determine if a company is right for you, or if you are right for a company.

Simply stated, there's no getting around it. If you want to be successful at a company, and enjoy where you work, you need to adapt to the company's corporate culture. The company won't adapt to you, unless you're hired as a CEO. Only then will you be in the position to change and shape the corporate culture.

In short, those who succeed are able to adapt to the company's ways. They learn and understand how to swim with the corporate tide while working toward the company's goals.

Notes

Ethnocentric	种族优越感的	affluence	富裕
remuneration	报酬；赔偿；补偿	Sharia	伊斯兰教教法
conglomerate	密集而固结的；成簇的	consensus	共识；一致；合意
bond	黏合剂		

universal ethical principle orientation　　价值观念取向

T-group (Sensitivity Training)　　敏感性训练，也称 T- 团体训练。目的是通过受训者在共同学习环境中的相互影响，提高受训者对自己的感情和情绪、自己在组织中所扮演的角色、自己同别人的相互影响关系的敏感性，进而改变个人和团体的行为，达到提高工作效率和满足个人需求的目标。

Encounter Tips

◎　在西方，一般来说对别人的热情报以一种无表情的沉默意味着不友好，对一个有身份的人来说更是如此。相反，在中国，一个普通的成员一般见到职位比自己高的领导时，往往有意无意地流露出谦卑的神态，甚至有意回避。

◎　美国人希望分工明确，并恪守其职，而日本人对职责的概念很不明确；美国人认为在其位谋其职并承担一定的风险，而日本人觉得三者的联系并不如此密切，他们更趋向于从长计议。

6.7　Exercises

6.7.1　Exercises A

Decide whether the following statements are true or false.

(1) Individuals from low power distance culture accept power as part of society. As a result, superiors consider their subordinates to be different from themselves and vice versa.

(2) Price can be affected by the product cost, customer's concept of product, and competition in the market.

(3) Cross-cultural design of advertising usually composes of two effects, language and culture.

(4) Coca Cola in Chinese means tasty.

(5) We can translate the original Chinese version into English to promote a new product in the international advertising.

(6) A good international advertising should embody background information and linguistic devices.

(7) In the low-power-distance culture, people in power often try to look less powerful than they really are.

(8) Punctuality is essential and important in all business situations.

(9) In business negotiations the eye contact is usually unnecessary.

(10) In Asian cultures, the honored guest is seated facing the door.

6.7.2 Exercises B

Discuss why the following marketing strategies don't work.

(1) A soft drink was introduced into Arab countries with an attractive label that had stars on it—six-pointed stars.

(2) Pepsodent tried to sell its toothpaste in Southeast Asia by emphasizing that it "whitens your teeth."

(3) A golf ball manufacturing company packaged golf balls in packs of four for convenient purchase in Japan.

(4) Mountain Bell Company tried to promote its telephone and services to Saudis. Its advertisment portrayed an executive talking on the phone with his feet propped up on the desk, showing the soles of his shoes.

(5) Locum is a Swedish company. As most companies do at Christmas they sent out Christmas cards to customers. In 1991 they decided to give their logo a little holiday spirit by replacing the "o" in Locum with a heart. You can see the result...

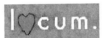

(6) One company printed the "OK" finger sign on each page of its catalogue and wanted to sell the products in Latin America.

6.7.3 Exercise C

Decide which country as a society is individualistic and which one is collectivist; explain why.

(1) New Zealand.

(2) Singapore.

(3) Italy.

(4) Japan.

6.7.4 Exercise D

Read the following case and discuss the questions. There may be more than one possible answer.

When Kellogg launched its breakfast cereals on the Brazilian market, it advertised on the "novellas," the popular type of local soap opera. The first campaign positioned cereal as a snack rather than as a part of a breakfast meal, but was soon withdrawn. Since an analysis of the Brazilian culture revealed a very high value placed on the family, with the male dominant authority, the next campaign focused on family breakfast scenes, with the father pouring the cereal into bowls and adding milk. Cereal sales increased, and Kellogg's achieved a 99.5% market share.

(1) In your opinion, why did the Kellogg first advertise the cereals on the "novellas"?

(2) What is the major difference between the first advertising campaign and the second one?

(3) What makes the second advertisement such a success?

(4) Suppose you are going to launch the same product on the Chinese market, how would you design the advertisement?

Chapter 6 Keys

References

包惠南. 文化语境与语言翻译 [M]// 毕思勇, 张成山. 商务谈判. 北京: 中国对外翻译出版公司, 2001.

BILBOW T G. 朗文商务致胜英文书信 [M]. 北京: 外语教学与研究出版社, 2001.

毕继万. 跨文化非语言交际 [M]. 北京: 外语教学与研究出版社, 1999.

曹文. 英语文化教学的两个层次 [J]. 外语教学与研究, 1998(3): 12-16, 82.

CHEN G M, STAROSTA J W. 跨文化交际学基础 [M]. 上海: 上海外语教育出版社, 2007.

陈艳红, 黄军辉. 跨国公司的文化差异与国际竞争优势 [J]. 陕西经贸学院学报, 2001(8):62-65.

戴凡, SMITH L J S. 文化碰撞: 中国北美人际交往误解剖析 [M]. 上海: 上海外语教育出版社, 2003.

邓炎昌, 刘润清. 语言与文化 [M]. 北京: 外语教学与研究出版社, 1995.

丁启红. 委婉语与禁忌语对比研究 [D]. 成都: 成都理工大学, 2006.

窦卫霖. 跨文化交际基础 [M]. 北京: 对外经济贸易大学出版社, 2007.

窦卫霖. 跨文化商务交际 [M]. 北京: 高等教育出版社, 2005.

窦卫霖. 跨文化商务交流案例分析 [M]. 北京: 对外经济贸易大学出版社, 2007.

封秀云, 刘晓雪. 生活在西方 [M]. 济南: 济南出版社, 2006.

郝静. 文化差异视角下的跨国企业交易费用 [J]. 广东财经职业学院学报, 2006(6): 43-45.

何维湘. 跨文化交际技巧 [M]. 广州: 中山大学出版社, 2004.

胡文仲, 高一虹. 外语教学与文化 [M]. 长沙: 湖南教育出版社, 1997.

胡文仲. 跨文化交际学概论 [M]. 北京: 外语教学与研究出版社, 1999.

胡英坤, 车丽娟. 商务英语写作 [M]. 北京: 外语教学与研究出版社, 2005.

贾玉新. 跨文化交际学 [M]. 上海: 上海外语教育出版社, 1997.

莱杰•布罗斯纳安, 毕继万. 中国和英语国家非语言交际对比 [M]. 北京: 北京语言学院出版社, 1991.

李君富. 跨文化交际背景下的中英文禁忌语对比研究 [D]. 大连: 东北财经大学, 2007.

刘凤霞. 跨文化交际教程 [M]. 北京: 北京大学出版社, 2005.

刘园. 国际商务谈判 [M]. 北京: 首都经济贸易大学出版社, 2007.

MEANS L T. 实用办公室英语 [M]. 唐述宗, 徐钟, 译注. 上海: 上海教育出版社, 2002.

POST L E. Etiquette[M]. 北京: 外语教学与研究出版社, 1997.

钱敏汝. 跨文化的经济交际 [M]. 北京: 外语教学与研究出版社, 1997.

钱清. 礼仪与风俗 [M]. 北京: 外文出版社, 2006.

石定乐, 彭春萍. 商务跨文化交际 [M]. 武汉: 武汉大学出版社, 2008.

SNOW D. 跨文化交际技巧——如何跟西方人打交道 [M]. 上海: 上海外语教育出版社, 2004.

吴进业, 王超明. 跨文化交际与外语教学 [M]. 郑州: 河南大学出版社, 2005.

吴晓露, 程朝辉. 说汉语、谈文化 [M]. 北京: 北京语言文化大学出版社, 2002.

吴新红. 商务礼仪 [M]. 北京: 化学工业出版社, 2006.

许兰贞. 时尚与休闲 [M]. 北京: 外文出版社, 2006.

许力生. 跨文化交际英语教程 [M]. 上海: 上海外语教育出版社, 2004.

许力生. 跨文化交流入门 [M]. 杭州: 浙江大学出版社, 2004.

徐小贞 . 国际商务交际 [M]. 北京：高等教育出版社，2005.

杨宏伟 . 英汉委婉语对比研究 [D]. 桂林：广西师范大学，2001.

尹丕安 . 跨文化交际：理论与实践 [M]. 西安：西北工业大学出版社，2007.

张爱琳 . 跨文化交际 [M]. 重庆：重庆大学出版社，2003.

张爱学 . 彼岸视点 [M]. 北京：外文出版社，2004.

张蓓，郑文园 . 跨文化意识 [M]. 北京：清华大学出版社，2003.

张春柏 . 商务英语写作 [M]. 北京：高等教育出版社，2001.

张从益 . 中西文化比较研究 [M]. 长沙：湖南人民出版社，2004.

张宏 . 英汉文化意象的对比与翻译 [D]. 上海：上海海事大学，2005.

张仁德，霍洪喜 . 企业文化概论 [M]. 天津：南开大学出版社，2001.

赵秀菊 . 精选商务英语阅读 60 篇 [M]. 北京：世界图书出版公司，2004.

周峰，朱冠群 . 成长在西方 [M]. 济南：济南出版社，2006.

庄恩平 . 跨文化商务沟通案例教程 [M]. 上海：上海外语教育出版社，2004.

MIECHELL C. A Short Course in International Business Culture[M]. Shanghai: Shanghai Foreign Language Education Press, 2000.

SNOW D. Encounters with Westerners: Improving Skills in English and Intercultural Communication[M]. Shanghai: Shanghai Foreign Language Education Press, 2004.

HALL T E. The Silent Language[M]. New York: Anchor/Doubleday, 1981.

DOLAN P J. Smart Negotiating: It's a Done Deal[M]. Cambridge, MA: Eliot House Productions, 2006.

SAMOVAR A L, PORTER E R. Communication between Cultures[M]. Beijing: Peking University Press, 2004.

DAVIS L. Doing Culture: Cross-cultural Communication in Action[M]. Beijing: Foreign Language Teaching and Research Press, 2001.

SAMOVAR A L, PORTER E R. Intercultural Communication[M]. California: Wadsworth Publications, 1988.

图书在版编目 (CIP) 数据

跨文化交际：英文 / 郑晓泉主编 . —3 版 . — 杭州：浙江
大学出版社，2021.6（2024.6 重印）
ISBN 978-7-308-19788-5

Ⅰ . ①跨… Ⅱ . ① 郑… Ⅲ . ①文化交流 — 英语 — 高等
学校 — 教材 Ⅳ . ① G115

中国版本图书馆 CIP 数据核字 (2019) 第 266679 号

跨文化交际（第 3 版）

郑晓泉　主编

责任编辑	李　晨	
责任校对	郑成业	
封面设计	春天书装	
出版发行	浙江大学出版社	
	（杭州天目山路 148 号　邮政编码 310007）	
	（网址：http://www.zjupress.com）	
排　　版	杭州青翊图文设计有限公司	
印　　刷	浙江新华数码印务有限公司	
开　　本	787mm×1092mm　1/16	
印　　张	14.25	
字　　数	426 千	
版 印 次	2021 年 6 月第 3 版　2024 年 6 月第 6 次印刷	
书　　号	ISBN 978-7-308-19788-5	
定　　价	48.00 元	